This book is due on the last date stamped below.
Failure to return books on the date due may result
in assessment of overdue fees.

FINES	.50 per day	

BLOOM'S

HOW TO WRITE ABOUT

The Brontës

VIRGINIA BRACKETT

BLOOM'S
LITERARY CRITICISM
An imprint of Infobase Publishing

Bloom's How to Write about the Brontës

Bloom's Literary Criticism
An imprint of Infobase Publishing
132 West 31st Street
New York NY 10001

Library of Congress Cataloging-in-Publication Data
Brackett, Virginia.
   Bloom's how to write about the Brontës / Virginia Brackett; introduction by Harold Bloom.
      p. cm. — (Bloom's how to write about literature)
   Includes bibliographical references and index.
   ISBN 978-0-7910-9794-6 (acid-free paper) 1. Brontë, Charlotte, 1816–1855—Criticism and interpretation. 2. Brontë, Emily, 1818–1848—Criticism and interpretation. 3. Brontë, Anne, 1820–1849—Criticism and interpretation. 4. Criticism—Authorship. 5. Report writing. I. Title. II. Title: How to write about the Brontës. III. Title: Brontës. IV. Series.
   PR4169.B73 2009
   823'.809—dc22   2008005709

Bloom's Literary Criticism books are available at special discounts when purchased in bulk quantities for businesses, associations, institutions, or sales promotions. Please call our Special Sales Department in New York at (212) 967-8800 or (800) 322-8755.

You can find Bloom's Literary Criticism on the World Wide Web at http://www.chelseahouse.com

Text design by Annie O'Donnell
Cover design by Ben Peterson

Printed in the United States of America

Bang MSRF 10 9 8 7 6 5 4 3 2 1

This book is printed on acid-free paper.

CONTENTS

*For those intrepid proofreaders, Sean Malone and Janice Gerke,
and the many additional students who continue to confirm
the joy of fine literature.*

SERIES INTRODUCTION

BLOOM's How to Write about Literature series is designed to inspire students to write fine essays on great writers and their works. Each volume in the series begins with an introduction by Harold Bloom, meditating on the challenges and rewards of writing about the volume's subject author. The first chapter then provides detailed instructions on how to write a good essay, including how to find a thesis; how to develop an outline; how to write a good introduction, body text, and conclusions; how to cite sources; and more. The second chapter provides a brief overview of the issues involved in writing about the subject author and then a number of suggestions for paper topics, with accompanying strategies for addressing each topic. Succeeding chapters cover the author's major works.

The paper topics suggested within this book are open-ended, and the brief strategies provided are designed to give students a push forward on the writing process rather than a road map to success. The aim of the book is to pose questions, not answer them. Many different kinds of papers could result from each topic. As always, the success of each paper will depend completely on the writer's skill and imagination.

HOW TO WRITE ABOUT THE BRONTËS: INTRODUCTION

by Harold Bloom

THOUGH AN always engaging novelist, Anne Brontë forever is in the shadows of her sisters Charlotte and Emily Jane. This is deplorable but inevitable, even as it is equally fated that to write about the Brontës is to juxtapose and compare two powerful narratives, *Jane Eyre* and *Wuthering Heights*. If you accept this, you can proceed to give your own description and estimate of these undying and canonical works.

Begin by reading George Gordon, Lord Byron's *Manfred*, an emblematic poem out of which Charlotte's Rochester and Emily's Heathcliff emanate. Byron's poetry and legend dominated the early girlhood of the Brontë sisters. They fell in love with him, and in complex ways they revenge themselves on their seducer through the physical suffering of Rochester and the erotic anguish of Heathcliff.

Jane Eyre achieves her happiness finally by dominating Rochester, in a mode from which sadomasochism certainly is not excluded. Far more subtly and even more sadistically, the dying Catherine Earnshaw provokes Heathcliff into a condition of death-in-life that ends only by his joining her in the grave.

Comparision of Rochester and Heathcliff is a useful way of writing about the Brontës and also introduces readers to the crucial process of juxtaposing literary characters to one another, both in Shakespeare and in the novel. Heathcliff is more inward than Rochester, just as Hamlet and Macbeth lead you on a deeper journey into the interior than do Othello and Antony.

HOW TO WRITE
A GOOD ESSAY

WHILE THERE are many ways to write about literature, most assignments for high school and college English classes call for analytical papers. In these assignments, you are presenting your interpretation of a text to your reader. Your objective is to interpret the text's meaning in order to enhance your reader's understanding and enjoyment of the work. Without exception, strong papers about the meaning of a literary work are built upon a careful, close reading of the text or texts. Careful, analytical reading should always be the first step in your writing process. This volume provides models of such close, analytical reading, and these should help you develop your own skills as a reader and as a writer.

As the examples throughout this book demonstrate, attentive reading entails thinking about and evaluating the formal (textual) aspects of the author's works: theme, character, form, and language. In addition, when writing about a work, many readers choose to move beyond the text itself to consider the work's cultural context. In these instances, writers might explore the historical circumstances of the period in which the work was written. Alternatively, they might examine the philosophies and ideas that a work addresses. Even in cases where writers explore a work's cultural context, though, papers must still address the more formal aspects of the work itself. A good interpretative essay that evaluates Charles Dickens's use of the philosophy of utilitarianism in his novel *Hard Times*, for example, cannot adequately address the author's treatment of the philosophy without firmly grounding this discussion in the book itself. In other words, any analytical paper about a text, even one that seeks to evaluate the work's cultural context, must also have a

1

firm handle on the work's themes, characters, and language. You must look for and evaluate these aspects of a work, then, as you read a text and as you prepare to write about it.

WRITING ABOUT THEMES

Literary themes are more than just topics or subjects treated in a work; they are attitudes or points about these topics that often structure other elements in a work. Writing about theme therefore requires that you not just identify a topic that a literary work addresses but also discuss what that work says about that topic. For example, if you were writing about the culture of the American South in William Faulkner's famous story "A Rose for Emily," you would need to discuss what Faulkner says, argues, or implies about that culture and its passing.

When you prepare to write about thematic concerns in a work of literature, you will probably discover that, as most works of literature do, your text touches upon other themes in addition to its central theme. These secondary themes also provide rich ground for paper topics. A thematic paper on "A Rose for Emily" might consider gender or race in the story. While neither of these could be said to be the central theme of the story, both are clearly related to the passing of the "old South" and could provide plenty of good material for papers.

As you prepare to write about themes in literature, you might find a number of strategies helpful. After you identify a theme or themes in the story, you should begin by evaluating how other elements of the story—such as character, point of view, imagery, and symbolism—help develop the theme. You might ask yourself what your own responses are to the author's treatment of the subject matter. Do not neglect the obvious, either: What expectations does the title set up? How does the title help develop thematic concerns? Clearly, the title "A Rose for Emily" says something about the narrator's attitude toward the title character, Emily Grierson, and all she represents.

WRITING ABOUT CHARACTER

Generally, characters are essential components of fiction and drama. (This is not always the case, though; Ray Bradbury's "August 2026:

There Will Come Soft Rains" is technically a story without characters, at least any human characters.) Often, you can discuss character in poetry, as in T. S. Eliot's "The Love Song of J. Alfred Prufrock" or Robert Browning's "My Last Duchess." Many writers find that analyzing character is one of the most interesting and engaging ways to work with a piece of literature and to shape a paper. After all, characters generally are human, and we all know something about being human and living in the world. While it is always important to remember that these figures are not real people but creations of the writer's imagination, it can be fruitful to begin evaluating them as you might evaluate a real person. Often you can start with your own response to a character. Did you like or dislike the character? Did you sympathize with the character? Why or why not?

Keep in mind, though, that emotional responses like these are just starting places. To explore and evaluate literary characters truly, you need to return to the formal aspects of the text and evaluate how the author has drawn these characters. The 20th-century writer E. M. Forster coined the terms *flat* characters and *round* characters. Flat characters are static, one-dimensional characters who frequently represent a particular concept or idea. In contrast, round characters are fully drawn and much more realistic characters who frequently change and develop over the course of a work. Are the characters you are studying flat or round? What elements of the characters lead you to this conclusion? Why might the author have drawn characters like this? How does their development affect the meaning of the work? Similarly, you should explore the techniques the author uses to develop characters. Do we hear a character's own words, or do we hear only other characters' assessments of him or her? Or does the author use an omniscient or limited omniscient narrator to allow us access to the workings of the characters' minds? If so, how does that help develop the characterization? Often you can even evaluate the narrator as a character. How trustworthy are the opinions and assessments of the narrator? You should also think about characters' names. Do they mean anything? If you encounter a hero named Sophia or Sophie, you should probably think about her wisdom (or lack thereof), since *sophia* means "wisdom" in Greek. Similarly, since the name *Sylvia* is derived from the word *sylvan*, meaning "of the wood," you might want to evaluate that character's relationship with nature. Once again, you might look to the title of the work. Does Herman Melville's "Bartleby, the Scrivener" signal anything about Bartleby himself? Is Bartleby adequately defined by his job as scrivener? Is this part of Melville's point? Pursuing questions like these can help you develop thorough papers about characters from psychological, sociological, or more formalistic perspectives.

WRITING ABOUT FORM AND GENRE

Genre, a word derived from French, means "type" or "class." Literary genres are distinctive classes or categories of literary composition. On the most general level, literary works can be divided into the genres of drama, poetry, fiction, and essays, yet within those genres there are classifications that are also referred to as genres. Tragedy and comedy, for example, are genres of drama. Epic, lyric, and pastoral are genres of poetry. Form, on the other hand, generally refers to the shape or structure of a work. There are many clearly defined forms of poetry that follow specific patterns of meter, rhyme, and stanza. Sonnets, for example, are poems that follow a fixed form of 14 lines. Sonnets generally follow one of two basic sonnet forms, each with its own distinct rhyme scheme. Haiku is another example of poetic form, traditionally consisting of three unrhymed lines of five, seven, and five syllables.

While you might think that writing about form or genre might leave little room for argument, many of these forms and genres are very fluid. Remember that literature is evolving and ever changing, and so are its forms. As you study poetry, you may find that poets, especially more modern poets, play with traditional poetic forms, bringing about new effects. Similarly, dramatic tragedy was once quite narrowly defined, but over the centuries playwrights have broadened and challenged traditional definitions, changing the shape of tragedy. When Arthur Miller wrote *Death of a Salesman*, many critics challenged the idea that tragic drama could encompass a common man like Willy Loman.

Evaluating how a work of literature fits into or challenges the boundaries of its form or genre can provide you with fruitful avenues of investigation. You might find it helpful to ask why the work does or does not fit into traditional categories. Why might Miller have thought it fitting to write a tragedy of the common man? Similarly, you might compare the content or theme of a work with its form. How well do they work together? Many of Emily Dickinson's poems, for instance, follow the meter of traditional hymns. While some of her poems seem to express traditional religious doctrines, many seem to challenge or strain against traditional conceptions of God and theology. What is the effect, then, of her use of traditional hymn meter?

WRITING ABOUT LANGUAGE, SYMBOLS, AND IMAGERY

No matter what the genre, writers use words as their most basic tool. Language is the most fundamental building block of literature. It is essential that you pay careful attention to the author's language and word choice as you read, reread, and analyze a text. Imagery is language that appeals to the senses. Most commonly, imagery appeals to our sense of vision, creating a mental picture, but authors also use language that appeals to our other senses. Images can be literal or figurative. Literal images use sensory language to describe an actual thing. In the broadest terms, figurative language uses one thing to speak about something else. For example, if I call my boss a snake, I am not saying that he is literally a reptile. Instead, I am using figurative language to communicate my opinions about him. Since we think of snakes as sneaky, slimy, and sinister, I am using the concrete image of a snake to communicate these abstract opinions and impressions.

The two most common figures of speech are similes and metaphors. Both are comparisons between two apparently dissimilar things. Similes are explicit comparisons using the word *like* or *as*; metaphors are implicit comparisons. To return to the previous example, if I say, "My boss, Bob, was waiting for me when I showed up to work five minutes late today—the snake!" I have constructed a metaphor. Writing about his experiences fighting in World War I, Wilfred Owen begins his poem "Dulce et decorum est" with a string of similes: "Bent double, like old beggars under sacks, / Knock-kneed, coughing like hags, we cursed through sludge." Owen's goal was to undercut clichéd notions that war and dying in battle were glorious. Certainly, comparing soldiers to coughing hags and to beggars underscores his point.

"Fog," a short poem by Carl Sandburg, provides a clear example of a metaphor. Sandburg's poem reads:

> The fog comes
> on little cat feet.
>
> It sits looking
> over harbor and city
> on silent haunches
> and then moves on.

Notice how effectively Sandburg conveys surprising impressions of the fog by comparing two seemingly disparate things—the fog and a cat.

Symbols, by contrast, are things that stand for, or represent, other things. Often they represent something intangible, such as concepts or ideas. In everyday life we use and understand symbols easily. Babies at christenings and brides at weddings wear white to represent purity. Think, too, of a dollar bill. The paper itself has no value in and of itself. Instead, that paper bill is a symbol of something else, the precious metal in a nation's treasury. Symbols in literature work similarly. Authors use symbols to evoke more than a simple, straightforward, literal meaning. Characters, objects, and places can all function as symbols. Famous literary examples of symbols include Moby Dick, the white whale of Herman Melville's novel, and the scarlet *A* of Nathaniel Hawthorne's *The Scarlet Letter.* As both of these symbols suggest, a literary symbol cannot be adequately defined or explained by any one meaning. Hester Prynne's Puritan community clearly intends her scarlet *A* as a symbol of her adultery, but as the novel progresses, even her own community reads the letter as representing not just *adultery,* but *able, angel,* and a host of other meanings.

Writing about imagery and symbols requires close attention to the author's language. To prepare a paper on symbolism or imagery in a work, identify and trace the images and symbols and then try to draw some conclusions about how they function. Ask yourself how any symbols or images help contribute to the themes or meanings of the work. What connotations do they carry? How do they affect your reception of the work? Do they shed light on characters or settings? A strong paper on imagery or symbolism will thoroughly consider the use of figures in the text and will try to reach some conclusions about how or why the author uses them.

WRITING ABOUT HISTORY AND CONTEXT

As noted earlier, it is possible to write an analytical paper that also considers the work's context. After all, the text was not created in a vacuum. The author lived and wrote in a specific period and in a specific cultural context and, as all of us are, was shaped by that environment. Learning more about the historical and cultural circumstances that surround the author and the work can help illuminate a text and provide you with productive material for a paper. Remember, though, that when you write analytical papers, you should use the context to illuminate the text. Do not lose sight of your goal—to interpret the meaning of the literary work. Use historical or philosophical research as a tool to develop your textual evaluation.

Thoughtful readers often consider how history and culture affected the author's choice and treatment of his or her subject matter. Investigations into the history and context of a work could examine the work's relation to specific historical events, such as the Salem witch trials in 17th-century Massachusetts or the restoration of Charles II to the British throne in 1660. Bear in mind that historical context is not limited to politics and world events. While knowing about the Vietnam War is certainly helpful in interpreting much of Tim O'Brien's fiction, and some knowledge of the French Revolution clearly illuminates the dynamics of Charles Dickens's *A Tale of Two Cities*, historical context also entails the fabric of daily life. Examining a text in light of gender roles, race relations, class boundaries, or working conditions can give rise to thoughtful and compelling papers. Exploring the conditions of the working class in 19th-century England, for example, can provide a particularly effective avenue for writing about Dickens's *Hard Times*.

You can begin thinking about these issues by asking broad questions at first. What do you know about the period and about the author? What does the editorial apparatus in your text tell you? These might be starting places. Similarly, when specific historical events or dynamics are particularly important to understanding a work but might be somewhat obscure to modern readers, textbooks usually provide notes to explain historical background. These are a good place to start. With this information, ask yourself how these historical facts and circumstances might have affected the author, the presentation of theme, and the presentation of character. How does knowing more about the work's specific historical context illuminate the work? To take a well-known example, understanding the complex attitudes toward slavery during the time Mark Twain wrote *Adventures of Huckleberry Finn* should help you begin to examine issues of race in the text. Additionally, you might compare these attitudes to those of the time in which the novel was set. How might this comparison affect your interpretation of a work written after the abolition of slavery but set before the Civil War?

WRITING ABOUT PHILOSOPHY AND IDEAS

Philosophical concerns are closely related to both historical context and thematic issues. As historical investigation does, philosophical research can provide a useful tool as you analyze a text. For example, an investigation into the working class in Dickens's England might lead you to a topic on the philosophical doctrine of utilitarianism in *Hard Times.* Many other works explore philosophies and ideas quite explicitly. Mary Shelley's famous novel *Frankenstein,* for example, explores John Locke's tabula rasa theory of human knowledge as she portrays the intellectual and emotional development of Victor Frankenstein's creature. As this example indicates, philosophical issues are somewhat more abstract than investigations of theme or historical context. Some other examples of philosophical issues include human free will, the formation of human identity, the nature of sin, or questions of ethics.

Writing about philosophy and ideas might require some outside research, but usually the notes or other material in your text will provide you with basic information and often footnotes and bibliographies suggest places you can go to read further about the subject. If you have identified a philosophical theme that runs through a text, you might ask yourself how the author develops this theme. Look at character development and the interactions of characters, for example. Similarly, you might examine whether the narrative voice in a work of fiction addresses the philosophical concerns of the text.

WRITING COMPARISON AND CONTRAST ESSAYS

Finally, you might find that comparing and contrasting the works or techniques of an author provides a useful tool for literary analysis. A comparison and contrast essay might compare two characters or themes in a single work, or it might compare the author's treatment of a theme in two works. It might also contrast methods of character development or analyze an author's differing treatment of a philosophical concern in two works. Writing comparison and contrast essays, though, requires some special consideration. While they generally provide you with plenty of material to use, they also come with a built-in trap: the laundry list. These papers often become mere lists of connections between the works. As this chapter will discuss, a strong thesis must make an assertion that you want to prove or validate. A strong comparison/contrast thesis, then, needs to comment on the significance of the similarities and differences you observe. It is not enough merely to assert that the works contain similarities and differences. You might, for example, assert why the similarities and differences are important and explain how they illuminate the works' treatment of theme. Remember, too, that a thesis should not be a statement of the obvious. A comparison/contrast paper that focuses only on very obvious similarities or differences does little to illuminate the connections between the works. Often, an effective method of shaping a strong thesis and argument is to begin your paper by noting the similarities between the works but then to develop a thesis that asserts how these apparently similar elements are different. If, for example, you observe that Emily Dickinson wrote a number of poems about spiders, you might analyze how she uses spider imagery differently in two poems. Similarly, many scholars have noted that Hawthorne created many "mad scientist" characters, men who are so devoted to their science or their art that they lose perspective on all else. A good thesis comparing two of these characters—Aylmer of "The Birth-mark" and Dr. Rappaccini of "Rappaccini's Daughter," for example—might initially identify both characters as examples of Hawthorne's mad scientist type but then argue that their motivations for scientific experimentation differ. If you strive to analyze the similarities or differences, discuss significances, and move beyond the obvious, your paper should bypass the laundry list trap.

PREPARING TO WRITE

Armed with a clear sense of your task—illuminating the text—and with an understanding of theme, character, language, history, and philosophy, you are ready to approach the writing process. Remember that good writing is grounded in good reading and that close reading takes time, attention, and more than one reading of your text. Read for comprehension first. As you go back and review the work, mark the text to chart the details of the work as well as your reactions. Highlight important passages, repeated words, and image patterns. "Converse" with the text through marginal notes. Mark turns in the plot, ask questions, and make observations about characters, themes, and language. If you are reading from a book that does not belong to you, keep a record of your reactions in a journal or notebook. If you have read a work of literature carefully, paying attention to both the text and the context of the work, you have a leg up on the writing process. Admittedly, at this point, your ideas are probably very broad and undefined, but you have taken an important first step toward writing a strong paper.

Your next step is to focus, to take a broad, perhaps fuzzy, topic and define it more clearly. Even a topic provided by your instructor will need to be focused appropriately. Remember that good writers make the topic their own. There are a number of strategies—often called "invention"—that you can use to develop your own focus. In one such strategy, called *freewriting*, you spend 10 minutes or so just writing about your topic without referring to the text or your notes. Write whatever comes to mind; the important thing is that you just keep writing. Often this process allows you to develop fresh ideas or approaches to your subject matter. You could also try *brainstorming*: Write down your topic and then list all the related points or ideas you can think of. Include questions, comments, words, important passages or events, and anything else that comes to mind. Let one idea lead to another. In the related technique of *clustering*, or *mapping*, write your topic on a sheet of paper and write related ideas around it. Then list related subpoints under each of these main ideas. Many people then draw arrows to show connections between points. This technique helps you narrow your topic and can also help you organize your ideas. Similarly, asking journalistic questions—Who? What? Where? When? Why? and How?—can develop ideas for topic development.

Thesis Statements

Once you have developed a focused topic, you can begin to think about your thesis statement, the main point or purpose of your paper. It is imperative that you craft a strong thesis; otherwise, your paper will likely be little more than random, disorganized observations about the text. Think of your thesis statement as a kind of road map for your paper. It tells your reader where you are going and how you are going to get there.

To craft a good thesis, you must keep a number of things in mind. First, as the title of this subsection indicates, your paper's thesis should be a statement, an assertion about the text that you want to prove or validate. Beginning writers often formulate a question that they attempt to use as a thesis. For example, a writer exploring the theme of family in Charlotte Brontë's *Jane Eyre* might ask, Why can't Jane remain in one home? While a question like this is a good strategy to use in the invention process to help narrow your topic and find your thesis, it cannot serve as the thesis statement because it does not tell your reader what you want to assert about friendship. You might shape this question into a thesis by instead proposing an answer to that question: In *Jane Eyre*, the title character as a child is forced to move from place to place against her wishes. However, upon graduating from school, she expresses her independence by leaving Lowood behind and taking a position at Thornfield Hall. Notice that this thesis provides an initial plan or structure for the rest of the paper, and notice, too, that the thesis statement does not necessarily have to fit into one sentence. After discussing the differences between Jane's actions at the various places where she lives throughout the novel, you may settle on two, Lowood and Thornfield, to help develop a discussion of her character through their contrast. At Lowood, Jane is a helpless child, forced into a difficult situation. Her determination allows her to use what she learns at Lowood to move on to Thornfield Hall, where she will become a strong and independent young woman.

Second, remember that a good thesis makes an assertion that you need to support. In other words, a good thesis does not state the obvious. If you tried to formulate a thesis about friendship by simply saying,

Where the main character lives proves important to *Jane Eyre,* you have done nothing but rephrase the obvious. Since the novel clearly features multiple households in which Jane resides, you have no thesis to support; you have simply stated a fact. You might try to develop a thesis from that point by asking yourself some further questions: How does Jane change as she moves from place to place? Which households seem most important to her development as a character? Would she be the same person had she not been forced to survive in several difficult locations? Who in the households made life difficult for her? Such a line of questioning might lead you to a more viable thesis, like the one in the preceding paragraph.

As the comparison with the road map also suggests, your thesis should appear near the beginning of the paper. In relatively short papers (three to six pages) the thesis almost always appears in the first paragraph. Some writers fall into the trap of saving their thesis for the end, trying to provide a surprise or a big moment of revelation, as if to say, "TA-DA! I've just proven that in *Jane Eyre,* the protagonist moves often in order to gain experiences necessary to her eventual success at Thornfield Hall." Placing a thesis at the end of an essay can seriously mar the essay's effectiveness. If you fail to define your essay's point and purpose clearly at the beginning, your reader will find it difficult to assess the clarity of your argument and understand the points you are making. When your argument comes as a surprise at the end, you force your reader to reread your essay in order to assess its logic and effectiveness.

Finally, you should avoid using the first person ("I") as you present your thesis. Though it is not strictly wrong to write in the first person, it is difficult to do so gracefully. While writing in the first person, beginning writers often fall into the trap of writing self-reflexive prose (writing *about* their paper *in* their paper). Often this leads to the most dreaded of opening lines: "In this paper I am going to discuss . . ." Not only does this self-reflexive voice make for very awkward prose, it frequently allows writers to boldly announce a topic while completely avoiding a thesis statement. An example might be a paper that begins as follows: Wuthering Heights is a novel that shows how Heathcliff changes from a boy to a man. In this paper I am going to discuss how Heathcliff makes that change. The author of this paper has done little more than announce a general topic for the paper (that Heathcliff begins the story as a boy, but later becomes a man). While the last sentence might be a thesis, the writer fails to present an opinion about the significance of the reaction. To improve this "thesis," the writer would need to back up a couple of steps. First, the announced topic of the paper is too broad; it largely summarizes events in the story, without saying anything about the ideas. The writer should highlight what she considers the meaning of the story: What is it about? The writer might conclude, for instance, that Heathcliff's youth ends in devastation when he overhears Cathy telling Nelly that she cannot marry him. He leaves without hearing the rest of her comments, believing that she does not love him. He allows the bitterness that follows to become the driving force in his adult life, when his desire for vengeance is based almost entirely on a simple misunderstanding.

Outlines

While developing a strong, thoughtful thesis early in your writing process should help focus your paper, outlining provides an essential tool for logically shaping that paper. A good outline helps you see—and develop—the relationships among the points in your argument and assures you that your paper flows logically and coherently. Outlining not only helps place your points in a logical order but also helps you subordinate supporting points, weed out any irrelevant points, and decide if there are any necessary points that are missing from your argument. Most of us are familiar with formal outlines that use numerical and letter designations for each point. However, there are different types of outlines; you may find that an informal outline is a more useful tool for you. What is important, though, is that you spend the time to develop some sort of outline—formal or informal.

Remember that an outline is a tool to help you shape and write a strong paper. If you do not spend sufficient time planning your supporting points and shaping the arrangement of those points, you will most likely construct a vague, unfocused outline that provides little, if any, help with the writing of the paper. Consider the following example.

Thesis: In Charlotte Brontë's novel *The Professor*, William Crimsworth has never trusted or loved a woman. The traditionally feminine symbols of the garden, the moon, and the mirror represent Crimsworth's development of a new attitude toward women. That attitude will allow him to find fulfillment in an unconventional marriage with Frances.

I. Introduction and thesis

II. Symbolism
    A. Garden
    B. Moon
    C. Mirror
    D. Love for Frances

III. Crimsworth
    A. Relationship with brother
    B. Quits job and moves
    C. Feels isolated
    D. Needs help to reach his goals

IV. Hunsden's friendship
    A. Hunsden counsels Crimsworth
    B. Crimsworth's attitude toward Hunsden
    C. Hunsden visits Belgium

V. Conclusion
    A. We understand Crimsworth better through Brontë's use of symbolism

This outline has a number of flaws. First, the major topics labeled with the Roman numerals are not arranged in a logical order. If the paper's aim is to show that the novel's symbolism helps readers understand how Crimsworth changes in order to reach his goals, the writer must establish the particulars of his feelings about women, and then relate those feelings to the symbols. Second, too many symbols are listed to prove manageable in a brief, five-paragraph paper. Third, the thesis does not refer to Crimsworth's acquaintance with Hunsden, but the writer includes that relationship as a major section of this outline. Quite possibly the friendship is important, but it does not have a place in this paper. Fourth, the writer includes Crimsworth's love for Frances as one of the items in section II. Letters A, B, and C all refer to specific symbols; Crimsworth's feelings for Frances do not belong in this list. While one might argue that Crimsworth can only act on his love for Frances after changing due to his exposure to the symbols, that argument would represent a topic for another paper. A fifth problem is the inclusion of only a section A in V. An outline should not include an A without a B, a 1 without a 2, and so forth. The final problem with this outline is the overall lack of detail. None of the sections provides much information about the content of the argument, and it seems likely that the writer has not given sufficient thought to the paper's content.

A better start to this outline might be the following:

Thesis: In Charlotte Brontë's novel *The Professor*, William Crimsworth has never trusted or loved a woman. Brontë uses the traditional symbol of the garden to trace Crimsworth's development of a new attitude toward women. Only after his old attitudes are tested through various garden meetings will he change. His new attitude toward women, revealed in the change seen in the various garden imagery shaped by Brontë, allows Crimsworth to find fulfillment in an unconventional marriage with Frances.

    I. Introduction and thesis

    II. Early view of garden
        A. The garden and Mlle Rueter
        B. The garden symbolizes order and control

    III. Later view of garden
        A. Represents betrayal
        B. Represents power

    IV. Final view of garden
        A. The garden and Frances Henri
        B. The garden symbolizes intellectual love and freedom

```
V. Conclusion
    The reader better understands Crimsworth's
    attitudes toward women through Brontë's use
    of garden symbolism and imagery
```

This new outline would prove much more helpful when it came time to write the paper.

An outline like this could be shaped into an even more useful tool if the writer fleshed out the argument by providing specific examples from the text to support each point. Once you have listed your main point and your supporting ideas, develop this raw material by listing related supporting ideas and material under each of those main headings. From there, arrange the material in subsections and order the material logically.

For example, you might begin with one of the theses cited above: In Charlotte Brontë's *Jane Eyre*, the title character as a child is forced to move from place to place against her wishes. She especially detests Lowood school, where she faces deprivation and the loss of those she loves. However, her experiences while at Lowood school enable her to face and conquer even greater conflict at Thornfield Hall. As noted above, this thesis already gives you the beginning of an organization: Start by supporting the notion that Jane gains strength through the challenges of Lowood, which suggests that she will be able to call upon that strength at a later time. You will want to supply several examples to support your claim in the subsequent paragraphs. You might begin your outline, then, with four topic headings: (1) Jane arrives at Lowood an innocent and defenseless child; (2) Jane is challenged by the stark physical conditions; (3) Jane is challenged by the harsh attitude of Lowood's administrators; (4) Jane is challenged by Helen's death. Under each of those headings you could list ideas that support the particular point. Be sure to include references to parts of the text that help build your case. While assembling an outline, you may gather more quotations than needed for the essay, which is preferable to not having enough supporting material. As you shape your essay, you may pick and choose to select the most effective quotation for your needs. Remember, your quotations should support your point. They shouldn't control the essay.

An informal outline might look like this:

Thesis: In Charlotte Brontë's *Jane Eyre*, the title character as a child is forced to move from place to place against her wishes. She especially detests Lowood school, where she faces deprivation and the loss of those she loves, Helen Burns and Miss Temple. However, her experiences while at Lowood enable her to recognize her own strengths and abilities and prepare for the future.

1. Jane is challenged by the stark physical and emotional conditions
   - Jane is lonely and keeps her distance from the students: "As yet I had spoken to no one, nor did anybody seem to take notice of me."
   - The children's physical needs are not met
     - "Our clothing was insufficient to protect us from the severe cold"
     - Shoes don't fit: "feet inflamed"
     - Not enough to eat: "scanty supply of food"
   - Long walks in the cold each Sunday to church
     - "set out cold, we arrived at church colder"; later felt "almost paralyzed"
   - Jane is in a "struggle" with "new rules" and "unwonted tasks"
   - Children must memorize catechism on Sunday night and listen to long sermons
     - The younger children faint from weariness and have to stand in the middle of the floor
   - The outrageous conditions at Lowood help Jane recognize the power of her strength and her survival instincts

2. Meeting Helen Burns helps Jane recognize her own goodness and strength

- Brocklehurst brings guests to the orphanage
  - He commands that all of the girls' "top-knots" must be cut off.
  - Jane drops her slate and is called "A careless girl!"
  - She is placed on a stool: "I felt their eyes directed like burning-glasses against my scorched skin."
- Helen looks at Jane, giving her hope: "What an extra-ordinary sensation that ray sent through me."
  - Courage lit her eyes "like a reflection from the aspect of an angel"
  - Helen wears a badge that marks her as "untidy"
- Jane does well in school and is accepted, but still feels "crushed and trodden on"
  - Helen helps Jane feel better by encouraging her to believe in God, rather than humans

3. Miss Temple protects Jane and serves as a role model
   - Miss Temple orders a healthy lunch after a horrible breakfast, although it will be expensive: "my responsibility"
   - Miss Temple stands up to Mr. Brocklehurst: "Miss Temple passed her handkerchief over her lips . . . to smooth away the involuntary smile."
   - Miss Temple comforts Jane at Helen's death and acts as a role model for her remaining years at Lowood
   - When Miss Temple leaves, Jane realizes she must also depart and test her independence

Conclusion:
- Jane's suffering helps her better understand the world and how to trust herself
- The novel suggests that hardships can help train one for the future
- Without conflict and loss, Jane could not have developed the strong character that stands her in good stead later in the novel

You would set about writing a formal outline with a similar process, though in the final stages you would label the headings differently. A formal outline for a paper that argues the thesis about Charlotte Brontë's *The Professor* cited above (that the protagonist's changing view toward women is represented by garden imagery and symbolism) might look like this:

Thesis: In Charlotte Brontë's novel *The Professor*, William Crimsworth has never trusted or loved a woman. Brontë uses the traditional symbol of the garden to trace Crimsworth's development of a new attitude toward women. Only after his old attitudes are tested through various garden meetings will he change. His new attitude toward women, revealed in the change seen in the various garden imagery shaped by Brontë, allows Crimsworth to find fulfillment in an unconventional marriage with Frances.

    I. Introduction and Thesis

   II. Early view of garden
      A. The garden and Mlle Reuter
         1. Mlle Reuter sits in a special nook
         2. First glimpse—controlled and orderly
         3. Previously "an unknown region"
      B. Falls in love with Zoraide Reuter
         1. Original romantic view of garden
         2. First enters the garden

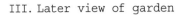

    III. Later view of garden
         A. Represents betrayal
            1. Faith in love and friendship lost
            2. Garden threatens illness
         B. Garden represents Crimsworth's developing
            power
            1. Crimsworth as gardener
            2. Garden as setting for confrontation
               of M. Reuter

    IV. Final view of garden
         A. Garden represents Frances Henri
            1. Untamed and unconventional, like
               their relationship
            2. Wild garden "nook" after marriage
            3. English garden has peculiar flowers
         B. Frances becomes the garden

    V. Conclusion
         A. Mlle Reuter's garden represents order,
            control, betrayal
         B. Frances's garden represents creativity,
            interdependence, loyalty

As in the previous example outline, the thesis provides the seeds of a structure, and the writer is careful to arrange the supporting points in a logical manner, showing the relationships among the ideas in the paper.

Body Paragraphs

Once your outline is complete, you can begin drafting your paper. Paragraphs, units of related sentences, are the building blocks of a good paper, and as you draft you should keep in mind both the function and the qualities of good paragraphs. Paragraphs help you chart and control the shape and content of your essay, and they help the reader see your organization and your logic. You should begin a new paragraph whenever you move from one major point to another. In longer, more complex essays, you might use a group of related paragraphs to support major

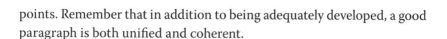
points. Remember that in addition to being adequately developed, a good paragraph is both unified and coherent.

Unified Paragraphs

Each paragraph must be centered around one idea or point, and a unified paragraph carefully focuses on and develops this central idea without including tangents. For beginning writers, the best way to ensure that you are constructing unified paragraphs is to include a topic sentence in each paragraph. This topic sentence should convey the main point of the paragraph, and every sentence in the paragraph should relate to that topic sentence. Any sentence that strays from the central topic does not belong in the paragraph and needs to be revised or deleted. Consider the following paragraph about how William Crimsworth's view of women is represented through the use of garden imagery:

> Some men view romance in the traditional way, desiring to feel an overwhelming passion and to control the women they decide to marry. Others seek the nontraditional path to romance and lifelong happiness, preferring a rational attraction and an intellectual partnership in which each partner finds contentment and love. William Crimsworth thinks he prefers the former, but he discovers he wants the latter. Some men can never decide which they desire, an example being Pelet. Then there's Hunsden, who says no woman will ever be enough for him. However, he does like Frances Henri and teases Crimsworth by asking, "What business have you to be suited so well with a partner?" (193). Mlle Reuter represents a type of romance that Crimsworth does not want. She is the one who wants to be controlling and is too paranoid to trust any man. Crimsworth is too blinded by passion to recognize that she is not a good match for him. The garden where she spends so much time will help reveal this to him. Gardens will also symbolize Frances later in the story. Crimsworth tells the reader, "I watched this change much as a gardener watches the growth of a precious plant" (116). Mlle Reuter's garden is organized

and designed so as to conceal a place for her to hide,
whereas the gardens identified with Frances are wild
and uncontained, symbolizing that she is better suited
to a nontraditional relationship with Crimsworth.

Although the paragraph begins well enough, and the second and third
sentences provide the central idea of the paragraph, the author soon
goes off on a tangent. If the purpose of the paragraph is to demonstrate
the importance of garden imagery to understanding Crimsworth's view
of women, many sentences are out of place. The sentences referencing
the two other men's attitudes do not belong here. They may find a place
later in the paper, but they should be deleted from this paragraph.

Coherent Paragraphs

In addition to shaping unified paragraphs, you must also craft coherent paragraphs, paragraphs that develop their points logically with
sentences that flow smoothly into one another. Coherence depends
on the order of your sentences, but it is not strictly the order of the
sentences that is important to paragraph coherence. You also need
to craft your prose to help the reader see the relationship among the
sentences.

Consider the following paragraph about the use of garden imagery
in *The Professor*. Notice how the writer uses the same ideas as the paragraph above yet fails to help the reader see the relationships among the
points.

William Crimsworth does not feel confident about his
ability to romance women. He believes that he is falling
in love with Mlle Reuter when she introduces him to
the garden. Her garden has been used to separate the
boys' and the girls' schools. Crimsworth discovers
it separates him from Mlle Reuter. She tells him to
walk ahead of her into the garden. He looks back to
determine whether she follows. Mlle Reuter asks him to
sit beside her on the bench in the forbidden garden
nook. Crimsworth responds with passion, and his hopes
rise that he and Zoraïde might develop a relationship.

He hears Pelet walking with Mlle Reuter, who makes light of Crimsworth's response to her, and he feels betrayed. The light is extinguished in the garden-house and he thinks "so, for a time, was my faith in love and friendship" (86). He regains that faith with Frances Henri. Crimsworth realizes that teaching is like tending a garden, an idea made clear in his thoughts. Crimsworth tells the reader about Frances, "I watched this change much as a gardener watches the growth of a precious plant" (116). He decides that Frances might be the better match.

This paragraph demonstrates that unity alone does not guarantee paragraph effectiveness. The argument is hard to follow because the author fails both to show connections between the sentences and to indicate how they work to support the overall point.

A number of techniques are available to aid paragraph coherence. Careful use of transitional words and phrases is essential. You can use transitional flags to introduce an example or an illustration (*for example, for instance*), to amplify a point or add another phase of the same idea (*additionally, furthermore, next, similarly, finally, then*), to indicate a conclusion or result (*therefore, as a result, thus, in other words*), to signal a contrast or a qualification (*on the other hand, nevertheless, despite this, on the contrary, still, however, conversely*), to signal a comparison (*likewise, in comparison, similarly*), and to indicate a movement in time (*afterward, earlier, eventually, finally, later, subsequently, until*).

In addition to transitional flags, careful use of pronouns aids coherence and flow. If you were writing about *The Wizard of Oz,* you would not want to keep repeating the phrase *the witch* or the name *Dorothy.* Careful substitution of the pronoun *she* in these instances can aid coherence. A word of warning, though: When you substitute pronouns for proper names, always be sure that your pronoun reference is clear. In a paragraph that discusses both Dorothy and the witch, substituting *she* could lead to confusion. Make sure that it is clear to whom the pronoun refers. Generally, the pronoun refers to the last proper noun you have used.

While repeating the same name over and over again can lead to awkward, boring prose, it is possible to use repetition to help your paragraph's coherence. Careful repetition of important words or phrases can lend coherence to your paragraph by reminding readers of your key points. Admittedly, it takes some practice to use this technique effectively. You may find that reading your prose aloud can help you develop an ear for effective use of repetition.

To see how helpful transitional aids are, compare the paragraph below to the preceding paragraph about the function of garden imagery in helping readers understand William Crimsworth. Notice how the author works with the same ideas and quotations but shapes them into a much more coherent paragraph whose point is clearer and easier to follow.

William Crimsworth does not feel confident about his ability to romance women. However, he believes that he is falling in love with Mlle Zoraïde Reuter when she introduces him to her garden. The garden has been used to separate the boys' and the girls' schools, and it arouses Crimsworth's curiosity, as does Mlle Reuter herself. At first, she tells him to walk ahead of her into the garden, and he looks back to determine whether she follows, not noticing that she has easily commanded him to do her will. Next, she asks him to sit beside her on the bench in the forbidden garden nook. Crimsworth responds with passion, and his hopes rise that he and Zoraide might develop a relationship. Unfortunately, a short time later, he overhears the womanizer Pelet walking with Mlle Reuter. She makes light of Crimsworth, and he feels betrayed. As he stares into the garden, the light is extinguished in the garden-house, and he thinks "so, for a time, was my faith in love and friendship" (86). Nevertheless, he later will regain that faith with Frances Henri, who represents a very different garden, one filled with promise.

Similarly, the following paragraph from a paper on the importance of role models to the development of Jane Eyre demonstrates both unity and coherence. In it, the author argues that without such role models, Jane could not have developed a sense of independence and quiet self-confidence.

In the first volume of *Jane Eyre*, Charlotte Brontë depicts Jane as a child desperate for affectionate, trustworthy role models to help her develop the independence and self-confidence she would need in order to survive in harsh surroundings. Her stint at Lowood Institution at first offers little hope of discovery of such figures. She arrives feeling confused and abandoned, confessing that after a few days, "As yet I had spoken to no one, nor did anybody seem to take notice of me" (59). Although she is used to the isolation, the physical trials of insufficient protection from the cold (causing her tiny feet to become inflamed and swollen), the lack of nutritious food, and a stern environment that also freezes and starves the souls of children all challenge her endurance.

Jane wonders how she can survive in such surroundings, particularly after the heartless Mr. Brocklehurst publicly declares her a liar and places her on a stool, exposed "to general view on a pedestal of infamy" (76). However, she meets Helen Burns, a girl criticized even more than Jane, and in observing Helen, Jane learns to tolerate such abuse and not to take it personally. When Jane tells Helen that she believes she should confront those who attack her, Helen responds, "It is not violence that best overcomes hate—nor vengeance that most certainly heals injury" (67). This philosophy, coupled with Helen's many kindnesses and spiritual strength in the face of adversity, teaches Jane to be confident in her own goodness and sense of justice. In turn, Helen worships Lowood's superintendent, Miss Temple, for her compassion and strength to confront Mr. Brocklehurst and occasionally break rules for the benefit of the students. Jane also comes to treasure Miss Temple, particularly after she challenges Mr. Brocklehurst's charge against Jane and announces Jane's innocence to the entire school. Miss Temple moves the ailing Helen into her own quarters to keep her comfortable in her final days.

Although Jane suffers greatly from Helen's death, Miss Temple remains her guide and comfort over the following years, with Jane stating, "her friendship and society had been my continual solace" (92). Upon Miss Temple's departure from the school, Jane stands ready to leave Lowood herself, recognizing that her mind no longer needs "what it had borrowed of Miss Temple" to flourish. She has undergone a change that awakens her own emotion, her own desire to go into the world "to seek real knowledge" (93). She would never have arrived at that promising juncture in life without the assistance of Helen Burns and Miss Temple.

Introductions

Introductions present particular challenges for writers. Generally, your introduction should do two things: capture your reader's attention and explain the main point of your essay. In other words, while your introduction should contain your thesis, it needs to do a bit more work than that. You are likely to find that starting that first paragraph is one of the most difficult parts of the paper. It is hard to face that blank page or screen, and as a result, many beginning writers, in desperation to start somewhere, start with overly broad, general statements. While it is often a good strategy to start with more general subject matter and narrow your focus, do not begin with broad sweeping statements such as Everyone likes to be creative and feel understood. Such sentences are nothing but empty filler. They begin to fill the blank page, but they do nothing to advance your argument. Instead, you should try to gain your readers' interest. Some writers like to begin with a pertinent quotation or with a relevant question. Or, you might begin with an introduction of the topic you will discuss. If you are writing about Brontë's use of role models for Jane Eyre, for instance, you might begin by writing about the fact that everyone benefits from having role models. Another common trap to avoid is depending on your title to introduce the author and the text you are writing about. Always include the work's author and title in your opening paragraph.

Compare the effectiveness of the following introductions.

1) Everyone needs role models in order to learn about their own strengths and talents. We hear that from our parents and counselors all the time: Get a role model. Sometimes it's hard to see how they help us, though. For instance, if I'm not planning to be a teacher, how can a teacher be my role model? Did you ever wonder whether you'll look back on a certain teacher or coach and think about what you learned from them? This happens with Jane Eyre when she learns about herself from first a friend and then a teacher.

2) Most people agree with the line from Shakespeare's *Hamlet*, "to thine own self be true." However, humans are not born knowing themselves. They often need role models who can teach them about life and how to deal with its challenges in order to recognize their own personal strengths. By watching and even imitating those we love and respect, we are able to practice sound life skills. Then when the time comes for us to separate from those models and confront life's challenges on our own, we have developed a keen sense of our own capacity to handle conflict. We have also learned to recognize our talents and skills through the encouragement of our role models, allowing us to step out of the confinement of our childhood and seek whatever knowledge life offers to us. In Charlotte Brontë's *Jane Eyre*, young Jane will do just that, empowered by the influence of a lost friend from her youth and by one very special teacher.

The first introduction begins with a vague, overly broad sentence; cites unclear, undeveloped examples; and then moves abruptly to the thesis. Notice, too, how a reader deprived of the paper's title does not know the title of the story that the paper will analyze. The second introduction works with the same material and thesis but provides more detail and is consequently much more interesting. It begins by offering an easily recognized quotation, discussing the widely accepted value of role models, and giving specific examples of the positive results of role modeling. The paragraph ends with the thesis, which includes both the author and the title of the work to be discussed.

The paragraph below provides another example of an opening strategy. It begins by introducing the author and the text it will analyze, and then it moves on by briefly introducing relevant details of the story in order to set up its thesis.

> Charlotte Brontë makes powerful use of the traditional symbol of the garden in her posthumously published novel *The Professor* (1857). Garden imagery reflects the developing attitudes held by the novel's protagonist, William Crimsworth, regarding women and romance. The garden has long been symbolic of women, suggesting beauty and life, but also representing temptation and danger. This dichotomy is suggested through the types of gardens associated with the novel's most prominent female characters, the confident schoolmistress, Mlle Zoraïde Reuter, and the hesitant foreign teacher turned student, Frances Henri. Mlle Reuter represents a cultured domestic flower, at home in her perfectly tended and controlled garden. In contrast, Frances Henri suggests a wildflower, willful and independent and determined to bloom and mature even in foreign surroundings. Crimsworth's realization that his future happiness lies with Frances develops through his exposure to both women and to the gardens they inhabit.

Conclusions

Conclusions present another series of challenges for writers. No doubt you have heard the old adage about writing papers: "Tell us what you are going to say, say it, and then tell us what you've said." While this formula does not necessarily result in bad papers, it does not often result in good ones, either. It will almost certainly result in boring papers (especially boring conclusions). If you have done a good job establishing your points in the body of the paper, the reader already knows and understands your argument. There is no need to merely reiterate. Do not just summarize your main points in your conclusion. Such a boring and mechanical conclusion does nothing to advance your argument or interest your reader. Consider the following conclusion to the paper about the importance of role models in *Jane Eyre*.

> To conclude, Jane discovers the importance of role models. Even though she won't have a great life for a while, at least she is able to stand up to all the abuse. After all the harshness of the school, I guess she learned that things could be worse. That's a lesson we all could use, as we face so many problems everyday.

Besides starting with a mechanical transitional device, this conclusion does little more than summarize the main points of the outline (and it does not even touch on all of them). It is incomplete and uninteresting (and a little too depressing).

Instead, your conclusion should add something to your paper. A good tactic is to build upon the points you have been arguing. Asking "why?" often helps you draw further conclusions. For example, in the paper on *Jane Eyre*, you might speculate or explain how Jane's experience speaks to what Brontë wants to suggest about individual survival in an often uncaring world. Another method for successfully concluding a paper is to speculate on other directions in which to take your topic by tying it into larger issues. You might do this by envisioning your paper as just one section of a larger paper. Having established your points in this paper, how would you build upon this argument? Where would you go next? In the following conclusion to the paper on *Jane Eyre*, the author reiterates some of the main points but does so in order to amplify the discussion of the story's central message and to connect it to other texts by Charlotte Brontë:

> Jane Eyre learns much from her role models, mainly how to survive within a system controlled by others.

Helen and Miss Temple exemplify self-control but also ingenuity and the ability to focus on goals as a life skill. Like other Charlotte Brontë heroines, including Lucy in *Villette*, Jane will find a way to express her independence in a world that does not welcome intelligence and creativity on the part of women. The significance of her role models is not in their creating an imitative robot out of Jane, but rather in their empowering her to tap into her own survival instincts and utilize talents that others might not encourage. Discovering the world to be an often cold and unwelcoming place proves an uncomfortable lesson; however, Jane's teachers offer additional lessons that will allow her to find success beyond the walls of Lowood Institution.

Similarly, in the following conclusion to a paper on the importance of garden symbolism in *The Professor*, the author draws an inference about the use of traditional symbols in nontraditional ways.

At last, Crimsworth found a woman he could not only love but also admire and trust. Frances offered far more than the traditional passion that Crimsworth first felt with Zoraïde Reuter in her garden. He discovered that, while beautiful and tempting, the Mlle's garden was dangerous in its controlled atmosphere, threatening to overshadow and ensnare him into a dangerous dependency. In contrast, Frances offered the promise of discovery and individuality; her association with natural gardens promised a nontraditional relationship, supported more by intellect and a desire for equality than containment and control. Like most people, Crimsworth found himself attracted at first to an image of beauty and desire, but then he discovered the image to be only that: a carefully arranged and orchestrated presentation designed to disillusion the viewer. Brontë's skill in employing garden imagery to represent her protagonist's conflict confirms her status as one of 19th-century England's most gifted authors.

Citations and Formatting

Using Primary Sources

As the examples included in this chapter indicate, strong papers on literary texts incorporate quotations from the text in order to support their points. It is not enough for you to assert your interpretation without providing support or evidence from the text. Without well-chosen quotations to support your argument, you are, in effect, saying to the reader, "Take my word for it." It is important to use quotations thoughtfully and selectively. Remember that the paper presents *your* argument, so choose quotations that support *your* assertions. Do not let the author's voice overwhelm your own. With that caution in mind, there are some guidelines you should follow to ensure that you use quotations clearly and effectively.

Integrate Quotations:

Quotations should always be integrated into your own prose. Do not just drop them into your paper without introduction or comment. Otherwise, it is unlikely that your reader will see their function. You can integrate textual support easily and clearly with identifying tags, short phrases that identify the speaker. For example:

> Crimsworth thinks, "I shall now at last see the mysterious garden."

While this tag appears before the quotation, you can also use tags after or in the middle of the quoted text, as the following examples demonstrate:

> "It is my garden," Mlle Reuter tells Crimsworth, "which makes me retain this house, otherwise I should probably have removed to larger and more commodious premises."

> After viewing the garden, which Crimsworth judges as "pleasant, very pleasant," he then turns his gaze

```
"back on herself," clearly identifying the garden with
Mlle Reuter.
```

You can also use a colon to formally introduce a quotation:

```
Crimsworth's change from viewing the garden as a place
of romance to one of possible disease is clear in his
comment to Mlle Reuter: "I hope that you took no cold
last night in consequence of your late walk in the
garden."
```

When you quote brief sections of poems (three lines or fewer), use slash marks to indicate the line breaks in the poem:

```
As the poem ends, Dickinson speaks of the power of the
imagination: "The revery alone will do, / If bees are
few."
```

Longer quotations (more than four lines of prose or three lines of poetry) should be set off from the rest of your paper in a block quotation. Double-space before you begin the passage, indent it 10 spaces from your left-hand margin, and double-space the passage itself. Because the indentation signals the inclusion of a quotation, do not use quotation marks around the cited passage. Use a colon to introduce the passage:

```
Crimsworth's change in his view of a garden is revealed
in his thoughts about the development of Frances's
intellectual capacity:
```

```
    To speak truth, I watched this change much as
    a gardener watches the growth of a precious
    plant, and I contributed to it too, even as the
    said gardener contributes to the development
    of his favourite. To me it was not difficult to
    discover how I could best foster my pupil, cherish
    her starved feelings, and induce the outward
```

manifestation of that inward vigour which sunless
drought and blighting blast had hitherto forbidden
to expand.

At this point, the reader easily observes the use of
the garden imagery as a metaphor for the change in
Crimsworth's attitude.

The whole of Dickinson's poem speaks of the
imagination:

To make a prairie it takes a clover and one bee,
One clover, and a bee,
And revery.
The revery alone will do,
If bees are few.

Clearly, she argues for the creative power of the mind.

It is also important to interpret quotations after you introduce them
and explain how they help advance your point. You cannot assume that
your reader will interpret the quotations the same way that you do.

Quote Accurately:

Always quote accurately. Anything within quotation marks must be the
author's exact words. There are, however, some rules to follow if you need
to modify the quotation to fit into your prose.

1. Use brackets to indicate any material that might have been
   added to the author's exact wording. For example, if you need
   to add any words to the quotation or alter it grammatically
   to allow it to fit into your prose, indicate your changes in
   brackets:

   At this moment, Crimsworth remains focused on
   the garden as representing the traditional view
   of love. He thinks, "It seem[s] as if the romantic

```
visions my imagination had suggested of this
garden, while it was yet hidden from me by the
jealous boards, [are] more than realized."
```

2. Conversely, if you choose to omit any words from the quotation, use ellipses (three spaced periods) to indicate missing words or phrases:

```
In this scene, Crimsworth thinks, "It seem[s]
as if the romantic visions my imagination had
suggested of this garden  . . . [are] more than
realized."
```

3. If you delete a sentence or more, use the ellipses after a period:

```
Crimsworth tells his readers, "In another minute
I and the directress were walking side by side
down the alley bordered with fruit-trees. . . .
Released from the stifling class, surrounded
with flowers and foliage, with a pleasing,
smiling, affable woman at my side, how did I
feel? Why, very enviably."
```

4. If you omit a line or more of poetry, or more than one paragraph of prose, use a single line of spaced periods to indicate the omission:

```
To make a prairie it takes a clover and one bee,
. . . . . . . . . . . . . .
And revery.
The revery alone will do,
If bees are few.
```

Punctuate Properly:

Punctuation of quotations often causes more trouble than it should. Once again, you just need to keep these simple rules in mind.

1. Periods and commas should be placed inside quotation marks, even if they are not part of the original quotation:

   > Crimsworth's negative feelings are strongly associated with the garden-house: "I perceived that its solitary light was at length extinguished; so, for a time, was my faith in love and friendship."

   The only exception to this rule is when the quotation is followed by a parenthetical reference. In this case, the period or comma goes after the citation (more on these later in this chapter):

   > Crimsworth's negative feelings are strongly associated with the garden-house: "I perceived that its solitary light was at length extinguished; so, for a time, was my faith in love and friendship" (86).

2. Other marks of punctuation—colons, semicolons, question marks, and exclamation points—go outside the quotation marks unless they are part of the original quotation:

   > Why is it important that Crimsworth "opened the often-mentioned boarded window"?

   > Crimsworth specifically asks his audience: "How did I feel?"

Documenting Primary Sources

Unless you are instructed otherwise, you should provide sufficient information for your reader to locate material you quote. Generally, literature papers follow the rules set forth by the Modern Language Association (MLA). These can be found in the *MLA Handbook for Writers of Research Papers* (sixth edition). You should be able to find this book in the reference section of your library. Additionally, its rules for citing both primary and secondary sources are widely available from reputable online sources. One of these is the Online Writing Lab (OWL) at Purdue University. OWL's guide to MLA style is available at http://owl.english.purdue.edu/owl/resource/557/01/. The Modern Language Association also offers answers to frequently asked questions about MLA style on this helpful Web page: http://www.mla.org/style_faq. Generally, when you are citing from literary works in papers, you should keep a few guidelines in mind.

Parenthetical Citations:

MLA asks for parenthetical references in your text after quotations. When you are working with prose (short stories, novels, or essays) include page numbers in the parentheses:

```
Crimsworth's change from viewing the garden as a place
of romance to one of possible disease is clear in his
comment to Mlle Reuter: "I hope that you took no cold
last night in consequence of your late walk in the
garden" (88).
```

When you are quoting poetry, include line numbers:

```
Dickinson's speaker tells of the arrival of a fly: "There
interposed a Fly— / With Blue—uncertain stumbling Buzz—
/ Between the light—and Me—" (12-14).
```

Works Cited Page:

These parenthetical citations are linked to a separate works cited page at the end of the paper. The works cited page lists works alphabetically by the authors' last name. An entry for the above reference to Brontë's *The Professor* would read:

```
Brontë, Charlotte. The Professor. Hertfordshire, England:
Wordsworth Editions, 1994.
```

The *MLA Handbook* includes a full listing of sample entries, as do many of the online explanations of MLA style.

Documenting Secondary Sources

To ensure that your paper is built entirely upon your own ideas and analysis, instructors often ask that you write interpretative papers without any outside research. If, on the other hand, your paper requires research, you must document any secondary sources you use. You need to document direct quotations, summaries or paraphrases of others' ideas, and factual information that is not common knowledge. Follow the guidelines above for quoting primary sources when you use direct quotations from secondary sources. Keep in mind that MLA style also includes specific guidelines for citing electronic sources. OWL's Web site provides a good summary: http://owl.english.purdue.edu/owl/resource/557/09/.

Parenthetical Citations:

As with the documentation of primary sources, described above, MLA guidelines require in-text parenthetical references to your secondary sources. Unlike the research papers you might write for a history class, literary research papers following MLA style do not use footnotes as a means of documenting sources. Instead, after a quotation, you should cite the author's last name and the page number:

> "*Jane Eyre* is enshrined in the canon as a sublime exemplification of the Romantic and feminist imagination" (Searle 36).

If you include the name of the author in your prose, then you would include only the page number in your citation. For example:

> According to Alice Searle, "*Jane Eyre* is enshrined in the canon as a sublime exemplification of the Romantic and feminist imagination" (36).

If you are including more than one work by the same author, the parenthetical citation should include a shortened yet identifiable version of the title in order to indicate which of the author's works you cite. For example:

> Sandra Gilbert writes, "Helen Burns, Miss Temple's other disciple, presents a different but equally impossible ideal to Jane" ("Plain Jane's" 481).

Similarly, and just as important, if you summarize or paraphrase the particular ideas of your source, you must provide documentation:

> *Jane Eyre* demonstrates how the biblical concept of hope supports use of the imagination (Searle 36).

Works Cited Page:

Like the primary sources discussed above, the parenthetical references to secondary sources are keyed to a separate works cited page at the end of your paper. Here is an example of a works cited page that uses the examples cited above. Note that when two or more works by the same author are listed, you should use three hypens followed by a period in the subsequent entries. You can find a complete list of sample entries in the *MLA Handbook* or from a reputable online summary of MLA style.

WORKS CITED

Gilbert, Sandra. *The Madwoman in the Attic.* New Haven: Yale, 1979.

——. "Plain Jane's Progress." *Jane Eyre by Charlotte Brontë.* Ed. Beth Newman. Boston: Bedford Books of St. Martin's Press. 475–501.

Searle, Alice. "An Idolatrous Imagination? Biblical Theology and Romanticism in Charlotte Brontë's *Jane Eyre.*" *Christianity and Literature.* 56.1 (Autumn 2006): 35–61.

Plagiarism

Failure to document carefully and thoroughly can leave you open to charges of stealing the ideas of others, which is known as plagiarism, and this is a very serious matter. Remember that it is important to include quotation marks when you use language from your source, even if you use just one or two words. For example, if you wrote, Helen Burns, Miss Temple's other disciple, presents a different but equally impossible ideal to Jane, you would be guilty of plagiarism, since you used Gilbert's distinct language without acknowledging her as the source. Instead, you should write: Miss Temple represents an "impossible ideal" for Jane, as does Helen, her "disciple" (Gilbert 481). In this case, you have properly credited Gilbert.

Similarly, neither summarizing the ideas of an author nor changing or omitting just a few words means that you can omit a citation. Beth Newman's article "A Critical History" contains the following passage about Brontë's publication of the novel:

> "Reviewers were struck by its refreshing unconven-tionalities, by its departure from the formulas of much other contemporary fiction, and by the new, different, and powerful voice of its author" (445).

Below are two examples of plagiarized passages:

> Reviewers found the novel to be invigorating and not conventional, and they praised its lack of the predictable approaches of other fiction of the day, as well as Brontë's original, interesting, and authoritative expression.

> Those who reviewed the novel liked its refreshing unconventional approach, as well as its difference when compared to much other contemporary fiction, and also the author's new and powerful voice (Newman 445).

While the first passage does not use Newman's exact language, it does contain the same ideas she proposes without citing her work. Since this description is Newman's distinct idea, this constitutes plagiarism. The second passage has changed some wording and included a citation, but some of the phrasing is Newman's. The first passage could be fixed with a parenthetical citation. Because some of the wording in the second remains the same, though, it would require the use of quotation marks, in addition to a parenthetical citation. The passage below represents an honestly and adequately documented use of the original passage:

> "Reviewers were struck by its refreshing unconven-tionalities, by its departure from the formulas of much

other contemporary fiction, and by the new, different, and powerful voice of its author" (445).

When *Jane Eyre* was published, it received positive reviews. Some reviewers admired the novel's "refreshing unconventionalities," while others enjoyed its variance from the plot and styles of "much other contemporary fiction," praising the unknown author's "powerful voice" (Newman 445).

This passage acknowledges that the interpretation is derived from Newman while appropriately using quotations to indicate her precise language.

While it is not necessary to document well-known facts, often referred to as "common knowledge," any ideas or language that you take from someone else must be properly documented. Common knowledge generally includes the birth and death dates of authors or other well-documented facts of their lives. An often-cited guideline is that if you can find the information in three sources, it is common knowledge. Despite this guideline, it is, admittedly, often difficult to know if the facts you uncover are common knowledge or not. When in doubt, document your source.

Sample Essay

GARDEN IMAGERY TELLS THE STORY IN *THE PROFESSOR*

Charlotte Brontë makes powerful use of the traditional symbol of the garden in her posthumously published novel *The Professor* (1857). Garden imagery reflects development of the attitude toward women and romance held by the novel's protagonist, William Crimsworth. The garden has long been symbolic of women, suggesting beauty and life but also representing temptation and danger. This dichotomy is suggested through the types of gardens associated with the novel's most prominent female characters, the confident schoolmistress, Mlle Zoraïde Reuter, and the hesitant foreign student, Frances Henri. Mlle Reuter represents a cultured domestic flower, at home in her perfectly tended and controlled garden. In contrast, Frances Henri suggests a wildflower, willful and independent and determined to bloom and mature even in foreign surroundings. Crimsworth's realization that his future happiness lies with Frances develops through his exposure to both women and to the gardens they inhabit.

Crimsworth first learns about Mlle Reuter from his landlord, Monsieur Pelet, and from her mother. An Englishman who has relocated to Belgium, he has been teaching in a boys' school opposite the girls' school that Mlle Reuter operates and where he also hopes to teach. Like Mlle Reuter's beautiful garden, she appears mysterious and remote to Crimsworth. After arranging to meet her and interview for a teaching position, Crimsworth looks at the boarded window in his room and thinks, "I shall now at last see the mysterious garden. I shall gaze both on the angels and their Eden" (57). The boarded window represents a safe barrier that has thus far protected Crimsworth. When he moves beyond its protection to enter Mlle Reuter's garden, he places himself in temptation's way, as signaled by the reference to the Garden of Eden. However, he remains oblivious of any danger and later exults in his "first glimpse of the garden" (58), after which he meets the fabled Zoraïde Reuter. When she finds him staring out of a "crimson curtain" framed window, trimmed by ivy with "some trendrils of vine . . . trained," admiring the garden, she announces "It is my garden, monsieur, which makes me retain this house" (59). She also assures him that she and, by extension, he could not find a more pleasant garden anywhere in town. The crimson color of the curtain symbolizes passion and also hints at the fact that the garden hides various secrets, while the tendrils trained to vine around the window signal that the garden, like all other living creatures that surround Zoraïde Reuter, do her bidding.

Invited to lean out the window to better enjoy the view, Crimsworth notes how "very pleasant" the garden appears, but he immediately shifts his gaze to Zoraïde Reuter, thinking, "when I had taken a view of her well-trimmed beds and budding shrubberies, I allowed my glance to come back to herself, nor did I hastily withdraw it" (60). While not a beautiful woman, the Mlle has an allure that Crimsworth compares to "the bloom on a good apple," on one "as sound at the core as it is red on the rind" (60). At this point, Brontë has clearly connected Mlle Reuter to the Garden of Eden, in which Adam lost everything to Eve's temptation. The suggestion remains clear that Crimsworth may also fall victim to the temptation of this modern version of Eve. Even when her talk turns to business and she presents the fact with a practicality and disinterestedness that should have alerted Crimsworth, he remains romantically drawn to her. He explains his attraction to the reader with foreshadowing when he remarks, "So impressionable a being is man" (61).

Crimsworth soon experiences her close scrutiny of everything and everyone connected with her school, particularly her most recently hired professor:

> She was searching for salient points, and weak points, and eccentric points. She was applying now this test, now that, hoping in the end to find some chink, some niche where she could put in her little firm foot and stand upon my neck, mistress of my nature. (68)

While Crimsworth states that the Mlle wishes to gain "no amorous influence" (68), he clearly does not believe this himself. He later is commanded to go into the garden and looks back at her, as if bidding her to follow. He tells his audience that "it seemed as if the romantic visions my imagination had suggested of this garden" (82) were coming true, and as the Mlle joined him to sit in a niche on a chair, "a revelation dawned" on him that he "was on the brink of falling in love" (83). Unfortunately, as he later leans out of his window, observing a "most-sheltered nook" where the flowers and lilacs grew thick, "its shrubs screen[ing] the garden-chair" (83) he had shared with the Mlle, he observes her arm-in-arm with Pelet, his landlord. He overhears a decidedly romantic conversation, in which marriage seems to be discussed. Pelet scolds her for enticing "that schoolboy Crimsworth" and says that Crimsworth has become infatuated with her. She laughs and explains that "Crimsworth could not bear comparison with you either physically or mentally. . . . Some may call him gentlemanlike and intelligent-looking, but for my part . . ." (85–86). As her voice fades, Crimsworth notes that the light in the garden-house is extinguished and thinks, "so, for a time, was my faith in love and friendship" (86). His hopes for romance crushed, he no longer views the garden as beautiful, nor Mlle Reuter as desirable.

When Crimsworth first meets Frances Henri, he reserves judgment about her. Hired to teach in Mlle Reuter's establishment, she has problems communicating in English. Raised in Switzerland with a Swiss father and English mother, she has, as the cynical Mlle Reuter describes it, "inevitable deficiencies" and "backwardness" (90). Crimsworth observes that Frances possesses little confidence in her abilities, appears shy and withdrawn, and speaks only hesitantly. He soon discovers much to admire in her creativity and intelligence and begins to encourage her. Once again, Brontë introduces traditional flower and garden imagery, this time to represent Frances. Under Crimsworth's tutelage, Frances has changed, having lost her "sunless" expression and enjoying a "bloom" of "clearness of skin" (116). Her movements evince "lightness and freedom" that "correspond with [Crimsworth's] idea of grace" (116). Suddenly he becomes a gardener, noting, "I watched this change much as a gardener watches the growth of a precious plant" (116), delighted that Frances has responded to "the benefits" of his "system" (117). At once the reader understands that Crimsworth has found a new garden, and in the fertile soil of praise and encouragement, Frances has matured like a well-tended rose. He begins to fall in love, not with any traditional romantic aspects of Frances, but with her courage and intelligence. He finds himself learning from her, as she learns from him.

When Frances disappears from the school for a time, Crimsworth fears that Mlle Reuter has dismissed her. He confronts the Mlle as he walks with her, and they approach "the garden-chair" (122). This time, when she beckons him to join her, he will not, instead simply resting one knee on the chair and leaning against "a huge laburnum" (122) covered with golden flowers. Crimsworth has become a part of the garden, while Mlle Reuter, who would rather command the orderly garden scene, remains literally beneath him. In this scene, he shows he has mastered this minutely detailed garden and its controlling mistress, and he moves on to find Frances. After a month's separation, he locates her in a cemetery, mourning the loss of her aunt. The cemetery is bordered by a "thickly planted nursery of yew and cypress," some of its graves covered by "a brilliant thicket of roses," and Frances sits on a garden bench in a sheltered nook (130–31). Much of this imagery is reminiscent of the place that Crimsworth had briefly shared with Mlle Reuter, when he falsely believed himself to be falling in love. This time, there is no doubt that he has found his future wife, and a short time later he declares his feelings for Frances. The garden imagery continues as the two find a long and happy life together. Frances is framed in a Belgian "wild garden nook" (197) following their marriage. When they move to England, the English garden at their home is "full of its own peculiar flowers" (205), so different from the carefully cultured flowers in Mlle Reuter's garden, but so like Frances. In a final use of garden imagery, Brontë equates Frances to a garden when Crimsworth says of his wife that "these flowers were still there, preserved pure and dewy under the umbrage of later growth and hardier nature" (199).

At last, Crimsworth finds a woman he can not only love but also admire and trust. Frances offers far more than the traditional passion that Crimsworth first felt with Zoraïde Reuter in her garden. He discovers that while beautiful and tempting, the Mlle's garden was dangerous in its controlled atmosphere, threatening to overshadow and ensnare him into a dangerous dependency. In contrast, Frances offers the promise of discovery and individuality, her association with natural gardens promising a nontraditional relationship, supported more by intellect and a desire for equality than containment and control. Like most people, Crimsworth found himself attracted at first to an image of beauty and desire, but then he discovers the image to be only that: a carefully arranged and orchestrated presentation designed to disillusion the viewer. Brontë's skill in employing garden imagery to represent her protagonist's conflict confirms her status as one of 19th-century England's most gifted authors.

Works Cited

Brontë, Charlotte. *The Professor*. Hertfordshire, England: Wordsworth Editions, 1994.

Starzyk, Lawrence. "Charlotte Brontë's *The Professor*: The Appropriation of Images." *Journal of Narrative Theory* 33.2 (Summer 2003): 143–162.

HOW TO WRITE ABOUT
THE BRONTËS

AN OVERVIEW

CHARLOTTE, ANNE, and Emily Brontë were born in Thornton, York-shire, and grew up in the early 19th century in the parsonage of nearby Haworth, near Bradford. Their family included one brother, Branwell; two older sisters, Maria and Elizabeth; their mother, Maria; and their father, Reverend Patrick Brontë. Following Charlotte's birth, Branwell, Emily, and Anne arrived in quick succession. Friends exclaimed over the close relationship between Emily and Anne, who were compared to twins, and both girls involved Branwell in their early dramas and fantasies. The many deaths that touched the Brontës probably informed the writing siblings' attitudes toward family and mortality in their novels.

Patrick wanted an education for all of his children, which proved to be a blessing, as girls of that era could not always count on receiving any schooling. Education often occupies a major focus in the Brontës' novels, through the use of schools and classrooms as settings and the vocation of governess and/or teacher for multiple characters. Charlotte and Emily were enrolled along with their two elder sisters, Maria and Elizabeth, in a school named Cowan Bridge. Tragically, Maria and Elizabeth became ill and returned home to die a short time later. That experience would prove crucial to Charlotte's first novel, *Jane Eyre*.

Charlotte and Emily were brought home to the parsonage and schooled for several years by Elizabeth Branwell, an aunt who had moved in to help raise the children after their mother's death four years earlier in 1821. Imaginative children, the four remaining siblings constructed stories and poetry—particularly their sagas about the imaginary kingdom of Angria and the world of Gondal—that foreshadowed the sisters' later output of literature. Their combined novels were among the few written by women to be accepted in the canon (literature approved for study in academia) prior to the 20th century. Because their works contain strongly autobiographical themes, understanding the lives of each of the three writing sisters will enhance any discussion of their literary output.

Charlotte Brontë

In adulthood, Charlotte Brontë (1816–55) proved to be the sister most willing to act as an advocate for her and her sisters when seeking publication of their poetry and novels. While attending Cowan Bridge school, she suffered from a strict discipline that involved withholding food and warm clothing from the students. She later fashioned the despicable Lowood school in *Jane Eyre* on her experiences at Cowan Bridge and based the character of Helen Burns on her sister Maria, whom she felt had been treated with unusual cruelty. An intelligent girl, Charlotte had an especially sharp memory and learned languages easily, winning a prize for French literature while later attending Roe Head School. Known for her lively imagination, she was said to have terrified the other students with her late-night tales. She worked with Branwell to write the Angria saga, stories filled with memorable heroes and heroines.

After remaining at home for three years, Charlotte later returned to Roe Head as a teacher, bringing Emily with her as a pupil. She eventually sent samples of her poetry to poet laureate Robert Southey, a member of the Lake School of romantic poets, a group of writers that had an extreme influence on all the sisters' writing, especially that of Emily. He admired Charlotte's work but cautioned her against setting her sights on a career in literature, as that was an unfitting pursuit for a woman. Such an admonition probably helped shape the character of Jane Eyre, whose defining creative outlet is art, rather than literature.

During the period prior to her writing success, Charlotte suffered doubts and feared death, due to what she perceived as her lack of holiness. She became very strongly attached to her good friend, the highly spiritual Ellen Nussey, and hated for the two to be separated. Some of Charlotte's doubts and questioning of spiritual matters can be seen in *Jane Eyre*. However, Jane never suffered the breakdown that caused

Charlotte to leave Roe Head and return home to recover. She detested her tendency toward depression, but did not know how to remedy it.

A marriage proposal from Ellen's brother, Reverend Henry Nussey, would also be reflected in *Jane Eyre* in St. John's proposal to Jane. Henry admitted that he should marry a pious, religious woman, not a romantic, imaginative personality like Charlotte. She did not accept that proposal, nor another by Reverend David Pryce, a man she had only met once. A frequent visitor to the parsonage, Reverend William Wightman, helped raise Charlotte's spirits, which could be quite buoyant, proving she did not possess a depressive personality. She later suffered greatly over William's early death, one of many in her close circle.

Charlotte eventually traveled to Brussels with her father and Emily to attend school and later to teach English. Emily taught music, and both girls earned their room and board as instructors. Charlotte became enthralled with Constantin Heger, husband of the school's mistress. She later based events in her novels *The Professor* and *Villette* on that period of her life.

Following their aunt's death, the sisters used their inheritance to open a school, but it failed. After Emily's poetry was discovered in 1846, Charlotte paid to have their poetry published under the pseudonyms of Currer, Ellis, and Acton Bell and began to prepare three of their novels, *The Professor, Agnes Grey*, and *Wuthering Heights*, for publication. Rejection of *The Professor* prompted Charlotte to begin work on her masterpiece, *Jane Eyre*. In 1847, her sisters' novels were accepted by Smith, Elder and Company, encouraging Charlotte to complete *Jane Eyre*. It was accepted immediately by George Smith and published in 1847.

Charlotte next set to work on *Shirley*, but her writing was marked by grief over the quick successive loss of all three of her siblings. Branwell succumbed in September 1848 to tuberculosis exacerbated by intense alcoholism and drug usage following a long and nightmarish decline witnessed by the entire family. He was followed a few months later by Emily, who died from tuberculosis as Anne also lay seriously ill. With the help of Ellen Nussey, Charlotte took Anne to Scarborough in hope of finding a cure, but Anne died there in May 1849, also from tuberculosis.

Wracked with grief, Charlotte returned to work on *Shirley*, which was published in October 1849. The last portion of the novel reflected her losses and caused later critics to remark on its harmful effect on the plot. In 1850, she reissued the novels by her sisters, except for Anne's *The Tenant of Wildfell Hall,* a story of a woman who takes her son and flees the abuse of her alcoholic and womanizing husband. Charlotte publicly stated that she felt the novel to be a mistake and not in tune with Anne's character. Critics have suggested the true reason was probably its association with the debilitation of Branwell, at one time Charlotte's best friend and confidant. She eventually enjoyed later visits to London and experienced additional romantic attachments, including a close friendship with George Smith. After the publication of *Villette* in 1853, her relationship with Smith cooled as he recognized himself and his mother in the characters of John Bretton and Mrs. Bretton.

Charlotte returned home to receive a proposal from Reverend A. B. Nicholls, which she at first refused, due to her father's violent reaction to the idea of her marrying and leaving him alone. She later accepted Nicholls, despite his lack of intellectual refinement. She confided to others that her affinity for Nicholls was based on his good nature and his obvious love for her. They married in 1854 and by all reports enjoyed a happy, if brief, life together. Ill during pregnancy, Charlotte died at the end of her first trimester in 1855.

Emily Brontë

Emily Brontë (1818–48) has long offered biographers a challenge, as they can base their writings only on fragments of "Diary Papers" that she coauthored with Anne, a few brief statements by her friends and family, her own poetry, and Charlotte's famous preface to the second edition of *Wuthering Heights.* That preface had the editorial intent of convincing a Victorian reading audience that, despite the shocking content of her sister's novel, Emily was not a rebel against society, but rather a romantic. While she possessed great physical strength, she also had "retiring manners and habits," according to Charlotte. Later biographers reluctantly followed Charlotte's lead, as it was the only substantial statement about Emily that existed.

The fifth of the six Brontë children, Emily lived all except her first two years at Haworth, suffering the early death of her mother but otherwise enjoying what appeared to be a fairly normal childhood. With her siblings as playmates and fellow fantasy aficionados, Emily early on found an outlet for her imagination. Especially close to her younger sister, Anne, her coauthor of the Gondal saga, she also interacted closely with Charlotte and with her brother, Branwell. She spent much time playing on the moors, once experiencing a dangerous and dramatic storm during which a 7-foot-high roiling mixture of mud, peat, and water roared through the valley. Her fascination with the awe-inspiring powers of nature and with the moors would greatly inform her only novel. As a child, she was educated by her father and Charlotte and, like the other children, given free access to her father's impressive library. Acutely reserved, Emily preferred to be alone much of the time, and her self-imposed isolation became a repeated theme in her lyric poetry. She attended school briefly, first at Cowan Bridge, where her two eldest sisters, Elizabeth and Maria, became ill and subsequently died, and then at Roe Head, where, as Charlotte described it, she was afflicted with acute homesickness. She longed to return to Haworth and the moors, where she might preserve her privacy. After only three months at Roe Head, she gained her wish, and Anne took her place at the school.

At age 20, Emily became a teacher at Miss Patchett's school at Law Hill, Halifax, despite Charlotte warning her against the long hours, lack of exercise, and poor diet that characterized such positions. Emily faced the challenges, managing to produce poetry while teaching 40 pupils. The Law Hill area contributed greatly to Emily's creative output, and her students were said to have liked her, although Emily told them frankly that she liked the dog more than them. When she returned for a second term, her health deteriorated, as did her creative output, and by March 1839 she was again home at Haworth. She continued studying Latin with her father and worked on translations of Virgil's *Aeneid* and Horace's *Ars Poetica.* Two years later, she joined Anne and Charlotte in an unsuccessful attempt to found their own school.

Emily continued drawing and studying works about nature, such as Thomas Bewick's *History of British Birds,* a favorite book of Jane's in Charlotte's *Jane Eyre.* Emily also studied works featuring the romantic poets, such as Thomas Moore's *Life of Byron.* Both her novel and her poetry bear traces of the romantics' influence, as well as that of the metaphysical poets. She spent one year in Brussels with Charlotte, a period that greatly influenced her intellectual development. She studied hard, particularly French, but did not get along with the master, M. Heger. However, she seemed to benefit from their interactions, discovering her argument for distrust of society and the destructive effects of nature that would strongly inform *Wuthering Heights.* As noted in Elizabeth Gaskell's *The Life of Charlotte Brontë,* Heger later wrote about Emily that "she should have been a man—a great navigator," praising her "powerful reason" and "her strong, imperious will." She continued her quiet revolution against society, at times refusing to speak or conform to fashion dictates, despite Charlotte's urging. Each sister inherited money from their Aunt Branwell upon her death, which allowed Emily to return home and to remain there, willingly shouldering various domestic duties and learning to shoot a pistol.

In 1844, Emily began composing two poetry notebooks, one filled with lyrics and the other with poetry that accompanied the Gondal stories. In 1845, she and Anne impersonated characters from the Gondal saga while on a train trip, but Anne indicated that such girlish activity held less attraction for her. The two did not share their former intense intimacy, partly because Emily saw little value in Anne's strong Christian beliefs. She viewed a relationship with God as a private matter, and her scorn for human creeds became obvious in her poetry.

Following Charlotte's discovery of Emily's poetry, she allowed selections to be published along with Anne's and her own poems. The publication proved a failure in terms of sales but introduced the sisters to the publishing world. Although the exact dates of the time Emily spent writing *Wuthering Heights* are not known, it was published in 1847 by Thomas Cautley Newby along with Anne's novel *Agnes Grey.* Newby waited until *Jane Eyre* enjoyed great success, hoping to confuse the public into believing the author of that novel had contributed to the later volumes. Emily became bitter over Charlotte's revealing the true identities behind the sisters' pseudonyms, and her sister later regretted telling the world that Ellis Bell was actually Emily Brontë. Despite some negative reviews at the time of publication, *Wuthering Heights* has remained in print, and it became a crucial part of the canon of English literature long before women authors were recently included.

An uncompromising personality, Emily expressed the belief that individuals must bear responsibility for their own actions. She had been honest with her brother, telling him early on that he was destined to become an unpleasant man. She did not grieve as her sisters did during Branwell's self-destructive use of alcohol and drugs, although she mourned his death in 1848. She still insisted on her own personal freedom even as she grew weaker from a tuberculosis infection, refusing treatment despite her sisters' dismay. She took no medicines and accepted her fate, agreeing to see a physician only a few hours before her death in 1848 at 30 years of age.

Anne Brontë

Anne Brontë (1820–49) was the youngest of the six Brontë children and described as having quite a different appearance from her siblings. Some believed her to be the prettiest, and her light brown curls and slender neck were remarked upon. The deaths at school of her sisters Maria and Elizabeth and Anne's delicacy and propensity for illness probably contributed to the decision to school her at home. Her aunt and father gave her lessons until 1832, when older sister Charlotte assumed responsibility for educating both Anne and her "twin" sister Emily.

Like Emily, Anne loved animals. That fact probably contributed to the violent reaction of her governess character Agnes Grey in the novel of that title to the cruelty to animals displayed by one of her young charges. Also like her sisters, Anne had an acute awareness of and appreciation for nature and included exquisitely detailed outdoor scenes in her novels. Along with Emily, she wrote as a child about the fantasy world of Gondal; 23 poems by Anne based on that saga exist.

At age 15, Anne enrolled in school, taking the ill Emily's place at Roe Head and joining Charlotte there. Like her sisters, she was determined to one day earn her own living, and thus she became a strong and serious student, receiving a prize for good conduct presented "lovingly" from her instructor, Miss Wooler. Not much else is known of Anne's time spent at Roe Head, other than an illness that greatly alarmed Charlotte but Miss Wooler judged as minor. Charlotte engaged Miss Wooler in a quarrel that led the teacher to write to Reverend Brontë, who called his daughters home the following day. Before leaving Roe Head, Anne's illness occasioned the visit of the Moravian bishop Reverend James La Trobe. He shared with Anne the Moravian doctrine of universal salvation, which became part of what may have been a religious crisis for Anne. That doctrine would appear in Anne's novel *The Tenant of Wildfell Hall*, espoused by its heroine, Helen Huntingdon. Anne recovered at home, and Charlotte returned to teach at Roe Head for an additional term.

In 1839, Anne began service as a governess, which she would immortalize in *Agnes Grey*. The stupidity and stubbornness of the fictional students were grounded in the real-life struggles Anne underwent with the family that first hired her. She endured great physical and emotional hardships until the year's end, when she returned home for January and February 1840. That spring, she took a new position with the family of Reverend Edmund Robinson at Thorp Green Hall near York, a position she held until 1845. At first exhausted and discouraged by her new assignment, she considered not returning following a three-week vacation at home. She suffered from a crisis of faith at that time that increased her feelings of guilt and dissatisfaction. The Robinsons' earnest pleas convinced her to return, and Anne came to love the children. She came home on several occasions, including after her aunt's death in 1842. She received a generous inheritance and continued to work and also to study Latin and German, languages that she and her sisters hoped to offer in a school of their own.

Sometime in 1843, Branwell joined the Robinson household to tutor the son, Edmund. Over time, Mrs. Robinson took a personal interest in Branwell, though Anne did not record any doubts as to the propriety of their relationship. Branwell was eventually dismissed by Mr. Robinson, who threatened to shoot him if he returned to the property. Anne did not dispute the account of a romantic relationship between Branwell and Mrs. Robinson when she returned home permanently in 1845.

For several months starting in August 1846, Anne and Emily had to care for the increasingly debilitated Branwell while Charlotte accompanied their father to Manchester for cataract surgery. The closest of the sisters to Branwell, Anne took most personally the devastating effects of his alcohol and drug use, expressing regret over the waste of talent and particularly over her brother's moral degeneracy. No doubt her defense of the realistic portrayal of human nature that prefaced the second edition of *The Tenant of Wildfell Hall* had its roots in her association with her brother and his disastrous personal choices.

When Charlotte discovered Emily's poems in 1845, Anne revealed her own writing, and the three published *Poems* by Currer, Ellis, and Acton Bell in 1846. The volume was reissued two years later by the publishers Smith, Elder and Company, following the success of the sisters' novels, and Anne enjoyed the publication of additional pieces in *Fraser's*

Magazine. She probably worked on *Agnes Grey* in 1845–46. Charlotte submitted Anne's novel to several publishers, and T. C. Newby accepted it in July 1847. Charlotte's *Jane Eyre* was published later that year, also by Smith, Elder and Company, and George Newby held back Emily and Anne's novels until the success of *Jane Eyre* was assured. Also in 1847, Anne suddenly received a number of letters from the Robinson daughters, who expressed their "endless esteem and gratitude" and never alluded to their mother's supposed misbehavior with Branwell. Critics suggest that the contrast between the Robinson's way of life and Branwell's self-destruction weighed heavily on Anne's mind as she wrote *Tenant*, a story about a woman who flees the abuse of her alcoholic husband, only to suffer the abuse of her new neighbors, due to lack of understanding her situation. A strongly religious woman, she eventually returns to the scene of her abuse to nurse her dying husband, inspiring him to seek her forgiveness before death.

Anne became ill again, but she pursued publication of *Tenant*, again with George Newby, despite his underhanded tactics in publishing her first novel. He misrepresented *Tenant* by informing American publishers Harper & Brothers that it was authored by Currer Bell, Charlotte's pseudonym. Because the next Currer Bell novel had been promised to another publisher, Charlotte and Anne visited London to surprise their editors with the revelation that the Bells were women. While they were in London, a review declared *Tenant* coarse and brutal, charges Anne addressed in the preface to its second edition, defending such characterization as necessary to make the harsh point of her realistic novel.

Anne was diagnosed with tuberculosis in 1849, a great blow to Charlotte following the deaths of both Branwell and Emily the year before. Anne continued to feel the need to stress her religious beliefs and used some of her final poems as a means of expressing her views. Charlotte and her friend Ellen Nussey took Anne to Scarborough in May 1849 in the hope that she would improve, but she died on May 28. Purportedly, her final words were of thanksgiving and appreciation for a gentle death.

The three Brontë sisters published seven novels and multiple poems, making stunning contributions to the world of English literature. Many possible topics and strategies are available to consider for writing essays about the Brontës and their works. The following suggestions are offered as models on which you can base your own ideas. Plan to allow your ideas to develop gradually as you engage in a close reading of your subject. Remember that biographical details do not substitute for an analysis or interpretation of the literary works, but they can inform your analysis or interpretation. Should you choose to write about topics that relate to the Brontës' lives, be sure to read one or more of the many in-depth biographical sources, some of which are listed at the end of this chapter.

TOPICS AND STRATEGIES
Themes

Every piece of literature offers multiple topics about which to write. Considering those topics may lead you to the theme or overall meaning of a work of literature. In thinking of the Brontës' lives and the concerns of their era, the topic of opportunities for women comes to mind. Women had few choices during the early 19th century if they wanted to contribute to their own support. Anne Brontë's *The Tenant of Wildfell Hall* features a woman left on her own to support herself and her son, which she attempts to do partly through painting. Her efforts do not gain the admiration of her neighbors; instead, they simply become suspicious of the reasons for her living arrangements.

Anne Brontë's *Agnes Grey* and Charlotte Brontë's *Jane Eyre* both feature young women who must endure the demanding life of a governess. That position leads to another possible topic for an essay: isolation. A governess felt constant isolation, often accepted by neither the family that retained her nor the servants of their households. Emily Brontë also examined the effects of isolation in *Wuthering Heights,* in which the featured characters live on the moors, far from contact with any community or urban center. Their lives thus have become insular, and they demand much of one another, finding few outlets for their frustration.

Nature appears as a topic in most of the Brontës' novels and in Emily's poetry, also discussed in this volume. In some instances, such as in *Agnes Grey,* nature offers beauty and redemption. In Charlotte's *The Professor,* the cultured nature found in gardens represents temptation and danger, while the more natural flora suggest honesty and security. Nature in *Wuthering Heights* can stand for independence and adventure, as when Heathcliff and Cathy escape to the moors. On the other hand, it is also forbidding and dangerous, evident when Lockwood loses his way in the fog and becomes injured while traveling between Thrushcross Grange and Wuthering Heights. As you consider these topics and others, attempt to relate them to the idea that you believe the author wants the reader to take away from her work.

Sample Topics:

1. **Opportunities for women:** What message about opportunities for women do the Brontës' works offer to the reader?

   After selecting a work on which to focus, examine details about the women who work. Have they chosen their work willingly? Is the fact that they can find work celebrated or denigrated by the characters themselves and by the author? You will want to be careful in declaring a particular idea about opportunities for women unless you can find specific passages that support your declaration. Always take care not to project today's attitudes on past eras.

2. **Isolation:** Do characters suffer from or enjoy their isolation? Does the isolation seem to be self-imposed, or is it inflicted on them by circumstance?

   Isolation is not always a negative condition. For instance, in *The Professor,* Crimsworth enjoys the separation from his brother and seems to welcome the challenges of living in a foreign country where he does not know the customs. For him, isolation from family and home is a matter of choice. Jane Eyre, however, must work as a governess in order to be able to support herself. She has no choice in the matter and cannot enjoy an isolation caused in part by her lack of family or friends. Her art helps protect her from an unbearable emotional isolation, as she waits to discover people with whom she wants to spend time and who will break through her loneliness. In *Wuthering Heights,* Heathcliff lives in isolation his entire life, despite being a member of two different families by the book's conclusion. Thus, isolation can have emotional and psychological ramifications.

3. **Nature:** What does the fact that the Brontës offer varying messages about nature mean?

If one accepts that nature is a static force, how could it be represented in so many different ways? Is nature evil or good, or is its value neutral? Perhaps the Brontës express a fear, common to all people, of a greater power, whether that power is nature, God, or a combination of both.

Characters

Characters often provide a fascinating focus for essays. All characters are important in how they relate to or support the author's message. Minor characters generally are important in the way they help readers better understand the main characters. You might search for certain patterns associated with individual characters or groups of characters in the Brontës' writings to begin your quest for a proper writing focus.

Sample Topics:

1. **Gender:** In which works are female characters the most important? How do they relate to male characters? In which works are male characters the most important? How do they relate to female characters?

Most of the Brontës' works feature strong female characters. This suggests that male characters either accept the women's strength and support it, or they battle against it. Such divergent courses of action reflect the personality of the male in question. *The Professor* features a male as its protagonist. You should be curious as to whether that novel also contains strong female characters, as it is a trademark of the other prose works.

2. **Family relationships:** In which novels does family membership most affect the protagonists? Are those families positive or negative? How do the different novels define family?

Family relationships proved extremely important to the Brontës in their private lives, and that value is reflected in their fiction. In *Jane Eyre,* Jane spends her life searching for a family and moving from one community to another until she identifies the group for which she feels a close affinity. In *Wuthering Heights,* family composition is a foundation for enormous conflict. As the outsider, Heathcliff belongs to neither family, yet he "owns" both families by the novel's conclusion. Agnes Grey must leave her own relations to work among two other families, neither of which wants to accept her. In *Shirley,* two brothers employ varying methods to search for family, each discovering that their lack of ability to correctly recognize and define family has made them blind to the best possibilities.

History and Context

The 19th century proved a time of great change for England, which enjoyed expanding trade with other countries and a growth in industry never before imagined. Change proved positive for some but negative for others, bringing conflict with it. Not everyone viewed change as progress. It resulted in a deepening class division and redistribution of property that guaranteed material wealth to the upper class, with little of that affluence trickling down to the working class. The working class received no benefits such as universal health care or wage guarantees, and collective bargaining had not yet been instituted. Gender issues also came into sharper focus as more women entered the workplace, all under the control of male management. Members of the middle and upper-middle classes would not perform factory work, which was deemed beneath them. Such women's choices for earning an income remained narrow, generally restricted to a governess position or serving as companion to a wealthier female. However, women could still gain power independent of society's dictates through their personal relationships with men. The Brontë novels most often examine that possibility.

Sample Topics:

1. **Class structure:** Which novels feature class structure as a major aspect? To which class does the heroine or hero belong? Are all the characters from each class level featured as "bad" or

"good"? How does being a member of either class ennoble or challenge that character? Do any of the characters appear to be stereotypes?

All of the Brontës novels feature members of the working class as main characters. Their interaction with upper-class members represents much of the conflict of the novels. In some cases, the material aspects of their lives cause difficulties for the main characters, who must make choices based on income. *Shirley* emphasizes class structure as a source of controversy in the work world, introducing an unusual female figure who has money and, thus, the type of power often reserved only for males. Her class background and material resources challenge the men around her who are accustomed to being the seat of power. In a different approach, *Jane Eyre* emphasizes the ways in which social and class differences affect the individual.

2. **Gender issues:** How does gender relate to success in the Brontë novels? Which novels explore the ways a character's success or failure is tied to gender?

The Brontës novels are overt in the ways they marshal support for women, so that idea alone will not make a solid thesis. Rather, you will want to analyze how their characters deal with the challenges to success within a traditionally male power structure. In *The Professor,* the male protagonist, Crimsworth, associates with a woman of independent character who manages her own business. His reaction to her offers an interesting focus for an essay. In *Jane Eyre,* the physically weak Jane possesses a mighty spirit, buoyed by her creative personality. This allows her to win over the wealthy Rochester despite her lower-class status.

Philosophy and Ideas

An era's philosophy regarding morality offers an interesting springboard to a potentially strong essay topic. In 19th-century England, morals were the cornerstone of the Victorian ethos. People were expected to attend church and practice Christianity in their daily dealings with one another. Yet some issues of morality were not always clear. Civic laws might seem moral to one group but not to another, in that they determined wealth and welfare, generally favoring the wealthier group. Because some groups had power over others, they could act in an immoral manner without fear of reprisal. With the growth of industry, ethics—or the lack of them— gained importance in business dealings. Factory owners could treat workers unethically in the name of profits, an acceptable approach as the Industrial Revolution changed England's social and financial structure.

Sample Topics:

1. **Morality:** Which novels contain blatantly immoral characters? How is that immorality depicted? How does their stance on morality help shape their characters?

   The basis for characters' moral choices may become a factor in defining their personalities. The Brontë sisters held varying views on morality, with Emily deeming religion of much less value in living a moral existence than Anne did. These contrasting attitudes are more pronounced in *The Tenant of Wildfell Hall* than in *Wuthering Heights*. Charlotte Brontë felt she had to defend both of her sisters' moral character in relation to those works. Her need to do so supports the claim that both Emily and Anne used their novels to make strong statements they would not necessarily voice in their private lives.

2. **Ethics:** Which novels emphasize ethics in business and society? Which group or groups appear to be the most ethical? Are those groups defined by gender, income, social status, or something different?

   Charlotte Brontë's *Shirley* most clearly examines ethics in business, emphasizing the Luddite revolution against mechanization that caused many factory workers to lose their jobs. Ethics are also important, however, on the individual level, such as in Agnes Grey's treatment by her employers. They wished to pay as little as possible yet expected her to achieve great results in shaping their children. The fact that they did not care to invest materially in their own children's future proves of interest and reflects their values. Even more interesting is the fact that they probably would not acknowledge that point of view.

Symbols, Imagery, and Language

As with most novels, those by the Brontës offer strong examples of symbols, images, and language effects for analysis. Although three very different women wrote the works featured in this volume, they share many common symbols. Nature proves crucial to several of the novels for symbolic value as well as for its detailed imagery. Houses and other buildings feature prominently as well. In addition, character names often prove symbolic. Language or word choice can project a particular tone, an aspect of style in any novel. That tone, or the author's attitude toward her subject matter, characters, and audience may shift over the course of the novel or even in a particular chapter or scene. When a writer like Charlotte or Anne Brontë produces multiple novels, the tone will vary from book to book, depending on the subject matter. An examination of any of these facets will supply strong possibilities for essay writing.

Sample Topics:

1. **Nature:** In which novels does nature prove a positive force and in which a negative force? How do the Brontës represent that positive or negative aspect symbolically? Which nature symbols are traditional and which are literary (symbolic only to that piece of literature)?

   The Brontë children grew up on the Yorkshire moors and witnessed nature to be as benevolent as it was destructive. *Wuthering Heights* depicts a moody, changeable natural environment that mirrors the temperament of its characters. Heathcliff and Cathy each reflect the landscape through metaphor, as when, for example, Cathy compares Heathcliff to an "arid wilderness" and Heathcliff compares Cathy to clouds and trees. *The Professor* emphasizes nature through the orderly imagery of the garden, a traditional female symbol, with two gardens representing the personalities of the two main female characters.

2. **Houses/buildings:** Which novels feature significant houses or other buildings? What is their significance? Do they symbolize the people or events attached to them? If so, in what ways?

Most of the Brontë novels contain significant buildings, some of which possess symbolic names. For instance, in *Jane Eyre*, Lowood represents a home in which a low value is placed on children, while Thornfield symbolizes a thorny, potentially harmful and threatening workplace for Jane. Wuthering Heights and Thrushcross Grange are important not only for their material value but for their symbolic family significance to Heathcliff. The two schools in *The Professor* represent simultaneously educational benefits for both boys and girls, as well as the separation and hierarchy of the two genders. Wildfell Hall's name signifies the potential for chaos for its inhabitants, despite their attempts to establish an orderly life. The factory in *Shirley* is aligned with systems of power and control, and the houses in *Agnes Grey* gain significance through their lack of the features that generally constitute a comfortable family home.

3. **Names:** Which novel contains the greatest number of symbolic names? How might symbolic names prove important to understanding characters?

Names may act as labels for characters, suggesting meanings to alert readers. For example, in *Jane Eyre,* Jane is a plain name as compared to names such as Adèle and Blanche. Blanche symbolizes something blanched, or colorless, which could help describe her personality, while Fairfax indicates that Thornfield's housekeeper possesses a high sense of justice. Reed is also the name of an undesirable weed, and Miss Temple's name suggests religious protection or refuge. One may also assign symbolic significance to the name Rivers, because when a character crosses a river in literature, that act generally suggests a new beginning.

4. **Tone:** How would you characterize the tone of each novel? What specific phrases would support your characterization? Does the tone change with the development of the protagonist? Does the author seem to value her characters and subject matter and to respect her audience?

When assessing tone, one might begin with simple general classifications, such as negative or positive viewpoints, and move on to more specific labels, including gloomy, hopeful, distraught, or joyful. Novels that contain didactic, or preachy, material, such as *The Tenant of Wildfell Hall,* may be seen as disrespectful of reader intelligence. However, when considering didacticism, a trait that sophisticated readers held in disdain after the 19th century, one must keep in mind that art's ability to emphasize a lesson was still valued during the era of the Brontës.

Bibliography and Online Resources

Allot, Miriam. *The Brontës: The Critical Heritage.* New York: Routledge, 1996.

The Brontë Sisters Web. http://www.lang.nagoya-u.ac.jp/~matsuoka/Bronte. html. Downloaded December 23, 2007.

Chapel, John, and Alan Shelton, ed. *The Letters of Mrs. Gaskell.* Cambridge, MA: Harvard UP, 1966.

———. *Further Letters of Mrs. Gaskell.* Manchester, England: Manchester UP, 2000.

Chitham, Edward. *A Life of Emily Brontë.* Oxford: Basil Blackwell, 1987.

Crump, R. W. *Charlotte and Emily Brontë.* 3 vols. Boston: G. K. Hall, 1982 –1986.

Eagleton, Terry. *Myths of Power: A Marxist Study of the Brontës.* London: McMillan, 1975.

Ewbank, Inga-Stina. *Their Proper Sphere: A Study of the Brontë Sisters as Early-Victorian Female Novelists.* Cambridge, MA: Harvard UP, 1968.

Frank, Katherine. *A Chainless Soul: A Life of Emily Brontë.* New York: Houghton Mifflin, 1990.

Gaskell, Elizabeth Cleghorn. *The Life of Charlotte Brontë.* New York: Penguin, 1998.

———. " The Life of Charlotte Bronte." The Brontë Sisters Web. Available online. URL: http://www.lang.nagoya-u.ac.jp/~matsuoka/EG-Charlotte.html. Downloaded December 26, 2007.

Gérin, Winifred. *Anne Brontë*. Nashville: Thomas Nelson & Sons, 1959.

———. *Charlotte Brontë: The Evolution of Genius*. Oxford: Clarendon Press, 1967.

———. *Emily Brontë*. New York: Oxford UP, 1978.

Gilbert, Sandra M., and Susan Gubar. *The Madwoman in the Attic: The Woman Writer and the Nineteenth-Century Literary Imagination*. New Haven: Yale UP, 1979.

Martin, Robert Bernard. *The Accents of Persuasion: Charlotte Brontë's Novels*. New York: W.W. Norton, 1968.

Nash, Julie, and Barbara Suess, ed. *New Approaches to the Literary Art of Anne Brontë*. Burlingame, VT: Ashgate Publishing, 2001.

Paddock, Lisa Olson, and Carl E. Rollyson. *The Brontës A to Z: The Essential Reference to Their Lives and Works*. New York: Checkmark Books, 2003.

Passel, Anne. *Charlotte and Emily Brontë*. New York: Garland Publishing, 1979.

Pinion, F. B. *A Brontë Companion*. London: McMillan, 1975.

The Poems of Anne Brontë. Available online. URL: http://mick-armitage.staff.shef.ac.uk/anne/poems/an-poems.html. Downloaded August 7, 2007.

Pykett, Lyn. *Emily Brontë*. London: Macmillan, 1989.

———. "Gender and Genre in Wuthering Heights: Gothic Plot and Domestic Fiction." *Wuthering Heights, New Casebooks*. Ed. Patsy Stoneman. London: Macmillan, 1993. 86–99.

Thomson, Douglass H. "Charlotte Brontë and Emily Brontë." *Gothic Writers: A Critical and Bibliographical Guide*. Ed. Douglass H. Thomson, Jack G. Voller, and Frederick S. Frank. Westport, CT: Greenwood Press, 2002. 69–75.

Tillotson, Kathleen. *Novels of the Eighteen-forties*. Oxford: Clarendon Press, 1965.

The Victorian Web. Available online. URL: http://www.victorianweb.org/. Downloaded December 23, 2007.

Visick, Mary. *The Genesis of Wuthering Heights*. 3rd ed. New York: Oxford UP, 1980.

Wilkes, Brian. *The Brontës*. London: Hamlyn, 1977.

———. *Illustrated Brontës of Haworth: Scenes and Characters from the Novels of the Brontë Sisters*. New York: Facts On File, 1986.

Winnifrith, Tom. *The Poems of Charlotte Brontë: A New Annotated and Enlarged Edition of the Shakespeare Head Brontë*. Oxford: Blackwell, 1984.

Wroot, Herbert E. *Sources of Charlotte Brontë's Novels: Persons and Places*. Oxford: Caxton Press for the Brontë Society, 1935.

JANE EYRE

READING TO WRITE

CHARLOTTE BRONTË's *Jane Eyre* (1847) changed contemporary society's ideas about female main characters. Seldom had an independent-minded young woman with no prospects served as a novel's protagonist and romantic heroine. Unlike the heroines of "domestic fiction" who sought to fulfill the accepted feminine ideal, Jane moved beyond the domestic sphere in search of adventure and intellectual and artistic stimulation. If you can imagine yourself living in early 19th-century England when reading this novel, you will understand why Brontë's audience found Jane such a remarkable main character. Not only had she read much of the Bible, challenging works by 17th-century writer John Milton, a good deal of history, and books about birds and nature by age 10, she applied much of what she learned to her own life. She remained silent, not because she was practicing proper behavior for a woman, like later Victorian heroines, but because she knew most of those around her would neither share nor understand her ideas if she spoke. You may even recognize a bit of yourself in Jane Eyre, if you have ever felt isolated and unappreciated by those around you.

As you read the novel in preparation for writing, you will want to take careful notice of what Jane notices; details important to her should also become important to you. You should ask frequent questions about her reactions to other characters and to the conflict she encounters. The answers to such questions may develop into a topic about which you want to write. The key to writing a strong essay is the choice of a topic in which you are interested; such a topic will motivate you to bring a lively energy to your writing. Once you have chosen a topic, you will develop a thesis statement to form the basis of your essay. A careful analysis of passages from the novel that reflect your theme is crucial. Your instructors and other readers of your essay will expect you to interpret such passages, explaining how they relate to your topic.

For instance, a scene in the first chapter, in which Jane interacts with her nasty cousin John Reed, might be a promising one to consider for important topics. Jane has been reading the Reed family books, and John objects to this, not because his family ever reads them, but because he does not want Jane to have them. He tells her,

> "You have no business to take our books; you are a dependant, mama says; you have no money; your father left you none; you ought to beg, and not to live here with gentlemen's children like us, and eat the same meals we do, and wear clothes at our mama's expense. Now, I'll teach you to rummage my book-shelves; for they *are* mine; all the house belongs to me, or will do in a few years. Go and stand by the door, out of the way of the mirror and the windows."

In this passage, you will immediately notice that John feels he is of a higher social class than Jane. You might ask, why is one's class important? John's rude behavior indicates that he does not respect others. Is this true of all members of the upper class? If so, what does that indicate about that group of people as Brontë presents them in this novel? You will also notice that John believes Jane should be turned out onto the street to beg. If she is related to him, why does he treat her so badly? Why does he wish her ill? He condemns Jane for having no money, a condition for which a child of 10 could not be responsible. John is also a child, but he sees nothing wrong with his dependency on his mother, something for which he indicts Jane. He also claims to own the house and takes for granted that he owns all of the possessions in it. Why would a child feel that way? These questions suggest the topics of class structure and differences between boys and girls as possible themes about which to write. They also lead to other questions, such as: How did class divisions come about during the pre-Victorian age in which the novel is set? What were the laws that determined inheritance? How might a poor girl make a life for herself? You will read a later section titled "History and Context" that will help you begin to answer such questions. As you answer your questions, your analysis begins.

To take another approach, the books in the scene might catch your interest, as the reader understands the importance of books to Jane. She not only learns from them; they supply the singular joy that she experiences as a child. In the scene following the one quoted above, John uses a book as a weapon, injuring Jane. What does this action tell you about John's attitude toward books? How does his attitude contrast with that of Jane? Does this action tell us more about the social class division, and if so, what? Another object in this scene is the mirror. Mirrors traditionally symbolize self-reflection, and when we read of characters looking into mirrors, we suspect they are in the process of developing a self-identity. Here John tells Jane to step away from the mirror. Does this mean that Jane will not develop a sense of self while in the Reed household?

Once you have asked such questions about scenes in this lengthy novel's early pages, you will look for other scenes that might help you answer those questions. You should also observe whether certain patterns begin to emerge as related events occur throughout the novel. For instance, Jane's movement from one household to another is a pattern. What is the importance of that constant movement? How do the households differ? What does Jane learn in each?

Being an active reader and asking questions about aspects of the novel that interest you will guide you toward a theme for your writing. A careful reading will help you recognize passages you can use as examples to support the idea you propose to your reader. Remember to write down your questions and answers and to take notes about the scenes that interest you. Otherwise, you will spend much time later searching for scenes that you want to discuss in your essay.

TOPICS AND STRATEGIES

In this section of the chapter, you will find discussions of several possible essay topics based on Charlotte Brontë's *Jane Eyre*. Please keep in mind that this section simply offers ideas, which will hopefully help jump-start your own brainstorming for topics or themes, and for ways to write about those themes. Remember: A strong, solid topic on which to base your essay is your starting point. Much additional work will follow.

When you have chosen a promising theme, you will develop it into a main point, or thesis statement. As emphasized earlier, you should think of the thesis statement as a foundation on which you must build your essay. The bricks you arrange on your foundation are the development paragraphs of your essay. A discussion of development comes later in this book. For now, just keep in mind that the development of topics into thesis statements represents a crucial early step in the essay-writing process. In order to arrive at possible topics, you should brainstorm, writing down any idea that comes into your head. Then you will ask yourself questions about the topics, and soon you will have several possible thesis statements in mind.

As is true of most novels published during the early to mid-19th century, *Jane Eyre* is divided into three volumes. (Such a division allowed publishers to make separate sales with each volume published.) The discussion of themes for *Jane Eyre* below match the novel's three divisions, as an example of how a reader could focus on only one volume in a novel of such length and complexity. Each volume covers a certain period of development in the life of the protagonist. You will find clearly indicated in your text the page on which each volume begins. You may apply any of the themes below to any of the three volumes, but those below especially suit the volumes for which they are suggested. This will be true of any of the novels discussed in this volume, but it will be applied as an example only to *Jane Eyre*. If you are asked to write a lengthy essay, consider whether you might follow one theme throughout all three volumes.

Themes:
Volume 1: Chapters 1–15: Themes

Like any superior work of literature, *Jane Eyre* suggests multiple themes and ideas that recur throughout the novel. Because they are repeated, you will probably find several strong examples of each theme about which to write. Because Jane begins the story as a small child, you watch her mature, and themes mature along with her. Thus, as themes such as the importance of art recur, the reader sees its particular importance change just as Jane sees it change. For instance, as a young child Jane is interested in the art that illustrates the books she reads because, as she notes, "Each picture told a story." Later, when Jane enters school at Lowood, she takes art as a school subject. One of the first pieces of her art is a drawing of her "first cottage." Still later, as Jane moves on to become a governess at Thornfield Hall, Mr. Rochester demands to view her portfolio, a collection of her watercolors. Jane describes one of her paintings as "but a pale portrait of the thing I had conceived."

Closely related to art as a theme would be literature and reading. Because what one reads tends to shape one's life, Jane's reading of Bewick's *History of British Birds* and Goldsmith's *History of Rome* as a young child, and later Richardson's *Pamela,* Swift's *Gulliver's Travels,* and Milton's *Paradise Lost,* may tell the reader much about the primary influences on her character.

A third instantly noticeable theme is that of family. As the first volume begins, Jane's family consists of an abusive aunt and some detestable cousins, as well as one kind servant for whom Jane feels more affection than her true family. When Jane moves to Lowood, she forms a new family consisting of herself, Helen, and Miss Temple. While at Thornfield Hall, she seems to lack family. Although she cares for the young Adèle, she does not yet feel true fondness for her. Mrs. Fairfax is not the type of person in whom Jane can confide, and she feels quite uncertain regarding the character of Mr. Rochester.

A fourth strong topic for the first volume is that of independence. Although in the novel's opening Jane remains controlled by various rules of the Reed household, she maintains an independent spirit. We see this revealed in her refusal to bend to the will of her cousin John. At Lowood, Jane and others must follow many rules, but she feels free to express her ideas to Helen and to Miss Temple. She also gains independence through her imagination and her growing knowledge. In Jane's early weeks at Thornfield, she enjoys the first sensation of independence as she earns her first income and is not a prisoner within the estate's walls.

The topic of hauntings can provide a fifth theme. While in the Reed home, Jane believes she sees a ghost, and she fears that the red room is haunted. At Lowood, Jane compares Mr. Brocklehurst to an "apparition," and at Thornfield Hall, she hears mysterious ghostly noises. In addition, a fire that cannot be explained to Jane's satisfaction almost kills Mr. Rochester.

Finally, the story's settings may also provide ideas for a thesis statement. Jane lives in multiple settings in the first volume. She moves from the Reed home to Lowood, and from Lowood to Thornfield Hall. Within those houses and buildings, specific spaces play a crucial role in her life.

Examples include the red room in the Reed house, Miss Temple's private quarters at Lowood, and Jane's own room at Thornfield Hall.

Once you select a theme that interests you, you should shape questions that focus on that theme. The answers to your questions may then yield a main point about the theme that you would like to emphasize in your essay. Some examples appear below.

Sample Topics:

1. **Art:** In what ways does art benefit Jane? When does she practice drawing and painting? Why is art important to Jane? Who else in the book engages in or enjoys art, such as painting or music? How does Jane's art reflect her personality? How does Jane's art affect her relationship with other characters in the novel?

   If you find the theme of art interesting, you will begin by noting at what points in the plot art appears. For instance, you will want to note whether it appears just before a scene of conflict or just after such a scene. If you observe that all of the main characters are depicted enjoying art, you can examine what else those characters have in common. In addition, you should examine the effect on Jane of not only her own art but that of others. Then you may proceed to develop a thesis statement about art's role in the novel.

2. **Literature and reading:** Why does Jane read? What does she read? How does reading affect her? When and where does she think about or comment on what she reads? What does the fact that Jane enjoys reading tell the reader and other characters about her?

   Literature and the act of reading enjoy important roles in the development of Jane's character. Observe what she says and how she behaves after a particular piece of literature is referenced. You might then consider how the act of reading influences Jane and those around her. Does it act as a bond that they share? Does it cause conflict? The fact that Charlotte Brontë includes so many references to reading allows her to transmit a certain message to the reader. That message may lead to your development of a strong thesis statement.

3. **Family:** How does Jane define the term *family*? What families are represented in volume 1? Why is family important to Jane? Do most children require the love and respect of a family? What effect might a loving family have on a child? What effect might the lack of family have on a child?

   An essay focusing on family would require that you review all of the scenes where groups that might be labeled family appear, then determine which groups Jane feels she can relate to as family and why she feels that way. Your paper could address the topic by considering whether Jane feels that family is important and whether or not she wants a family. You should notice how many times issues of family appear in volume 1 to help you determine whether it remains important to Jane.

4. **Independence:** Jane badly desires independence—why? Exactly what does Jane desire freedom from? Does she seek physical or spiritual independence? If she cannot achieve physical independence, does she achieve any other type of freedom? If so, how does she achieve it?

   Your essay about independence would define that concept from Jane's point of view as she matures throughout volume 1. You would want to examine how the concept changes for her and also why she finds it so important. You also need to determine whether she finds freedom at any point in volume 1, and if so, how she manages to do so.

5. **Hauntings:** This novel contains many references to ghosts, shadows, dreams, mysterious occurrences, and hauntings. These references begin in the first chapter. How do these references seem to affect the novel's tone? How do the various hauntings affect Jane as a child? How do they affect the reader?

As with all topics, you will want to ask how the hauntings advance the plot and identify the overall mood they bring to the story. You should also investigate the idea of metaphorical hauntings—that is, hauntings that are not physical. An example would be the manner in which various characters seem to suffer from mental or emotional hauntings, perhaps by their past or their future.

6. **Setting:** What types of settings, or spaces, does Jane occupy? How does she react to those spaces? What type of space does she desire? Does she ever find such a space? Does Jane want to share her space with others? How do you know?

An essay that discusses the importance of setting or space to a novel will first define the term *setting*. The settings that different groups occupy can tell the reader much about those groups. When Jane becomes a part of each group, she will necessarily be influenced by their use of the space she shares. The room Jane does not have to share, such as her chamber at Thornfield Hall, is also important. Because rooms and buildings are constructed of common materials in common dimensions, they have no positive or negative value on their own. Rather, the people who occupy them and the manner in which those people use the space in their houses, schools, and businesses determine the special mood that seems to inhabit their bedrooms, hallways, kitchens, libraries, classrooms, and so forth.

Volume 2: Chapters 16–26: Themes

In the second volume, Jane's relationship to Mr. Rochester continues to develop. Danger becomes more prominent as a topic, as members of the household appear to be under threat by an unseen force. In volume 1, when Jane was in emotional and mental danger and suffered the threat of disease, she could identify the sources of her threat, something she cannot do in volume 2. Jane's personality is such that she does not become hysterical but rather seeks the source of the danger. Closely related is the topic of courage, which Jane must have in order to face the threat of danger at Thornfield Hall. Rochester recognizes her courage when he selects her to assist him in managing the results of the mysterious occurrences in the house.

Imagination might also supply a topic. Jane's imagination has been previously depicted in her art as well as in her dreams, so the reader understands how important "fancy" is to her. In the second volume, she questions whether her imagination might be the source of the strange noises she hears. After she decides that she does not imagine the happenings at Thornfield, others continue to try to convince her that she does. Closely related to imagination is the topic of dreams, a common occurrence in the classical quest plot. In quest stories, such as that of Odysseus in Homer's *Odyssey,* visions and dreams play a crucial part, as the hero on his journey often confronts his fears and imagines his future through visions and dreams.

In this second volume, home remains an important topic. Although Jane has lived in several residences, she has never felt as though any were her home. While at Thornfield Hall, she begins to consider herself at home, and then suffers feelings of conflict when Mr. Rochester brings a beautiful woman into the house. Mrs. Fairfax discusses his possible marriage to Miss Ingram, suggesting that Jane might lose her home. Just as she again feels comfortable at Thornfield following Mr. Rochester's marriage proposal to her and their impending wedding, she again loses that comfort with the revelation of Rochester's marriage to Bertha Mason.

Sample Topics:

1. **Danger:** Who appears to be involved with danger? What type of danger is it? Are those who are involved victims? Who needs rescue? Who helps rescue them? How do they react? How is Jane involved? How do dangerous occurrences advance the plot?

   Readers can relate to the topic of danger, as some have experienced it firsthand, and everyone has seen physically dangerous situations depicted in the media and in books. In addition, most have suffered some feeling of danger, whether or not it actually exists. Sometimes we fantasize about being caught in certain dangerous situations. We will generally ask ourselves how we might react in such a situation. In the novel, those involved analyze the level of danger and react accordingly. However, one cannot react correctly until all facts are known. When humans share and conquer a dangerous situation together, certain bonds form between them due to the shared experience, which will influence the nature of their relationship. If you choose to write about this topic, you will want to apply these ideas to those facing danger in volume 2. You will also want to examine all involved: perpetrators, victims, and rescuers.

2. **Courage:** Who shows courage? How do they demonstrate it? Do you observe more than one type of courage? Is one person's reaction to a situation requiring courage more "correct" than another's? If so, what does this tell the reader about that character's personality? Does Jane show courage? In what ways? Is her courage like that of those around her? Does she consider herself courageous?

   Courage offers a challenging topic in that it may be defined in so many ways. What one person labels courage, another might not. For instance, sometimes leaving a situation requires more courage than facing its challenges. A person may not be able to act courageously in one instance, but in another appear completely brave. While one character shows courage through certain actions, another shows courage in a different manner. The nature of courage thus becomes crucial to your essay. You will want to determine whether characters change after facing a situation that requires courage. Such a change will often be evident in their later thoughts, feelings, and decisions.

3. **Imagination:** Who uses imagination in the novel? How can the reader recognize that use? In what forms does it appear? Can we label all characters who use their imagination as leading a more admirable life than the others? Why or why not? What does use of the imagination provide for Jane? Does she experience conflict over the use of her imagination?

   Charlotte Brontë shared many of the opinions of the romantic age, one of those being the importance of the imagination. Imagination was believed superior to reason because it led to self-awareness and promoted one's spiritual life. Should you select imagination as your topic, you will need to identify examples of Jane's use of the imagination and how it benefits her. Imagination can lead to dreams and fantasies, and it can produce works such as art, music, and literature. Some consider such activities a waste of time; others consider them the best way to occupy one's time. You will want to examine that conflict and consider why people might disagree so vehemently.

4. **Dreams/visions:** When does Jane experience dreams and visions in volume 2? Why does she have them at those particular moments? Are there any set patterns to the dreams and visions? Does Jane learn from them? Do they help guide her actions?

Dreams and visions remain crucial aspects of the traditional hero's journey. Classical heroes gained wisdom from their dreams and visions; often, while in a dream state, they received important messages that helped to guide their future actions. While Jane does not seem a traditional hero, she engages in a rich dream and vision life. If you choose to focus on this topic, identify all of the dream and vision episodes, and then ask yourself how they relate to one another. Most importantly, decide their importance to Jane and her future.

5. **Home:** How does one define *home*? How does Jane seem to define it? Is it important to her? If so, why, and how does the reader know?

Traditionally, the return home is an important aspect of the hero's quest. In Jane's case, she has never had a home within the framework of the novel. She moves from house to house, but none becomes her own, proving the adage "a house is not a home." In order for a house to become a home, certain elements must be present. One might even venture that a home is as much a psychological construction as a real brick-and-mortar building. The reader wonders whether Jane will ever find her home and all of the elements necessary to her feeling at home in any one location.

Volume 3: Chapters 27–38: Themes

In the third volume, the plot begins to escalate toward the crisis of the conflict—the climax—as Jane makes many discoveries that will change her life. She gains experience in various social and educational matters and knowledge about her family, other characters, and herself. In addition, Jane gains strength in her physical, emotional, and spiritual life. Gender roles are also challenged as a result of seeing who exhibits strength and who exhibits weakness. Thus, knowledge and strength could each be strong topics to consider.

Internal peace also offers an excellent possible topic. Jane comments on the similarity between herself and St. John Rivers in regard to spiritual peace, and they each eventually discover peace in a different fashion.

Separation offers another interesting topic. Jane is not the only character who must separate from those she loves. The fact that separation may lead eventually to reunion is important to consider.

Finally, death offers an excellent point of focus. Should you select that topic, you will want to consider physical death and spiritual and emotional death. You will also want to think about whether death for some results in rebirth for others.

Sample Topics:

1. **Knowledge:** Who is knowledgeable and in what areas? Is one type of knowledge superior to another? What type of knowledge seems to lead to true wisdom? What knowledge does Jane gain from others? How does she use that knowledge?

   In the final pages of any novel, the protagonist usually gains further knowledge that will culminate in an epiphany, a life-changing realization. An essay that focuses on knowledge will investigate different types of knowledge, keeping in mind that just because we learn new facts, they do not necessarily lead to wisdom. Only the sound application of knowledge leads to wisdom. Jane remains young, so readers will not expect her to suddenly become a wise old woman. However, she should discover answers to many questions she has asked herself throughout the novel, the most important one being about her own self-identity. This essay can examine that discovery.

2. **Strength:** Who shows strength? Do different types of strength exist? Which is more desirable? Is the reader surprised by which characters exhibit strength and which ones exhibit weakness?

Much of the novel has focused on strength, with characters representing various types of strength, including physical, emotional, and spiritual. Jane's interactions with new members of her family allow readers to see further examples of these types of strength, as does her return to Rochester. An essay that focuses on strength will consider preconceptions and first impressions regarding strength that may be misleading. In addition, one person's weakness can inspire strength in others. Because we can only understand strength by understanding weakness, a discussion of both aspects of human nature and character will be necessary to this essay.

3. **Internal peace:** Why is internal peace important? Who exhibits internal peace? How can the reader ascertain which characters have achieved internal peace? What causes Jane to find internal peace?

The traditional hero's quest always includes the protagonist finding a reward for his or her efforts. In many instances, that reward is in the form of material treasure or goods. In modern plots, the reward may also be in emotional or spiritual form. Modern sensibilities hold that in order to enjoy material reward, an individual must find an emotional peace, the reward of having the courage to practice one's convictions. Not all characters can achieve internal peace, due to their personalities. An essay discussing the topic of internal peace might examine why the characters that seem to reach this state are able to do so when

other characters cannot. It will also want to focus on the satisfaction of material versus spiritual rewards.

4. **Separation:** Who is separated from whom? How might separation be perceived as a positive state rather than a negative one?
   Who reunites with whom? Who does not reunite? Is separation
   necessary to reunion?

   All readers will understand the difficulty in being separated
   from those they love. Thus, they will relate to the various
   separations that occur in the third volume of *Jane Eyre*. Most
   humans experience multiple separations throughout their
   lives. In order to write about this topic, you will want to consider both the causes and the effects of such separations. One
   often must gain the perspective that separation allows in order
   to then be able to successfully reunite with those left behind.
   Others never experience the reunion, and while this seems at
   first consideration a sad circumstance, the results prove to be
   the best for all involved.

5. **Death:** Who dies a physical death? Why do they die? How do
   their deaths affect Jane and other characters? Who dies an
   emotional or spiritual death? Does that character experience
   a rebirth? Are the deaths necessary to character development
   and fulfillment?

   The plot's action, including a death scene, escalates to a climax, after which there is little action until the novel's conclusion. While deaths occur throughout the novel, those in the
   final section prove crucial due to the nature of story plotting.
   Readers may first think only of physical death, but other types
   of death are also necessary in order for the protagonist to
   reach her full potential. Jane may need to experience a death
   of some type, becoming a new person after her epiphany. This
   death and rebirth should be obvious due to her thoughts and
   actions. When writing an essay on the topic of death, you will
   need to identify which types exist and then discuss the scenes

in which those thoughts and actions occur to help support your claim.

Character

Your essay may focus on one or more characters in *Jane Eyre*. You may consider characters by first dividing them into groups of *major* and *minor* characters. Determine which are the major characters by observing which ones receive the most page space. Typically, the major characters include the *protagonist,* or main character, and an *antagonist,* a character causing conflict for the protagonist. Many additional characters may be considered minor. Remember, just because a character falls into the minor group does not mean the character is unimportant. Minor characters help advance the plot or support the main character's development. Most stories could not exist without minor characters.

If you choose to consider the major characters, you might begin by examining the conflict that exists between them and how, or whether, it is resolved. The manner by which conflicts are resolved will lend clues to important aspects of the characters' personalities. In this novel, clearly the protagonist is Jane. While she has many antagonists, Mr. Rochester would be the main antagonist.

You may also analyze how the major characters change from the beginning to the end of a novel. In general, a book's protagonist is the only one who undergoes a significant change. You should be able to identify that moment of *epiphany,* or realization of something on the part of the protagonist that changes his or her view of life, and thus his or her actions. This need not be a life-or-death moment, but its importance to the character's future will also tell you something about that character's personality and needs.

If you choose to consider minor characters, you may use several approaches. You might want to focus on the character who acts as a *foil* to the main character. A foil reflects characteristics opposite to those of the protagonist in order to help the reader better understand the protagonist. Examples of foils in this novel would be Helen and Bertha Mason Rochester. You might also consider all of the authority figures, such as Aunt Reed, Mr. Brocklehurst, Miss Temple, and St. John Rivers as a group. Another group of minor characters consists of the teachers at Lowood. They hold varying opinions about the purpose of an education for girls. Some, such as Miss Temple, are more devoted to their young charges than others. The servants and hired help also contribute to the story and form meaningful relationships with Jane. Finally, individual characters adding conflict for both Jane and Mr. Rochester, such as Jane's cousins, Adèle, Mr. Mason, Grace Poole, and Miss Ingram, offer promise as essay topics.

Sample Topics:

1. **Development of Jane's character:** In what ways does Jane change from the beginning of the novel to the end? What is her most important change? What do other characters think of Jane? What does Jane think of herself? What does Jane's silence tell readers about her?

   Obviously Jane changes a great deal, because she grows from a child into an adult. You need to identify among all of her many changes the one you believe is the most important to Jane's development. You might examine the way she reacts to certain situations when young, and then note the way her reactions to similar situations change as she matures. Your thesis would reflect why you believe that change to be important. You might also examine passages that refer to Jane's small size, both from her point of view and that of others. An analysis of any discrepancy between Jane's view and that of others could lead to development of a thesis statement. Her tendency to remain silent suggests various ideas about Jane's personality. You could discuss those and support which idea you believe to be the most accurate, based on the evidence.

2. **Rochester as a character:** How does Mr. Rochester represent the traditional hero? How does he differ from the traditional hero? In what ways is he able to change his approach to life? What causes him to change? Does his change seem consistent with his personal beliefs? In which relationship does Rochester encounter the greatest amount of conflict? Why?

   An essay about Mr. Rochester would necessarily consider his interactions with Jane, Adèle, his guests, Bertha, her brother, and his servants to reveal his personality. You would want to notice both differences and similarities in his behavior with each individual. As you analyze the conflict he suffers in dealing with others, you may arrive at a thesis statement about the origin of that conflict and why he deals with it as he does.

3. **Characters serving as foils for Jane:** How many foils appear in the novel? Who are they? What is the purpose of each? How do they help the reader better understand Jane? How do they help Jane better understand herself?

   In this type of essay, you need to be specific about which aspects of Jane's character each foil brings to light. You might consider her reactions to those characters and whether they tap into deep-seated conflict for her, as well as how she handles that conflict. If you can analyze each foil's effect on Jane, you may be able to develop a thesis statement as to the importance of their collective presence in the novel.

4. **Characters who serve as authority figures for Jane:** Who are the novel's authority figures? Do Jane's reactions to authority figures change as she matures? Why does Jane react to them as she does? At what point does Jane no longer need authority figures?

   Like all of us, Jane must interact with people who hold positions of authority. Some will have positive effects on her, and some will have negative effects, but she learns from each. As you consider the ways in which she accepts or rejects their guidance, you will learn more about Jane herself. You can then develop a thesis statement as to their importance in Jane's life.

5. **The teachers at Lowood:** Which teacher does Jane like best? Why does she like that teacher? What long-lasting effect does that teacher have on Jane? What effect do any other teachers have on Jane?

When Jane departs the Reed house to attend school, she leaves behind the only family she has. Her adjustment to Lowood will depend on how she reacts to a new community composed of students and teachers. The ability of the teachers to help the children and Jane's response to the various teachers' personalities and styles of teaching will prove crucial to her future. An essay that focuses on the teachers could assume a cause-and-effect approach.

6. **The servants and hired help:** How does Jane interact with the servants and hired help? Can she become close friends with them? What is her attitude toward them? How does her attitude compare with that of others in the novel?

As the book opens, Jane is living in a house that belongs to wealthy members of her family. That family has a number of servants, including Bessie. All of the members of the household seem secure with regard to their social class and position, except for Jane. Later in the novel, when she moves to Thornfield Hall, she again interacts with servants, as well as the master of the house. An essay might investigate Jane's position in these households and how she relates to members of both groups.

7. **Additional characters:** How do Jane's cousins treat her? Why do they treat her as they do? How does Jane react to their treatment? How does Jane feel about Adèle? How does Mr. Rochester feel about the child? How does Adèle help shape Jane's relationship with Mr. Rochester? How does Mr. Mason's appearance change the mood of the story? What does Jane think of him? How does Rochester react toward Mason? What does the reader think of Mason? What does Jane learn about Grace Poole? How does she react toward Grace? How do her reactions to Grace change throughout the book? What is Mrs. Fairfax's attitude toward Miss Ingram? How does Miss Ingram treat Jane? What is the purpose of Miss Ingram to the plot?

As the questions above demonstrate, minor characters cause readers to ask some of what we call the journalistic questions: Who? What? When? How? After answering those questions, you may move on to answer the most important question of all, which is: *Why* are those characters present in the story? The answer to that crucial question should lead to a thesis statement.

History and Context

The history and context that act as a backdrop to *Jane Eyre* can also supply excellent essay topics. As you will recall, Jane herself reads history texts even as a young child, which helps emphasize the importance of history to understanding one's life and times. The number of readers exploded in the 19th century with the increasing popularity of newspapers, thanks to new printing techniques. The coffeehouses and clubs that had appeared in the 18th century offered a place for people to gather and discuss important political and social issues. Inexpensive novels could be sold to the expanding middle class, now reading in greater numbers than ever before. Many people who had gained new wealth as a result of the Industrial Revolution valued private collections of books, whether they read them or not. Books became status symbols for that group.

As contemporary writers such as Margaret Fuller in *Woman in the Nineteenth Century* (1845) make clear, the "woman question" continued to thrive, as the British culture held stubborn views of how "proper" women used their time and energies. A middle-class woman like Brontë had few choices for making a living, and she had experienced the hardships involved with trying to do so. Teaching in a school or in a private home as a governess was one of the few professions open to women. Brontë had tried both approaches and failed. While the group of women writers continued to grow, they were viewed as less than desirable. Labeled immodest and unfeminine and demonized for what the public saw as their attempt to escape domestic duties, many women writers chose to publish anonymously in order to escape such negative public outcry. Writing was considered "brain work," and women who occupied themselves with such work were seen as not fit to raise children. The medical establishment supported the idea that women were the "weaker sex" who could not tolerate any vigorous physical or mental activity.

The woman who did marry lost all legal rights. She was viewed as forming "one body" with her husband. In most cases, she could not own property or have custody of her children. Most women remained completely dependent on men—their fathers, husbands, brothers, or sons—to support them. In turn, they were expected for the most part to stay at home, their proper "sphere," as England's poet laureate Robert Southey described it. Mary Lyndon Shanley discusses these attitudes, which became even stronger as the century advanced, in *Feminism, Marriage, and the Law in Victorian England, 1850–1895* (1989). Men possessed power over women by controlling the family's income. In return, they expected certain behavior, defined by society, from the women who lived in their homes. On occasion, women gained financial independence, perhaps through inheriting money or property usually controlled by men. Thus, social expectations for the roles of both women and men could offer an interesting approach to an essay about this novel.

A related essay could focus on the types of novels for women published in Brontë's time. Most were labeled "domestic fiction," placing their heroines firmly in the home to act as what was later called "the angel in the house." This fiction played an important role in the control of middle-class women by helping to shape what society considered the perfect woman, who was self-sacrificing and completely unselfish—an ideal of what men wanted women to be. Few novels when Brontë wrote featured independent working women in a positive light. Most working characters in fiction were servants who remained passive, adding little to plot development. Work is another topic related to class structure that gives substance to the novel. The wealthy did not have to work, due to inheritance, but unattached middle-class women and all lower-class men and women had to work. However, the opportunities for work for women remained limited.

In addition, the growth of imperialism—the idea that England should rule the world—is reflected in the novel. Although no date for the time period in which Jane lives is given, clues throughout the novel indicate it is set at about the same time that Brontë wrote it. Britain had developed various colonies throughout the world and imported goods from them. The nation also began to force its own culture on these colonies, insisting they give up their own languages to speak English and adopt British laws and customs. The British Empire expanded to Canada, the West Indies,

Australia, New Zealand, and India. Wealth gained by many through the famed East India Company would later be lost, but investment in foreign trade grew in popularity. Susan Meyer discusses how imperialism affected women's fiction of the time in her book *Imperialism at Home: Race and Victorian Women's Fiction* (1996).

At the same time England saw its duty as colonizing and controlling other countries, at home its people were suffering from food shortages. As a consequence of the Industrial Revolution, people left farms to settle in the cities. In 1811, for the first time, nonagricultural activities employed more people than did farm work. Laws called the Enclosure Acts took away what had been land used "in common" by the poor to be appropriated and fenced by large landowners. The dispossessed land workers, or yeomen, once considered the heart of England, had to assume low-paying day-labor jobs. Most of those jobs lacked benefits such as health care, and much of the housing for workers and their families was dirty and dangerous. Many of the negative changes effected by the Industrial Revolution moved the romantics, the group of poets writing just before and during Brontë's time, to celebrate nature and the imagination as paths to emotional freedom.

Religion is an additional essay topic. In the early 19th century, those practicing Catholicism could not hold political office, and they suffered other penalties as well. Members of the Jewish religion were held in low esteem and often stereotyped in literature and in the press. Various Protestant groups known as "dissenters" rebelled against what they saw as hypocrisy and greed in the Church of England. With the rise in power of the middle class, the church became increasingly unpopular. Members of the growing class that made money by serving as go-betweens for producers and buyers, the bourgeoisie, viewed the Church of England as representing only the very wealthy. Many novels published in England in the first few decades of the 19th century focused on religious dissent or refusal to conform to the old way of worship. Such reformers exported religion as others exported goods, sending missionaries abroad. Many of these missionaries were religious zealots, believing their approach was the only acceptable one. They stood ready to force their ideas on others in the name of Christianity. Various religious sects believed strict living equated with spirituality. Thus, the schools they managed offered spartan conditions, emphasizing thriftiness, practicality, and self-sacrifice as essentials of a spiritual life.

Sample Topics:

1. **Class structure:** Jane is born into a certain social class, and she interacts with and observes those from other social classes. What does Brontë want the reader to think about that social-class structure? How does Jane's position in her social class help move the plot forward? Which social class does each character represent? How do Jane's speech and actions change as she interacts with different groups?

   In order for your essay to adequately consider how social-class division relates to *Jane Eyre,* you would need to find sources that discuss those divisions, such as Boyd Hinton's *A Mad, Bad, and Dangerous People?: England 1783–1846.* That source could explain how difficult it might be for a person to move from a lower social-class division to a higher one, as well as how one's social class could affect the development of a positive or negative self-image. These topics might lead you to consider Jane's emotions and reactions more closely. How does her social position make her feel?

2. **Gender roles:** How does Jane feel about the various men with whom she interacts? Does Brontë shape the male characters as positive or negative characters? Why does she make those choices? What does the novel seem to say about the fact that men had power over women? In which scenes do women or men claim others as their property? Who is allowed to own property?

   The reader meets several male characters in the novel. All of them have self-identities shaped by their roles and their social class. All live with or control women, and they are both positive and negative characters. Because Jane must relate to each of these men, they affect plot as well as reveal her character. Minor women characters must also relate to men, as well as to older women who may see the young women as property. Entailment and laws governing inheritance caused women to behave in certain ways. Examination of these factors will help the reader better understand Jane's position as a member of a community of women caught up in the gender dictates of a certain era.

3. **Work:** In what types of work do both major and minor characters engage? Is some work better than others? What do the characters earn for their work? In what type of work does Jane engage? What additional types of work does Jane consider? How do members of the same work group relate to one another? What different attitudes toward work are expressed in the novel? How do/can the novel's women find relief from work?

A consideration of work as an essay topic requires you to survey all of the novel's characters. You might then place them into groups according to the work they pursue, as well as by their attitudes toward their work. In some instances, work seems to be related to religion or personal beliefs and ethics. Jane's attitude toward her own work gives readers a clue to her personality and the content of her character. Also crucial to understanding Jane is a consideration of what she does to find relief from work, not only within the time span of one day, but for longer periods as well. A source such as *The Industrial Revolution and Work in Nineteenth-Century Europe,* edited by Leonard R. Berlanstein, could bring insight to these issues.

4. **Social welfare:** Which characters see themselves as saviors of the lower classes? How do they go about accomplishing this salvation? Are they positive or negative characters? In what ways do they affect Jane and other characters in the book?

This topic relates to topic 1, but it can be considered using a different approach. No research is required. You need only describe the idea of social welfare—the caretaking of one group of society by another—as you see it in the novel. Consider whom the caretakers benefit more, as well as their motivations in assuming this role.

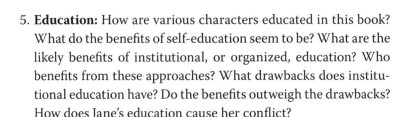

5. **Education:** How are various characters educated in this book? What do the benefits of self-education seem to be? What are the likely benefits of institutional, or organized, education? Who benefits from these approaches? What drawbacks does institutional education have? Do the benefits outweigh the drawbacks? How does Jane's education cause her conflict?

A consideration of each character's education is appropriate. Such an essay must clarify whether those characters benefit from that education. The novel clearly depicts Jane's educated state as causing her and others conflict. Deprivation appears to be an important part of some institutionalized education. Make clear why some characters assume that such harsh approaches are necessary. Also discuss what happens to cause change in this system.

6. **Imperialism/colonialism:** In what ways does the plot of *Jane Eyre* support the idea of Britain imposing its ideas on other countries? Which characters have traveled to foreign countries, and what did they do there? Which characters come from foreign countries, and how do they accept life in England? Why did they leave their homes to come to England? Where do exotic items from other countries appear? Who owns them? Do they have symbolic value?

Because *Jane Eyre* does not actually discuss Britain's conquering of other nations, you would need to look for ways in which the novel questions one culture's domination of another. You could do this by examining the relationships that various characters have with those who are from another country. You may also note and draw conclusions about the many exotic items that you see mentioned throughout the novel.

7. **Religion:** What is Jane's attitude toward the institution of religion? Which characters in the novel represent this type of religion? What remarks are made about religions? What are other characters' attitudes toward religion?

How various characters refer to religious groups will lend insight into the typical British viewpoint of those groups in the 19th century. Because reading is such an important activity for Jane, whether or not she reads the Bible will give some insight into her attitude about religion. Also, the way she interacts with those in the book who represent religion will help readers understand what she thinks of religion as a formal institution.

Philosophy and Ideas

Essay topic possibilities may also be discovered by examining the philosophy that supports the novel. Charlotte Brontë lived during a time of great change, following the romantic period and at the beginning of the Victorian era, the long period in which Queen Victoria occupied the throne. Attitudes toward proper behavior, what constituted self-fulfillment, personal values, and public behavior were constantly shifting. Thus, doubt over self-identity proved a problem for the culture and could form a solid basis for an essay. While Brontë matured in isolation like her character Jane, she read a great deal and was well informed regarding current philosophical discussion. Much of that discussion grew from new ideas about culture, science, and the economy. Adam Smith had published *Wealth of Nations* in 1776, and many in the industrial society at the beginning of the next century adopted his attitude that business would flourish if simply left alone. The idea that individual wealth and profit was positive, regardless of how many in the culture suffered from poverty and disease, helped legitimate the philosophy of self-interest. It also legitimated the fact of some possessing great wealth while others served as servants and slaves as a naturally occurring result of smart business practices. Workers began to unite to express their dissatisfaction and to develop a rhetoric of protest, as outlined in Marc W. Steinberg's *Fighting Words: Working-Class Formation, Collective Action, and Discourse in Early Nineteenth-Century England.*

Poets at the turn of the century also rebelled against rampant self-interest. The group later known as the romantic poets started their own counterrevolution against the industrialization of England by celebrating nature as pure, the ideal for producing positive emotions. William Wordsworth famously wrote that poetry resulted from "the spontaneous overflow of powerful feelings." Poets of the day celebrated the power of one's imagination as superior to the rational logic that supported the development of commerce and industry. Due to the increase in worldwide trade, the Orient—what we know as South and East Asia—gained prominence, particularly India. Its products and people were believed to be exotic. One Oriental product was opium, a legal medical drug at that time. The view of the imagination as the ultimate power for self-realization and self-expression led many to use the drug in an attempt to broaden their imagination. Those who did not use opium saw the imagination—and, with it, passion—as a type of natural drug that could expand their sense of self and their observational abilities, enhancing art and personal expression. Brontë lived in the decades between that permissive culture and the height of the strict Victorian morality that would stress conventional behavior and discourage the celebration of the individual.

Faith is an important topic that can be considered separately from organized religion. One's faith represents an overall philosophy of life, while formal religion represents a cultural institution. Aunt Reed states that she is religious, yet she proves to be a hypocrite in practice; this is also true of Mr. Brocklehurst. On the other hand, Helen holds an unshakable faith, but she does not resemble any of the religious figures in the novel. An investigation of these contradictions can result in an essay that distinguishes the idea of faith from formal religion.

An additional approach is to search the novel for the general life philosophy of its various characters. For instance, do some characters engage in stereotyping other characters? Do they stereotype members of certain social, economic, or religious groups? Do they engage in gender stereotyping? Because stereotypes consist of general concepts applied to specific individuals, they often signal the unwillingness of an individual or group to carefully consider important aspects of their own or others' cultures and environment. Do some characters take their place in society for granted? What does this assumption of privilege tell you about those characters and about contemporary English culture in general?

Sample Topics:

1. **Development of self-identity:** What is Jane's attitude toward herself at the beginning of the story? How does that attitude

change as the plot moves forward? Why does it change? How can the reader recognize scenes in which Jane considers self-identity? Does imagination play a part in her development of self-identity? What does she think of herself at the novel's conclusion?

The development of ideas about self remains strong with Jane. As a child, she considers herself in relation to others. She has not thought of herself as her own person in nearly so serious a manner previously as she does while first in residence at Thornfield Hall. One develops ideas about self partly through comparison to others and also as a result of shouldering new responsibilities and roles. Authors provide signals that indicate characters are undergoing self-realization, such as their looking into a mirror as a means of both literal and symbolic self-reflection, or as daydreaming about possible changes in their lives.

2. **Morality:** What choices about morals do various characters make? On what do they base their systems of morality? How does Jane distinguish right from wrong? How is Jane affected by other characters' ideas about morality? Who voices their moral code most strongly?

In order to write about morality in the novel, you must first decide how to define the terms *moral* and *immoral.* You must consider how each of the cultures in which Jane lives defines morality. You can figure this out by observing how each character behaves and then comparing their actual behavior to what they tell others about moral thought and action. Then you may judge whether they are moral characters, hypocritical characters, or immoral characters. Some may appear immoral at first, but they may later seem to have changed and adopted morality. Or they have acted in a way that causes other characters and you, the reader, to misjudge them. You will also determine why their moral codes prove important to Jane in developing her own code of moral behavior.

3. **Faith:** How do the characters define faith? Are the characters who see themselves as religious also filled with faith? How can the reader determine who has spiritual faith? How does Jane act toward those with faith versus those without faith? Does Jane have spiritual faith? Do some characters have faith in something other than God?

Institutional religion offers its followers rituals they may perform. Some substitute ritual for faith or spirituality. Individuals who have faith tend to behave differently from those who simply follow the steps of rituals. People who live a principled, or moral, life may not necessarily have faith in God, but they may still be "good" people. People who do not seem "religious" may have strong faith in God, turning to a divine being, rather than to religion or a church, to help them when in need.

4. **Materialism:** Which characters own many material objects and have great wealth? What is their attitude toward those objects or wealth? How do they act toward others? What do they assume about those lacking wealth? Do some characters have "new" wealth, as opposed to "old" wealth, money that has been in their family for some time? Does Jane change after she becomes an heiress?

Materialism is a philosophy in which people place great importance on acquiring wealth. Not many people were wealthy prior to the beginning of the 19th century, but that changed as Britain became a major center of trade. In order to write an essay about this topic, you should examine the attitudes of those in the novel who are wealthy and own property. Do they seem to feel that indicates something, not only about their own worth but also that of others? If you can answer that question with supportive material from the novel, you will arrive at an excellent focus for your paper.

5. **Stereotypes:** What are examples of stereotypes that you see in the novel? Who exemplifies the stereotypes? Which of those

characters are able to change their stereotypes? What are the results of the change?

Some people choose to apply stereotypes to others as a matter of convenience, or simply because they remain ignorant about the subject. They may feel that if they have knowledge of one person of another gender or race, they have insight into all such individuals. You may find characters and situations in the novel that disprove this idea. That will allow you to propose a thesis statement about those in the novel who engage in false generalities.

Form and Genre

Consideration of the form and genre of a work of literature can lead to an excellent thesis topic. *Jane Eyre* is a novel, written in prose. It has often been referred to as a gothic novel. Gothic stories involve mystery, ghosts, visions, spooky structures, such as houses and castles, heroines in danger, and mysterious heroes. You may also want to consider what *Jane Eyre* is *not* as you think of the time period in which it was written. For instance, it is not domestic fiction or a novel of manners, types of literature popular close to Brontë's time. If you adopt this approach, you will need to discuss the novel as one specifically written by a woman that focuses on matters important to women in a manner different from other fiction of its day. This topic would require research into popular literature at the beginning of the 19th century using a source such as Louis James's *Fiction for the Working Man, 1830–1850: A Study of the Literature Produced for the Working Classes in Early Victorian Urban England* (1974). An additional approach to the discussion of fiction would center on its narrative elements. Two of those, character and setting, are discussed above. You might also decide to focus on another narrative element, plot—the story's action—and the effect of the novel's division into three sections on that action. Other approaches may concern the plot's use of the Byronic hero as embodied by Mr. Rochester.

Sample Topics:

1. **The gothic novel:** What are characteristics of the gothic novel? Which gothic characteristics might a reader find in *Jane Eyre*? What expectations do readers bring to a novel considered

"gothic"? Does this novel fulfill or disappoint those expectations? What about this novel's plot makes its gothic elements particularly effective?

Because the gothic novel displays a number of specific plot, character, and setting characteristics, it is simple to classify this novel as gothic. In order to develop an essay topic from this approach, you must go beyond the fact that the novel is gothic to discuss why that fact is important to the reader. Examine the manner in which the gothic elements help the author to suggest an overall message she wants the reader to carry away from her story. Make clear that she could not have so clearly transmitted this message without these specific fictional elements. A text such as David Punter and Glynnis Byron's *The Gothic* can provide an overview of gothic elements and the history of that subgenre.

2. *Jane Eyre* **as new fiction:** How might you describe the "typical" novel of the period in which *Jane Eyre* was published? Did specific fiction for women exist? What were its characteristics? How was *Jane Eyre* "new" or different to its readers? What did Brontë do to prepare her readers for this new approach?

In order to write about the novel as new fiction, you need to focus carefully on matters important to women living at the time the book was published, rather than modern women. Your thesis statement must venture a claim as to the importance or effect of new fiction on readers of its era. Any new approach to writing changes traditional characteristics of a genre, and it must make clear to readers why it changes them. They should be able to see the benefit of such changes; otherwise, the author will seem to have little purpose in making such change.

3. **Plot:** Does Brontë build momentum quickly or slowly? Why does she make that choice? Does she balance description with

action? What might have been the effect of her inclusion of more action? How might the plot have been changed to reach the same effect? How does she retain readers' interest in Jane's situation? How does the novel's organization into three sections affect the plot and the reader?

In order to write an essay whose theme centers on plot, you must focus more on the novel's action than its meaning. This does not mean that you will ignore meaning. On the contrary, you should state what you believe to be Brontë's message to the reader and then demonstrate how that guides her shaping of the action. The novel's division into three sections makes it necessary for Brontë to help readers make the transition from one section to the next through the ebb and flow of the action in each part. Action should also build steadily toward a climax, then rapidly diminish following that climax. The protagonist's major epiphany must occur close to the climax, in order to allow the author to bring all elements to a rapid resolution by the novel's conclusion.

4. **The Byronic hero:** What is meant by the term *Byronic hero*? Why is this type of character particularly appropriate for *Jane Eyre*? Why is this type of character appropriate for the era in which the novel was written? How might use of another type of hero alter the story and its effect on readers?

You must begin this essay approach by making clear the characteristics of the Byronic hero, then showing how Mr. Rochester embodies those characteristics. This will not be enough for an essay, however, as you must use these facts to support a thesis statement regarding how this vision of Rochester affects the reader. Brontë specifically selected this type of character for the effect he might have on Jane. Thus, you must consider both characters in order to arrive at a claim as to why the Byronic hero is or is not the best characterization for Rochester.

Language, Symbols, and Imagery

Like all fiction, *Jane Eyre* is filled with language, symbols, and imagery, all adding clues that aid readers in understanding Jane and the story of her life. The author's choice of language, or vocabulary, is an element of fiction known as *style*. A closely related aspect of style is the author's tone, or attitude, toward her characters, subject matter, and readers. For instance, a writer might adopt a sarcastic, gentle, joyful, or forlorn tone in her narrative (that is, all of the words that are not character dialogue). The tone in a character's dialogue also remains crucial for helping readers understand the character. Point of view is an additional aspect of style. The author must choose whether to narrate from a first- or third-person point of view, and some use both. While the first-person point of view may be limiting, it does allow access to the protagonist's thoughts and emotions that she keeps hidden from other characters. Both traditional and literary symbols exist in abundance in *Jane Eyre.* Traditional symbols, which have held the same meaning over time, include the Sun, Moon, water, fire, flowers, birds, trees, the seasons, clothing, and colors. Literary symbols in this novel—those that gain additional meaning through their use in a specific work—include art, specific characters such as Helen and Bertha Mason, food, and locations. Names also offer a source of symbolism, as seen in both character and place-names.

Sample Topics:

1. **Vocabulary and tone:** How do Brontë's word choices affect the reader? What does she do to make her novel more interesting? Can you see patterns in her word choices? How does the characters' dialogue help shape their personalities? How does the characters' dialogue help shape readers' opinions of those characters? In what tone does Jane, the narrator, begin the novel? How do you know? In what scenes and sections of the novel does Jane's tone in narration change? How does the tone change affect the reader? How does the reader detect Jane's attitude toward setting, herself, and other characters?

   In an essay focusing on vocabulary, you will supply examples of words and phrases from the novel's narrative that support your claim. Keep in mind that you must not confuse the author,

Brontë, with the narrator, Jane. For instance, you may claim that Jane always adopts a certain tone when commenting to her audience about one setting. But you may also claim that Brontë makes specific choices in shaping Jane's character through tone. You may also examine Brontë's use of irony throughout the novel. An ironic tone insinuates that things are not as they seem. Fiction may contain both spoken irony, when the characters say one thing but mean another, and dramatic irony, a situation in which the reader may understand something that the characters do not. For all claims regarding tone, you should include examples of descriptions and general commentary in dialogue or narrative that support your contention. You will also want to examine how a character's dialogue tone changes from scene to scene, explaining why that change remains important.

2. **First-person point of view:** What risks does Brontë assume in crafting her novel from a first-person point of view? How does this point of view enhance or detract from the story? Is Jane an adequate narrator?

Brontë chooses to write in the first person, allowing her protagonist Jane to tell the story. A first-person point of view limits what the reader may know, because the narrator's knowledge is also limited. She learns from others by watching them act and listening to them speak, as do readers. Though readers are unable to access other characters through their thoughts, we remain privy to all of the protagonist's thoughts and ideas, which keeps attention trained on that character. Jane even speaks directly to the reader at various points in the novel. In writing about point of view, you will analyze both the positives and negatives associated with a first-person narrative. In order to write an essay on this topic, you will need to thoroughly discuss the limitations, as well as the advantages, of the use of the first person. If you wish to convince readers that this is the "correct" point of view for this particular novel, you will need to imagine it told not only in a third-person voice but also from the point of view of another character. Then you may defend your claim that its present narrative structure remains superior.

3. **Traditional symbols:** Which traditional symbols appear in the novel? How do these symbols aid in reader understanding? Are any traditional symbols used in a nontraditional manner?

   In order to write about traditional symbols, first identify those that you believe are particularly important to the novel. In formulating a theory as to why they are important, you will probably develop a thesis statement on which to base an essay. There are many traditional symbols familiar to the feminist critic, such as birds and the moon, both representing women. Also note clothing changes, as they often signal a symbolic donning of a new identity on the character's part.

4. **Literary symbols:** What literary symbols do you identify in the novel? How might the reader determine what they symbolize? Which specifically represent Jane? Does Brontë connect literary symbols with traditional symbols? If so, what is the effect of these connections on the reader?

   In addition to traditional symbols, almost all fiction contains symbols specific to it alone. These symbols are often generalized, but characters may also symbolize a certain type of objects or place, person or condition of person, such as poverty or ruthlessness. Jane's art is highly symbolic; you could develop an entire essay that focuses on the pictures Jane reluctantly shows Rochester shortly after her arrival at Thornfield Hall. In a combination of the literary with the traditional, the red room in which Aunt Reed orders Jane confined in the first chapter symbolizes danger, due to the red color, and confinement.

5. **Symbolic names:** Which names are symbolic, and what do they specifically symbolize? Why is that symbolism important? What might a reader miss in the novel by not recognizing it? Does anyone change her/his name?

Names need not always be symbolic, but most in *Jane Eyre* do represent the nature of their bearer. Miss Temple, for example, is a figure worshipped by Jane and Helen for her goodness, while Aunt Reed stands straight like a reed, but like that flimsy grass she is easily bent and broken. In addition to character names, the names of locations may also be symbolic. The orphanage of Lowood indeed represents a lowly place, devoid of wealth and warmth; Thornfield Hall presents Jane with many challenges and much pain, while Moor House offers her safe harbor, like a ship adrift that finds a mooring to hold it safely for a time. Name changes often symbolize a shift in self-identity or knowledge. The symbolic meaning of names is easy to identify; your challenge comes with ascertaining its importance to the reader.

Compare and Contrast Essays

If you choose to write a comparison/contrast paper, you will first compare and contrast characters or other narrative elements with one another. Comparisons reveal similarities, while contrasts reveal differences. The differences will generally yield a topic about which you can write. Take care not to simply list your findings in sentence form. While of some interest to the reader, those findings alone do not constitute a claim. You must examine your list closely to find a sound thesis statement on which to base your essay. An excellent way to begin to work toward a thesis is to ask questions about the characters or elements that seem to be opposites of one another. An overall question to begin with is why the author shaped the elements to contrast with one another.

A simple approach to this type of essay is to find contrasts among characters. Ask why Brontë chose to include both Aunt Reed and Miss Temple as mother figures for Jane. In what specific ways do each of these figures represent mothers? Is one superior to the other? How does the reader see that superiority? In what ways? Another pair of strongly contrasting figures is Rochester and St. John Rivers. How does Jane react to each of these figures? What measures does she use in choosing between them? Remember to move beyond the characters' differences to develop a statement that clearly indicates how those differences help the reader better understand the particular characters, Jane, or the story itself.

While characters lend themselves easily to contrast, so do additional topics. The communities that offer Jane surrogate families also contrast greatly in their specific attitudes toward her and the purpose of the family unit. You may also choose to contrast the characters in multiple novels by the same author.

Sample Topics:

1. **Families in *Jane Eyre*:** What family communities exist in the novel? What is each family's attitude toward Jane as a member? What values does each family practice? Which family is the more desirable? What does Jane desire in a family? In which family does Jane seem most comfortable?

   In order to compare and contrast family communities in the novel, you must identify those groups. After identifying them, note how Jane feels when thrust into each group. Whether she feels well received or not may lead to a thesis idea for you. You may also consider how the various families help support what you believe to be Brontë's main point.

2. **Jane Eyre from *Jane Eyre* and Lucy Snowe from *Villette*:** How do Lucy and Jane differ physically? How do they differ emotionally? What life experiences do they have in common? How does each react to conflict? How will their conflicts be solved? Is one more appealing to the reader than another? Why or why not? Do they share the same values and ideals? Do they each realize their dreams or desires?

   While readers expect heroines in different novels to be different, those in novels written by the same author may also be similar. That is because the author may have intended different novels to carry similar messages to readers. Thus, considering the differences between protagonists can lead to a thesis proposal based on how different main characters can relay similar ideas. You may also want to consider setting in the two novels, contrasting the characters' abilities to move from one setting to another and noting what that ease or difficulty tells us about their personalities. The same may be true for the way we see them interacting with others.

Bibliography and Online Resources for *Jane Eyre*

Berlanstein, Leonard R., ed. *The Industrial Revolution and Work in Nineteenth-Century Europe*. New York: Routledge, 1992.

Brontë, Charlotte. *Jane Eyre*. Ebooks of Essential English Literature. Available online. URL: http://www.bronte.netfury.co.uk/jane-eyre/. Downloaded June 14, 2007.

"Charlotte Brontë." About.com: Women's History. Available online. URL: http://womenshistory.about.com/library/bio/blbio_bronte_charlotte.htm. Downloaded August 7, 2007.

"Charlotte Brontë." The Victorian Web. Available online. URL: http://www.victorianweb.org/authors/bronte/cbronte/bronteov.html. Downloaded April 10, 2007.

Chen, Chih-Ping. "'Am I a Monster?': Jane Eyre Among the Shadows of Freaks." *Studies in the Novel* 34 (2002): 367–384.

"Christophine Site on the History and Literature of the Caribbean." The Imperial Archive, School of English at the Queen's University of Belfast. Available online. URL: http://www.qub.ac.uk/schools/SchoolofEnglish/imperial/carib/carib.htm. Downloaded April 10, 2007.

Dickerson, Vanessa. "Spells and Dreams, Hollows and Moors: Supernaturalism in *Jane Eyre* and *Wuthering Heights*." *Victorian Ghosts in the Noontide*. Columbia, MO: University of Missouri Press, 1996. 48–79.

Fraser, Rebecca. *Brontës: Charlotte Brontë and Her Family*. New York: Ballantine Books, 1990.

———. *Charlotte Brontë*. London: Methuen, 1988.

Fuller, Margaret. *Woman in the Nineteenth Century*. 1845. Mineola, NY: Dover Publications, 1999.

Gaskell, Elizabeth. *The Life of Charlotte Brontë*. Ed. Angus Easson. New York: Oxford UP, 2002.

Gilbert, Sandra M. "*Jane Eyre* and the Secrets of Furious Lovemaking." *Novel: A Forum on Fiction* (Summer 1998): 351–372.

Gordon, Lyndall. *Charlotte Brontë: A Passionate Life*. New York: W.W. Norton & Co., 1996.

Heller, Tamar. "Jane Eyre, Bertha, and the Female Gothic." Ed. Diane Hoeveler and Beth Lau. *Approaches to Teaching Brontë's Jane Eyre.* New York: Modern Language Association of America, 1993. 49–55.

Hilton, Boyd. *A Mad, Bad, and Dangerous People?: England 1783–1846.* New York: Oxford UP, 2006.

Imlay, Elizabeth. *Charlotte Brontë and the Mysteries of Love: Myth and Allegory in Jane Eyre.* New York: St. Martin's, 1989.

Keefe, Robert. *Charlotte Brontë's World of Death.* Austin: University of Texas Press, 1979.

Kees, Lara Freeburg. "'Sympathy' in *Jane Eyre.*" *Studies in English Literature, 1500–1900* 45.4 (Autumn 2005): 873–898.

Kreilkamp, Ivan. "Unuttered: Withheld Speech and Female Authorship in *Jane Eyre* and *Villette. Novel: A Forum on Fiction* 32.3 (Summer 1999): 331–354.

Linder, Cynthia A. *Romantic Imagery in the Novels of Charlotte Bronte.* New York: Barnes and Noble, 1978.

Melani, Lilia. "Charlotte Bronte: *Jane Eyre.*" Brooklyn College. Available online. URL: http://academic.brooklyn.cuny.edu/english/melani/cs6/bronte.html. Downloaded April 10, 2007.

Meyer, Susan L. "Colonialism and the Figurative Strategy of Jane Eyre." *Victorian Studies* 33.2 (1990): 247–268.

Michie, Elsie B., ed. *Charlotte Brontë's Jane Eyre: A Casebook.* New York: Oxford UP, 2006.

Moglen, Helen. *Charlotte Brontë: The Self Conceived.* New York: Norton, 1976.

Myer, Valerie, Grosvenor. *Charlotte Brontë: Truculent Spirit.* Totowa, NJ: Barnes and Noble, 1987.

Nandrea, Lori G. "Desiring Difference: Sympathy and Sensibility in *Jane Eyre.*" *Novel: A Forum on Fiction* 37.1–2 (Fall 2003–Spring 2004): 112–134.

Punter, David, and Glynnis Byron. *The Gothic.* Malden, MA: Blackwell Publishing, 2004.

Rockefeller, Laura Selene. "*Shirley* and the Politics of Personal Faith." *Brontë Studies* 32.2 (July 2007): 106–115.

Searle, Allison. "An Idolatrous Imagination? Biblical Theology and Romanticism in Charlotte Brontë's *Jane Eyre.*" *Christianity & Literature* 56.1 (Autumn 2006): 35–61.

Senf, Carol A. "Jane Eyre and the Evolution of a Feminist History." *Victorians Institute Journal* 13 (1985): 67–81.

Shannon, Edgar F. "The Present Tense in *Jane Eyre.*" *Nineteenth-Century Fiction* 10 (1956): 141–145.

Starzyk, Lawrence J. "'The Gallery of Memory': The Pictorial in *Jane Eyre.*" *Papers on Language and Literature* 33 (1997): 288–309.

Steinberg, Marc W. *Fighting Words: Working-Class Formation, Collective Action, and Discourse in Early Nineteenth-Century England.* New York: Cornell UP, 1999.

Stone, Laurie. "Why Charlotte Dissed Emily." *Literary Review* 49.3 (Spring 2006): 63–70.

Stoneman, Patsy. *Brontë Transformations: The Cultural Dissemination of Jane Eyre and Wuthering Heights.* Hemel Hempstead, England: Prentice Hall, 1998.

Taylor, Susan B. "Brontë's *Jane Eyre.*" *The Explicator* 59.4 (Summer 2001): 182–185.

Tyler, Irene. *Holy Ghosts: The Male Muses of Emily and Charlotte Bronte.* New York: Columbia UP, 1990.

Winnifrith, Tom. *A New Life of Charlotte Brontë.* New York: Palgrave McMillan, 1998.

Winnifrith, Tom, and Edward Chiltham. *Macmillan Literary Lives: Charlottë and Emily Brontë.* New York: Palgrave Macmillan, 1994.

THE PROFESSOR

READING TO WRITE

CHARLOTTE BRONTË wrote *The Professor* early in her career, proba-bly during the years 1845 and 1846. It was not published, however, until 1857, two years following her death. Some believe that *The Professor* provided valuable experience for Brontë, who would publish *Jane Eyre,* her most famous and acclaimed novel, in 1847. In both novels Brontë employs a first-person narrator, but in *Jane Eyre* that narrator is the female title character, while in *The Professor* it is the male pro-tagonist, William Crimsworth. Because few women had written novels other than romantic popular fiction narrated from a woman's point of view, Brontë's approach proved remarkable. *The Professor* is often com-pared to her 1853 novel *Villette,* as the two deal with similar subjects. Both are based on her personal experiences as a student and teacher in Belgium.

While critics often judge *Villette* to be the stronger of the two novels, *The Professor* is an important work because it shattered reader expec-tations. Readers accustomed to lengthy, plot-driven novels found this book's brevity and its use of realism startling. Brontë reveals in the pref-ace that she has overcome the "taste" she once had "for ornamented and redundant composition," preferring what she describes as "plain and homely." She wants her protagonist to represent "real living men" for whom no "sudden turn" (the coincidence so common to romantic novels) should suddenly transform him into a wealthy powerful person. She also feels that he would not marry a beautiful woman of high social position. This would result in his enjoying "a mixed and moderate cup" of success, rather than the clichéd happy ending required by traditional romance.

One aspect of the novel that may put some readers off is its inclusion of abundant French phrases. This is necessary to the novel's realism, as William Crimsworth moves from England to Belgium to teach in two schools where French is the spoken language. Belgium, and especially Brussels, then represented the epitome of multilingualism due to the country's history. Brontë remained true to that history in her novel. Readers might employ a French dictionary, but many meanings may be guessed from the context in which the phrases occur.

Brontë uses her novel in part to reflect on the restrictive social class structure that prevents the common working man from improving his lot in life. She also examines gender stereotypes, the weakness of the human character, and the conflict between Protestantism and Catholicism. These themes would reappear in much stronger form in *Jane Eyre,* making *The Professor* a crucial early novel in which Brontë first displays her personal beliefs in fiction. She also includes imagery that would prove vital to the work of later feminist critics, demonstrating a use of many symbols important to gender studies. Most importantly, she shatters stereotypes of both men and women, shaping a man who is not the typical romantic hero and a woman who can confront problems in a logical fashion, rather than requiring a male to solve them for her. As you read, you will want to recognize these elements, keeping track in a notebook of when and where they appear. This type of active reading helps prepare you to write an essay about *The Professor* and is sound practice when reading any assigned literature. After you observe and record, you can begin to analyze aspects of this novel that you find interesting and may want to write about. Following that analysis, you will develop a main point that seems to capture the meaning that your observations suggest.

For example, in one scene that occurs in chapter 12, the main character, William Crimsworth, feels a bit depressed. He decides to open a window and lean out to look into the garden that is between a girls' school and a boys' school, in both of which he teaches. He has recently met the proprietress of the girls' school, Mlle Reuter, and believes himself to be in love with her, but he has not yet told her:

> Above me was the clear-obscure of a cloudless night sky; splendid moonlight subdued the tremulous sparkle of the stars; below lay the garden, varied with silvery luster and deep shade, and all fresh with

> dew; a grateful perfume exhaled from the closed blossoms of the fruit-trees; not a leaf stirred; the night was breezeless. My window looked directly down upon a certain walk of Mademoiselle Reuter's garden, called *l'allée défendue*—so named because the pupils were forbidden to enter it on account of its proximity to the boys' school. It was here that the lilacs and laburnums grew especially thick. This was the most sheltered nook in the enclosure; its shrubs screened the garden-chair where that afternoon I had sat with the young directress.

This passage offers much to analyze, including paradox, foreshadowing, irony, imagery, and symbolism.

The term *clear-obscure* offers a perfect example of paradox, a phrase in which paired terms or ideas act as opposites. The sky could not actually be both clear and obscure, but the description is useful for what it suggests about William. Because the garden is so closely associated with Mlle Reuter, his vision of that garden represents his vision of her. While he believes that his feelings for her are real, he bases his feelings on a half-truth, something that seems clear but is actually obscure. This description is also ironic, suggesting a disparity between what seems to be true and what is actually true. *Irony* means basically that things are not as they seem. Might this phrase act as foreshadowing, predicting that William will later discover his lack of knowledge, that what seemed clear and truthful is actually obscure and false?

The moon and the garden traditionally symbolize the female, as do flowers and perfume. In this case, the moon's light blocks that of the stars, suggesting female power. Notice that the fruit-tree flowers are closed; they do not remain open or accessible to William. What do these symbols suggest about William's developing relationship with the mademoiselle? William believes he is on the verge of a new relationship with the mademoiselle, but symbols can cause the reader to believe she remains inaccessible to him. For example, the dew can symbolize a new beginning, yet that interpretation conflicts with the message the reader gleans from the closed blossoms.

Western literature—that is, literature written in English or in European languages—draws much of its symbolism from the Christian-Judaic tradition, which is based on teachings of the Bible. In the Bible, a tree symbolizes not only knowledge but also temptation, as in the Tree of Knowledge in the story of the Garden of Eden. The tree bore fruit that would make one wise, but that fruit was forbidden to Adam and Eve, and they were punished for sampling it. You might ask, does Brontë suggest that William should not give in to the temptation to pick fruit from the tree he observes? The imagery she provides connects the fruit flowers with Mlle Reuter, thus causing readers to believe that a relationship with her might prove dangerous.

We see continuing contrast in the imagery of "silvery luster" and "shade," the first phrase suggesting light, the other suggesting darkness. Traditionally, light can symbolize knowledge (think of the lightbulb used above a cartoon character's head to show that he has an idea), and darkness can symbolize a lack of knowledge and even evil. No movement exists in the garden, suggesting that William may be imagining what he sees; it is unworldly and still, like a calm preceding a storm. Thus, the lack of movement may also act as foreshadowing that William will soon experience an interruption of his calm meditation. Finally, he observes that Mlle Reuter remains hidden away from everyone, although William was allowed to share her chair. The garden is clearly described as "forbidden" to men, symbolizing the mademoiselle's removal from William's male sphere. Does the evidence indicate that he will be punished for entering that dangerous area? Notice that William remains separated from the garden; he is behind a wall in a building looking down on a scene that belongs to Mlle Reuter; it does not include him. One might anticipate the fact that, despite their previous interaction, the two will never enjoy a romantic relationship.

William observes that the mademoiselle's path is marked with thick "lilacs and laburnums." What does their density suggest? Might they be seen as protection against outsiders like William? You should read about those flowers to learn whether they might symbolize something more specific than just the female. For instance, an important fact about lilacs is that they must be allowed to grow with complete freedom. If they are pruned or cut back, as many plants must be, they will not bloom. What does that fact suggest about Mlle Reuter?

With practice, you will become adept at noticing such clues in literature. Think of the elements demonstrated here, such as foreshadowing, irony, symbolism, and imagery, as tools to help you deduce meaning from a reading. As you read, notice details in the description and narrative that call attention to themselves. You will not necessarily deduce meaning upon first noticing an element or idea. Meaning may come later, as you read more of the text and see those elements repeated.

TOPICS AND STRATEGIES
Themes

Fiction may contain multiple topics, but it generally emphasizes only one major theme or message. You should take notes as you read, recording topics and also questions that you might have about specific topics. You will find sample questions below focusing on several different topics found in *The Professor.*

The Professor contains an abundance of topics, many of which can be found in all of Charlotte Brontë's novels. This novel in particular stresses social issues, such as class structure and education. The restrictions of social structure are clearly evident in William's relationship with his brother Edward. Edward's position as the elder son places William in a subordinate position, further emphasized when he must work as a lowly clerk for his brother, who makes no special allowance for their blood relationship. Because William chooses to interact with relatives of whom Edward does not approve, Edward can use his social position as a wealthy businessman to treat William in a manner one would expect from an employer dealing with his servant. The mill owner Mr. Hunsden makes clear in chapter 4 that William has no power, blaming that lack of power on the fact that William is not a tradesman. Hunsden is a voice for the downtrodden and all members of what contemporary English society considers the "lower classes."

The conflict within the Crimsworth family suggests family as another topic. William's uncles, with whom Edward does not see eye to eye, had supported William's education. Edward takes out his frustration over this arrangement on William, choosing not to allow his younger brother to stay in his home. He even sets his wife's mind against the man she should welcome as her brother-in-law. By the novel's conclusion, Hunsden becomes like family and is more welcomed at William's home than is his own brother. Eventually, upon the Crimsworths moving to England, Hunsden becomes like an uncle to William's son, Victor. William, Frances, and Victor spend much time at Hunsden's home, as does Hunsden at their home. The topic of family is also stressed in the relationship between Frances and her aunt. Although not an active character, Frances's aunt serves as a foil to Edward Crimsworth. In her position as substitute parent for Frances, she supports her niece's bid to improve her social and professional position, being much more interested in Frances's welfare than Edward is in William's.

Gender offers an excellent essay topic for consideration—for example, the contrast in the nature of education between girls and boys. In Brontë's time, expectations for girls were decidedly lower than those for boys. The girls attend school as training for marriage. Genders are also carefully separated during education, symbolized by Mlle Reuter's garden, which acts as a physical barrier between the boys' and girls' schools.

Closely related is the equally strong topic of gender stereotypes, or expectations of behavior for both boys and girls. An example would be Monsieur Pelet's attitude toward women as objects to be used for his own pleasure. William initially thinks of Mlle Reuter as a woman who, surprisingly, seems to possess good sense and reason, while Frances possesses both reason and feeling; either case works against gender stereotypes. Frances's insistence on working and then progressing to owning and managing a school of her own also acts to strongly counter stereotypes of women as being unfit for careers.

Religion presents a strong topic for discussion, particularly the conflict between Catholicism and Protestantism. The narrator speaks of the judgmental nature of his Catholic students, particularly Sophie, who reports everything he says to her priest. Frances, clearly a good and worthy person, is considered a "heretic" within Mlle Reuter's Belgian school due to her practice of Protestantism. While the narrator claims not to be a religious bigot, he firmly blames the mental depravity of his female students on the Church of Rome.

Language and communication offer rich ground for exploration, particularly in light of the frequent use of French. Belgium, and Brussels in particular, offers an excellent setting in which to emphasize multilingualism (see History and Context, below). While Frances's use of English is less than technically perfect, she communicates more clearly than other students do. The narrator, Crimsworth, focuses not only on his students' use of English and his own use of French but also on his own body language. He is careful in how he communicates because of possible error.

Not surprisingly, due to her own experience as a student and teacher in Belgium, Brontë calls the reader's attention to the proper relationship between student and teacher in chapter 14. Hunsden and Frances have a rousing argument regarding the nature of humanity and their two countries, and William frequently remarks on her communicating with him in two languages, each symbolizing a different emotional state for her. When he asks her to call him William rather than monsieur, she refuses, noting the *W* is too difficult to pronounce and that *monsieur* is the term that better fits him.

The French language also makes clear that the setting is not England. Because setting can greatly affect the action and conflict in fiction, an essay could easily focus on the location of the story. Crimsworth must adjust to many aspects of his adopted Belgian culture, but he ends up finding both love and work there. Frances desires to leave Belgium to relocate to England, while Hunsden criticizes England and travels Europe to temporarily escape from what he views as English oppression. These facts suggest an additional topic for a possible essay, that the term *home* must be defined as something more than a simple geographic location.

Isolation is another important topic in *The Professor*. William feels physically, emotionally, and mentally isolated from everyone around him until he meets Frances. She is also isolated from family, friends, and home, causing her to be a perfect match for William. In chapter 25, following the wedding, William notes that the two enjoy a "pleasant isolation," which might be viewed as a paradox, as can the idea that they can be isolated together against the world.

Finally, Brontë asks readers to consider the importance of literature not only to one's mind but to one's physical and emotional well-being. Multiple works of literature are mentioned in the novel, and their reading and translation seem to improve Frances's health. She is literary in another sense as well: By including most of a short story and a complete poem written by Frances, Brontë calls attention to her own act of writing. She also emphasizes for the common reader the superiority of realistic writing over the more traditional romantic approach, especially in chapter 19, which she begins, "Novelists should never allow themselves to weary of the study of real life." Her emphasis on the possible negative effects of romance on readers reappears in several passages. Clearly she believes that romance has played a role in convincing women that they should not enjoy the same privileges and occupations as men. It also transmits damaging messages to men, who may assume the worst of themselves if they are not heroic and materially and physically superior to others. William tells Hunsden that his friend has seen only the "title page" of his happiness, calling the reader's attention to the book's similarity to a story of life.

You may find additional topics in the novel. Pursue them as has been done above, and locate multiple examples. The next step is to ask questions about those topics.

Sample Topics:

1. **Social/class issues:** Which social or class issues are most strongly emphasized? Which characters may be classified into what social class? How do the working class and the aristocratic classes differ? How does the relatively new class of the bourgeoisie relate to other classes? Which class seems to be favored by Brontë? How can you tell? Why does Hunsden so despise the aristocracy?

   Discussions of social and class issues generally focus on a group's level of income. The government who takes best care of its poor is often judged to be the most benevolent and ethical. This view also applies to its citizens. By observing various characters' views about wealth and poverty, and about other characters who fall into those categories, a reader could form a strong thesis statement for an essay. Such issues are not time-bound, so readers of any era may empathize with the class struggle that results.

2. **Family:** How many families are featured in *The Professor*? Are they traditional families, with a father, mother, and children? Are any families deemed more desirable than others? Why? Which family would today's readers judge the "better" family? Why? How do some families in the book succeed at forming strong relationships?

   William is left without a family at the novel's beginning. The portraits of his parents are more meaningful to him than his relationship with his brother. His eventual forming of a family involves much conflict, and at the story's beginning he is blind to the promise of Hunsden's becoming a surrogate relative. An examination of his change in attitude about family based on observation of those around him and on his own self-realizations offers excellent promise for an essay.

3. **Gender:** What gender stereotypes, or expectations for behavior according to one's gender, can you identify? Who matches those stereotypes and behaves in the expected manner? Who does not? How are gender and class issues related? How does that relationship reveal itself in the characters' relationships?

Expectations of behavior for men and women varied little over the centuries prior to Brontë's writing. During her era, a shift toward equality had begun but had not made much progress. However, gender expectations could change within a relationship when those involved decided to make that change. An examination of a character's variance from typical expectations aids in understanding that character's personality. It also influences that character's relationships with everyone around him or her.

4. **Religion:** William states he is not opposed to Catholicism; how, then, should a reader interpret his negative remarks about the faith? In what ways does religion prove important to individual characters? Does one's religion confer important social status? In what ways might a person not practicing the majority religion be vulnerable? How are religion and intellectualism linked?

Through William, Brontë strongly suggests a relationship between religion and freedom. By so doing, she makes the point that independence exists on not only a physical level but also mental and spiritual planes. Certain personalities in the novel seem more suited to being controlled than being independent, and their religion may help explain why that is true. The prevalent European tension between Protestantism and

Catholicism represents other tensions in the novel between people who are "different" from others. Analysis of that effect could make a promising essay.

5. **Language/communication:** Why does the use of multiple languages on the part of Belgians impress William? Why does Brontë include so many French-language phrases in a book written for English speakers? What is the effect on the reader of the use of a foreign language? How might that effect relate to a reader's understanding of the characters? How does the dual language affect the characters? Who has problems communicating? Are the problems related only to the language, or are other aspects involved? What type of communication in addition to spoken language does Brontë emphasize?

When a person must communicate in a language different from their natural language, the effect can be exciting but also disorienting. Self-confidence can be affected. Native language speakers develop certain impressions of foreign speakers based on their use of the language that may prove false. Thus, miscommunication may involve more than spoken language. Communication may vary depending on whether two speakers are alone together or within a larger group. An individual may be an expert in languages, but not necessarily in communication.

6. **Setting:** How does setting shift throughout the novel? What is the effect of a setting change on characters? Who hopes to escape his or her setting? How does setting affect the tone or mood of the story?

When writing about setting, one should consider not only geography but also culture and time period. In *The Professor*, William, Frances, and Hunsden all change settings several times. An essay writer could adopt a cause/effect approach in writing about setting. What are the effects of the setting, and how do those effects prove important to reader understanding?

7. **Isolation:** Who feels isolated? How would the characters define *isolation*? Is it bad? In what circumstances might it be seen as positive?

Generally isolation is considered a state contrary to human nature. However, in *The Professor* Brontë turns many such assumptions on their head. She makes the point that isolation is not bad in all cases, and also that it does not necessarily last forever. That two people can share isolation, as she suggests about William and Frances, makes a most interesting point to consider.

8. **Importance of literature:** Which works of literature does the narrator mention? What do they have in common? Which characters read them? What effect does the literature have on the novel's readers? What is the purpose of Frances's short story and poem? Why does William view realism as superior to romance?

Brontë has referred to so many specific works of literature that she must deem them crucial to character development. She may intend that readers judge characters based on their attitudes toward reading. William believes that romance weakens one's character and ability to reason; we learn this in his comments about Mlle Reuter at the end of chapter 10.

Character

Characters from fiction provide a wealth of possibilities as essay topics. One may examine the relationship between the protagonist and antagonist, but equally interesting is an analysis of the part played by minor characters. As the protagonist, William encounters various antagonists. Astute readers understand that the protagonist and antagonist cannot be labeled "good" and "bad" or "hero" and "villain," as human nature is seldom that simple. The minor characters of the girl students to whom William refers so often offer an interesting focus for analysis. In addition, an essay could compare and contrast the male or female characters, or analyze each group in respect to the gender stereotypes they represent. For instance, William, Edward, Hunsden, and M. Pelet offer several different types of male personalities, each supporting Brontë's message for readers. Characters may be examined in foil relationships as well. An example in this novel would be Mlle Reuter and Frances Henri, who are both teachers, ambitious regarding their futures, and attracted to William. However, they also have crucial differences, adding texture and edge to the novel's plot.

Sample Topics:

1. **The protagonist and the antagonist:** Who represents the antagonist? If more than one antagonist exists, how does each one cause conflict for the protagonist? How does the protagonist act toward each? Can an antagonist also support a protagonist? If so, how? Is the protagonist heroic? Is the antagonist evil? Is their conflict realistic and believable?

   The purpose of any antagonist is to provide conflict for the protagonist. If multiple antagonists exist, they probably do not all contribute to the same source of conflict. A skilled writer generally makes clear each character's motivation for his or her action, in order to make that action believable to the reader. Thus, we should understand exactly why Edward, Mlle Reuter, and M. Pelet challenge William. The reader observes all of the main characters confronting conflict and their reactions to that conflict. How one handles conflict reflects much about his or her personality. Whether or not the character's approach to conflict changes over time can define that character as dynamic or flat. Conflict generally causes the protagonist to experience an epiphany, or life-changing realization, which is important to identify when one writes an essay.

2. **Minor characters:** Who are the minor characters in *The Professor*? What is their purpose? How do they interact with the major characters? Do they change their approach from the beginning to the end of the story? What seem to be the motivations for their actions?

The term *minor* does not equate to the term *unimportant*. Most minor characters prove crucial to action in fiction, and most support the conflict in which the protagonist becomes ensnared. The young girls all challenge William in his position as teacher, and his comments about them reveal much about his personality and his beliefs. Their interaction and contrast with Frances is also important as William notices and eventually comes to value her. Edward represents a minor character due to his short tenure in the plot, but he proves vital to William's future. Students can consult Alex Woloch's *The One vs. the Many: Minor Characters and the Space of the Protagonist in the Novel* (2004) for a better understanding of the traditional relationship between major and minor characters.

3. **Characters as gender stereotypes:** What is a stereotype in fiction? Which characters represent stereotypes in *The Professor*? Are they so stereotypical as to be unbelievable? What purpose do they serve for Brontë? How do they support the meaning or theme of the novel?

Lewis Turco's *The Book of Literary Terms* (1999) may be helpful in understanding the use of stereotypes in fiction. A stereotype is based on a generality, and many gender stereotypes arise from fairy tales, written to teach traditional gender behavior to boys and girls. One gender stereotype example is the wicked stepmother, seen in such stories as "Snow White" and "Hansel and Gretel." Another fairy-tale stereotype is that of the hero, commonly a prince on a white horse, which suggests ideals very difficult for a real male to uphold. These stereotypes often prove difficult to overcome in fiction, and some writers, especially those referred to as feminist writers, use them in order to subvert, or work against, the stereotype. In *The Professor*, Brontë creates a protagonist who acts "against type"—that is, one who behaves in a way that counters the stereotype of the ever-victorious and successful male. The same could be said for the character of Frances Henri, a woman who is neither beautiful nor wealthy, yet is most admirable. Even Mlle Reuter, while playing the manipulating "other woman," goes against type in the rational "male" approach to achieving success. However, as she conquers M. Pelet, he being another gender stereotype as the misogynist French lover, she remains the stereotypical controlling woman.

History and Context

Historical events or movements occurring during any novel's writing and the context, or surroundings, in which those events and movements occur can provide excellent topics for essays about fiction. At the time Brontë was writing, Britain was becoming a formidable world power. The Industrial Revolution was in full swing, and trade had become essential to the success of many in the country. Adam Smith's *An Inquiry into the Nature and Causes of the Wealth of Nations* (1776) had claimed that business should be allowed to function with no controls, and England took that claim literally. Business as a concept remained morally and ethically neutral for Smith. However, Brontë makes evident that financial success may challenge one's ethics and affect one's morality. Hunsden provides a vehicle through which Brontë can express this idea in his conflict with the materialistically successful Edward. Hunsden has benefited from England's growth as a trade power, but he is not blind to the negative effects such growth has had on workers and the lower classes. While some like Frances idealize England, Hunsden's realization about its despicable treatment of the poor causes him to travel the world, as if in search of a better place to live.

Poverty also suggests a solid topic for an essay. None of the novel's main characters is wealthy, and William and Frances both experience poverty. As the narrator, William makes clear that poverty does not suggest slovenliness or evil; on the contrary, many of the poorest individuals work hard to better their lives. One way lives could be bettered was through education, an obvious topic for this novel. An education could qualify one for employment, but Brontë suggests it can do more, even affect one's physical condition.

The religious dispute between Protestants and Catholics forms another background for the novel. Belgium, the setting for most of the novel, was divided on the basis of language and religion. Following the Napoleonic

Wars, Belgium was created when Dutch-speaking Flemings and French-speaking Walloons formed a new state; residents of the very small eastern area were predominantly German. As the country's capital, Brussels was bilingual. The Industrial Revolution emphasized a linguistic north-south division in the country. Wallonia, in the south, became an early industrial boom area, affluent and politically dominant; it favored the French and their language, as well as Catholicism. Flanders, in the north, where most residents spoke Dutch and many practiced Protestantism, remained agricultural. Because industry gained such importance, Brussels and Wallonia both enjoyed superior economic and political systems to those of Flanders. After 1830, the formation of the two political parties, the Catholic and the Liberal (an anti-Catholic party), symbolized the conflict caused by religious and linguistic practice.

While religion and the social and class issues mentioned in this section have been previously discussed as possible topics, that discussion would center on the characters involved in religious, social, and class experiences. Such matters could also be discussed in the broader context of history and society. One might gain insight into the effect of culture on Charlotte Brontë by reading Tom Winnifrith's *The Brontës and Their Background*. Additionally, a more general source about 19th-century Europe would be required for support in this type of essay. You might consult Michael Rapport's *Nineteenth-Century Europe* or Michael S. Melancon and John C. Swanson's *Nineteenth Century Europe: Sources and Perspectives from History*. Excellent Internet sources include Paul Halsall's site, "The Long Nineteenth Century," found at http://www.fordham.edu/halsall/mod/modsbook3.html.

Sample Topics:

1. **England as a world power:** Which characters comment about England's place in the world? How do you interpret Hunsden's statements in chapter 24 about England's significance as a world power? Which characters benefit from English trade power? How might you describe their personalities? How do they define success? How do they interact with others?

   The characters in *The Professor* are easily divided into two groups: those who benefit from England's industrial expansion and those who do not. Brontë establishes the two groups as types, suggesting her feelings toward the groups. Through William, she asks how one should define success. William must leave England in order to find personal success, a fact that would form an excellent thesis statement. A strong approach to an essay would be to analyze Frances's attitude toward England. In addition to noting her wish to move to England, a study of her debate with Hunsden over the advantages and disadvantages of various nationalities, including her own Swiss culture, would offer insight into this topic.

2. **Poverty:** How does one define *poverty*? Does that definition differ from one culture to another? Which characters are poor? What makes them sympathetic or unsympathetic characters? What types of support are made available to those in poverty? Should a government care for its poor? If not, where should the poor turn for care and help?

At the time Brontë wrote, her nation had not yet developed social programs. Those who possessed material goods had certain attitudes toward those who did not. Often a government's attitude toward socioeconomic groups affected individual attitudes. Adam Smith's ideas about business did not encompass poverty, giving the newly formed industrial manufacturing class an excuse to do the same. A review of Smith's ideas regarding business would be helpful prior to writing an essay on this topic.

3. **Religion:** Why does William hold Catholics in low regard? How does Catholicism distinguish one person from another in the Belgian culture? How does Hunsden's cultural background prepare him for the Belgian attitude toward religion? Is William judgmental about spirituality or organized religion? How does one distinguish between the two?

Religion is important in *The Professor* due to its connection to national issues in Belgium, whose citizens divided their country according to cultural and religious background. William enjoys the relative protection of his Protestant faith in his mostly Protestant country of England. However, he finds himself displaced to the French section of Brussels, which supports Catholicism. Religion represents one of several cultural barriers in the novel, all of which prove important in shaping its characters.

Philosophy and Ideas

In Brontë's time, English society faced enormous challenges to traditional philosophy and ideas as unprecedented changes took place due to factors associated with the Industrial Revolution. That revolution created an entirely new social class in the form of the bourgeoisie, that group of business people and manufacturers who worked to transfer an ever-increasing array of goods from the worker to the consumer. They became the newly wealthy, adopting ideas from Adam Smith's *Wealth of Nations* as their philosophy. While they grew wealthy, the poor workers became more impoverished, faced with appalling and dangerous working conditions as well as a lack of medical care. Gender issues continued to cause conflict, as women increasingly desired a new place out of the domestic sphere. Ironically, poor women could easily find work in factories, while women of the middle class like Brontë had few choices. They could work as governesses or companions, but class restrictions meant any other type of work was considered vulgar.

One support for what would later become the women's movement was the great increase in the reading audience. Although still often denied a formal education, women could turn to printed matter, which was suddenly in abundance due to the development of cheap printing methods, for information and models. Classic works, such as those by John Milton, were often used for self-education. But the increase of popular publishing could prove a disadvantage to the reading public. Some works were used to control women by presenting material that instructed them in "proper" obedient behavior. Popular romances offered unrealistic scenarios, which promoted fantasies of a better life for both men and women through love and relationships that most would never experience. Nancy Armstrong's *How Novels Think: The Limits of Individualism from 1719–1900* (2005) and Garrett Stewart's *Dear Reader: The Con-*

scripted Audience in Nineteenth-Century British Fiction (1996) deal with such phenomena.

The value of work also offers an excellent topic for an essay. If women of the middle class could work, their efforts promoted a sense of self-value. Many saw work as a type of religion, to be practiced regularly and to be looked upon not merely as a source of income but as inherently valuable in itself. Others found through work a way by which they might improve the lives of those around them and, ultimately, their national environment.

Sample Topics:

1. **The philosophy of wealth:** Which characters have wealth? How did they gain their wealth? Do they regard it as a reward? Do they feel they should put the wealth back into their community? What happens if they lose their wealth? What do those living in poverty do to try to gain wealth? What makes some succeed while others fail? Which wealthy characters practice an ethical approach to enjoying or using their wealth?

   For many in the cultures described by Brontë, wealth came when they recognized an opportunity and actively pursued it. Others simply inherited wealth or manipulated the system to their own benefit. Self-identity could be affected by wealth and poverty. Some characters gain wealth and power and use it to help others, while other characters simply desire more wealth. Brontë stresses matters of materialism so often in the novel that she must be attempting to transmit a particular message to her readers.

2. **The philosophy of gender:** What forces seem to determine the manner in which men and women were expected to behave? By what means did those forces operate? Were they forces of civil or social law? Why did some men and women seem to overcome those forces? What did society think of them?

   In most instances in Western culture, gender roles are dictated by social forces, rather than by civil law. However, in some instances women were restricted from a certain occupation or activity. For instance, in the 19th century, women in England could not take degrees in medicine or law and could not serve as clergy. The women in *The Professor* cannot break free of civil restrictions, but they can challenge social restrictions. Such challenges often incur specific consequences. In order to write an essay about the philosophy of gender, one would need to identify the source of the forces acting to control men and women.

3. **The power of the written word:** How did reading serve to control certain groups of people? What evidence of this do you find in *The Professor*? Can one differentiate between control of the spirit and control of the mind? Why would such differentiation prove important in analyzing a culture's reading habits? Why is Brontë concerned with the idea of one group taking power over another through reading? Why should you be concerned about this today?

This topic remains closely related to the one discussed in the opening section on themes. However, one may take a different approach to reading habits among the common man and woman of the 19th century as part of an ongoing attempt by the upper classes to control the working classes. Much research has been done on this fascinating topic, and that research could support an excellent essay focusing on Brontë's reflection regarding such controls. By utilizing characters in *The Professor* as representatives of various classes and analyzing the contemporary messages that popular literature delivered to them, one can produce a microcosm of the reading public of Brontë's day. Although much of the plot is set outside England, because those with whom William deals are learning English through reading, the microcosm theory can hold. One can also relate such control to today's popular books, as well as to additional media materials.

Form and Genre

The Professor is a novel in form, its genre being fiction. This genre allows an author to build a story around his or her own experiences, filling it with characters who did not really exist, but who represent true characters. The novels most read by women of Brontë's time were labeled domestic fiction or romantic fiction. Critics believe that both were used to teach readers, especially women, their proper place in the world. The introduction to Janice A. Radway's study of contemporary readers of fiction, *Reading the Romance: Women, Patriarchy, and Popular Literature* (1991), recounts the effects of romance in Brontë's era and goes on to show that some of those desired effects in controlling women still linger. As a woman who yearned for more freedom for her sex, Charlotte Brontë sought to counter the traditional novel by writing one with a more realistic approach. She expresses her opinion within the novel that romance can poison and weaken the mind that must face challenges in a difficult daily existence. She also adopts a male first-person point of view that proved a new experience for her readers. Her plot incorporated traditional elements, such as a foreign setting and adventure, but it also introduced not so traditional elements, such as an unheroic hero and a heroine who was intelligent and wise rather than beautiful. One might write about form by examining any of the formal elements of fiction, with plot providing a strong focus. In the case of this novel, point of view also provides a strong focus due to a female writer's adoption of a male point of view.

Sample Topics:

1. ***The Professor* as realistic fiction:** What is meant by the term *realism* when applied to fiction? What is meant by the term *romantic* when applied to fiction? What does Brontë state in the novel's preface about her use of realism? Why does she view realism as preferable to romanticism? What were some obstacles she had to overcome in order to appeal to her audience? How does the novel itself comment about its realistic approach? Is its conclusion predictable?

   When writing about approaches in fiction such as realism and romanticism, one must first define terms. Books such as Duncan Heath's *Introducing Romanticism* (2006) and Pam Morris's *Realism* (2003) can be helpful. Brontë dared to depart from the typical approach to fiction, especially fiction for women. An essay investigating and defending possible reasons for that departure would require sources not only about the genre but also about reading preferences of the era. You may want to consult online sources, including the series "Learning to Write in Nineteenth Century England," found at http://www.nrdc.org.uk/index.asp (search for "Learning to Write").

2. **Plot:** What conflicts are most evident, and between which characters? How does the conflict help define the protagonist and antagonist? How does the rising action propel the plot forward?

A most important consideration when analyzing plot, the series of events that constitute a story, is to examine conflict. Conflict supplies the momentum for plot, building tension to a crucial point known as climax. Following the climax, the *falling action* should be far briefer than the *rising action* that heightened the tension prior to climax. In an essay that focuses on plot, one might declare the plot to be fast- or slow-moving and then explain how that rate of movement supports the author's style and message. In novels, *mini-climaxes* may occur in each chapter, all of which build to the major climax; tracing those smaller climaxes can illustrate the author's technique in plot building. Some conflicts will be resolved in the climaxes, others will not, particularly in *The Professor.* One might defend the idea that this is due to the fact that the novel represents realism.

Language, Symbols, and Imagery

Brontë is a master of language, symbolism, and imagery. Her skillful use of the topic of language has been discussed previously, as has the judgmental tone that results from her personal vocabulary. Other important terminology includes the many uses of figurative language, or comparisons, by Brontë. Examples include William's description of his childhood as containing some "overcast" days with "cold" and "stormy hours" in chapter 7. He later compares himself to a spiny porcupine when describing his reaction to M. Pelet, whom he believes to have stolen the attention of Mademoiselle Reuter at one point. Brontë also employs personification, as when referring to a cloud as a woman by using the pronoun *her.*

As discussed in the opening to this chapter, many symbols found in this novel are common to those termed *feminist* by later critics. One example is the moon, long a symbol of the female. The moon reflects the light of the sun, a traditional symbol of the male, thus establishing the hierarchical relationship between the genders. Gardens and flowers, which prove crucial to *The Professor,* also symbolize the female and are often seen as connected to the Garden of Eden. Thus, the imagery of Mademoiselle Reuter's garden suggests the temptation of Adam (male) by Eve (female) that occurred in the biblical story about Eden. Birds are also female symbols, as is any type of sewing, including needlework and knitting. Various birds, such as the cormorant, are featured in *The Professor*; Brontë also highlighted this melancholy creature in *Jane Eyre*. Both of the main female characters in this novel engage in sewing, which can represent the creative side of the woman who engages in that activity. More often, it symbolizes woman's plight to sit quietly and work alone in isolation. When William describes Mlle Reuter's knitting, he notes, "Her humble, feeble mind is wholly with her knitting," adding that if she can only complete her project, that will be "enough for her." When characters gaze into a mirror, or see their reflection, this symbolizes questions of self-identity; although in literature, women usually are the ones using the mirror, owing to society's emphasis on their physical appearance, William is described more than once with a mirror. Other traditional symbols include the rain followed by a rainbow as signaling a purification and hope for the future. The seasons also symbolize the stages of new life (spring) through death (winter).

Sample Topics:

1. **Figurative language:** Why do authors employ figurative language? How does Brontë employ it? Does it emphasize any particular message? Does it add or detract from the story?

   Authors never use language without thought; they carefully plan word choice. Thus, when they select figurative language rather than simple objective description, that approach is done consciously. Figurative language not only helps the reader to better visualize the events, setting, and characters, it also may reflect a character's personality, intellect, or creativity if she or he uses such references. In this instance, William as the narrator employs all the narrative language the reader sees. An essay might suggest what Brontë wants readers to think of William, citing his use of language as evidence.

2. **Symbols:** Which symbols are traditional? Which symbols are literary? Which symbols appear most often? Which symbols are used in an unusual way? What is the effect of that use?

An essay about symbolism may argue that a work is quite traditional, or that it departs from a traditional approach, by noting for support the symbols the author employs. As mentioned above, William's reflection is seen in a mirror in this novel. You might propose a reason why Brontë departs from shaping the traditional use of the mirror by women, supporting that claim to write an essay. You may also write about how symbols support certain topics, such as that of temptation, greed, poverty, or power.

Bibliography and Online Resources for *The Professor*

Alexander, Christine, ed. *The Early Writings of Charlotte Brontë.* New York: Blackwell Publishers, 1982.

Armstrong, Nancy. *How Novels Think: The Limits of Individualism from 1719–1900.* New York: Columbia UP, 2005.

Bock, Carol. *Charlotte Brontë and the Story Teller's Audience.* Iowa City: University of Iowa Press, 1992.

Brontë, Charlotte. *The Professor.* Ebooks of Essential English Literature. Available online. URL: http://www.bronte.netfury.co.uk/professor/. Downloaded June 14, 2007.

"Charlotte Brontë." The Victorian Web. Available online. URL: http://www.victorianweb.org/authors/bronte/cbronte/bronteov.html. Downloaded April 10, 2007.

Duthie, Enid. *The Foreign Vision of Charlotte Brontë.* New York: Barnes and Noble, 1975.

Fuller, Margaret. *Woman in the Nineteenth Century.* Mineola, NY: Dover Publications, 1999.

Gaskell, Elizabeth. *The Life of Charlotte Brontë.* Ed. Angus Easson. New York: Oxford UP, 2002.

Halsall, Paul. "The Long Nineteenth Century." Internet Modern History Sourcebook. Available online. URL: http://www.fordham.edu/halsall/mod/modsbook3.html. Downloaded June 25, 2007.

Linder, Cynthia A. *Romantic Imagery in the Novels of Charlotte Brontë.* New York: Barnes and Nobel, 1978.

The Literature Network. "The Professor." Available online. URL: http://www.online-literature.com/brontec/the_professor/. Downloaded June 14, 2007.

Maynard, John. *Charlotte Brontë and Sexuality.* New York: Cambridge UP, 1984.

Melancon, Michael S., and John C. Swanson. *Nineteenth Century Europe: Sources and Perspectives from History.* New York: Longman, 2007.

Rapport, Michael. *Nineteenth-Century Europe.* New York: Palgrave McMillan, 2005.

Rockefeller, Laura Selene. "*Shirley* and the Politics of Personal Faith." *Brontë Studies* 32.2 (July 2007): 106–115.

Rosengarten, Herbert J. "The Brontës." *Victorian Fiction: A Second Guide to Research.* Ed. George H. Ford. New York: Modern Language Association, 1978.

Starzyk, Lawrence J. "Charlotte Brontë's *The Professor*: The Appropriation of Images." *Journal of Narrative Theory* 33.2 (Summer 2003): 143–162.

Stewart, Garrett. *Dear Reader: The Conscripted Audience in Nineteenth-Century British Fiction.* Baltimore: Johns Hopkins UP, 1996.

Winnifrith, Tom. *The Brontës and Their Background: Romance and Reality.* 2nd ed. Houndsmill, Basingstoke, Hampshire: Macmillan, 1988.

———. *A New Life of Charlotte Brontë.* New York: Palgrave McMillan, 1998.

Winnifrith, Tom, and Edward Chiltham. *Macmillan Literary Lives: Charlottë and Emily Brontë.* New York: Palgrave Macmillan, 1994.

SHIRLEY

READING TO WRITE

BEFORE CHARLOTTE Brontë wrote *Shirley, A Tale,* she had decided to create something completely different from the popular *Jane Eyre* (1847). She reacted to criticism of *Jane Eyre*'s fantastic aspects and determined to write a novel that was realistic to the last detail. She had hoped that book would be *The Professor,* but following its multiple rejections, she settled down to work on the manuscript that would be *Shirley.* Many authors produce fragments of manuscripts that remain incomplete but clearly reflect aspects of later published works. Charlotte Brontë did so with a manuscript tentatively titled "John Henry" that bears many similarities to both *The Professor* and *Shirley.* "John Henry" features two brothers, the older of the two being unsympathetic to the younger one, resembling the Crimsworths of *The Professor.* It also contains many plot and character similarities to *Shirley,* including a mill owner named Moore and a plot focus on the Luddite problems of West Yorkshire. Critics recognize "John Henry" as Brontë's attempt to revise and improve *The Professor,* but one that instead looked forward to *Shirley.*

Brontë struggled through multiple tragedies to produce *Shirley,* including the death of her brother Branwell in September 1848. Emily followed him, dying that December, shortly after which Anne became fatally ill. Charlotte served as Anne's nurse, continuing to write and finishing volume 2 of the three-volume *Shirley* just before her sister's death on May 28, 1849. Most critics believe that Brontë's experiences influenced *Shirley*'s plot, despite her determination to remain focused on the working people of Yorkshire and the historical 1812 Luddite riots. Brontë titled the first chapter of *Shirley*'s third volume "The Valley of the Shadow of Death," centering it on the extended illness of the character Caroline. The balance of the novel seems to be a tribute to Brontë's dead sisters, although the novel as a whole exuded detailed familiarity with the Yorkshire landscape and its people. Writing the novel proved a much-needed distraction from Brontë's grief, and it was published during the months following Anne's death.

Brontë spent more time and effort revising *Shirley* than she had *Jane Eyre*, a fact that may reflect her state of mind following the loss of her siblings and best friends. The novel received mixed reviews, frustrating Brontë, who had written her realistic story in order to please those who had criticized *Jane Eyre* as too sensational. To her recorded dismay, she read reviews by those same critics who stated they longed for the excitement of *Jane Eyre*, noting that *Shirley* put them to sleep. A few critics did praise *Shirley* for being of a higher "womanly" character than *Jane Eyre*, a reflection, Brontë thought, of the fact that by that time, many critics and readers knew the true identity behind her publishing pseudonym, Currer Bell. Even the review by George Henry Lewes, a great champion of Brontë/Bell's work, stressed Brontë's gender, noting that her treatment of the curates in *Shirley* was "offensive, uninstructive, and unamusing" in light of the fact that she was the daughter of a clergyman. However, one review that did please Brontë marked *Shirley* as a strong examination of woman's place in English society and described the novel as rebellious without demeaning its author's gender.

Shirley is not read with the frequency of Brontë's other novels, but it does offer students an interesting opportunity to write about the historical facts that inspired it. Brontë handles details of Luddite riots and the suffering of factory workers with care. Such conflicted stories best satisfied her, and she willingly admitted that she could not bear to write simply of social or fashionable matters of the day, as did some of her fellow novelists.

When searching for essay ideas, one should approach *Shirley* just as any other novel, keeping a sharp outlook for detail that suggests an interesting topic. All good essay writers are also good observers. While reading a story for thesis statement possibilities, keep a record of key observations that may prove invaluable later. As you read, note the page numbers of any passages that appear rich with possibilities for analysis and interpretation. Few writers immediately recognize their essay topics. Rather, careful reading and note-taking inspire them to ask questions that may lead to strong thesis statements.

Consider, for instance, the following passage from chapter 10, "Old Maids." This chapter is the last entry in the first of the three volumes that compose *Shirley*. In this scene, Caroline, young cousin to Robert Moore and quite in love with him, recalls times they had spent together outdoors; the landscape of spring and summer provides a fitting backdrop for her romantic notions. Now in autumn, closed up in a quiet house, she understands that such intimate moments spent with Robert remain nothing but memories:

> Robert's features and form were with her; the sound of his voice was quite distinct in her ear; his few caresses seemed renewed. But these joys being hollow, were, ere long, crushed in: the pictures faded, the voice failed, the visionary clasp melted chill from her hand, and where the warm seal of lips had made impress on her forehead, it felt now as if a sleety rain-drop had fallen. She returned from an enchanted region to the real world: for Nunnely wood in June, she saw her narrow chamber; for the songs of birds in alleys, she heard the rain on her casement; for the sigh of the south wind, came the sob of the mournful east; and for Moore's manly companionship, she had the thin illusion of her own dim shadow on the wall.

To begin an analysis of this paragraph, one might choose to examine its tone. Tone, an aspect of style, illustrates the author's attitude toward her subject and characters. Because *style* may be defined at its simplest as vocabulary choice, you could examine the paragraph for words that imbue the scene with a particular mood or feeling. Examples include the words *hollow, crushed, faded, failed, chill, sleety, real, narrow, sigh, sob, illusion, dim,* and *shadow*. A quick analysis suggests that all of these words taken together give the scene a somber tone, one that is not completely depressed, yet is devoid of hope. Questions that could lead to a thesis statement might include, first, why did Brontë select so many words with negative connotations, and second, why did she compress them all into this one paragraph? Tone proves crucial to revealing details about main characters, and perhaps that is Brontë's intent. Thus, the answers to your questions will lead to statements that could form the basis of writing about how tone supports character development.

Another approach to interpretation of this strongly imagined scene would be to concentrate on imagery and symbolism. Caroline thinks Robert is with her in feature and form, meaning she can clearly recall his physical appearance and also the intimacy of their verbal exchanges and slight physical contact, but that memory does not satisfy her. For one thing, his caresses, while obviously cherished, were "few" in nature, suggesting that he does not return her feelings. She draws joy from the memory, but again, she qualifies her description by adding the adjective *hollow,* and we discover immediately the result of the hollow effect, because the memory "crushed in." It lacks substance and so is easily destroyed. The voice is not only indistinct, it actually fails, meaning that she can no longer hear it distinctly as she first imagined. She must accept her imaginings for what they are, nothing more than a vision. The conjured touch from Robert that at first seemed warm becomes "chill." The adept reader will note that the touch does not freeze with any abrupt change in temperature but loses its warmth, as autumn gradually loses the warmth of summer. However, in the next image, Robert's warm kiss on her forehead feels more like a drop of sleet, lowering the temperature from a chill to true cold. Sleet does not project the nurturing symbolism of rain, although both bring moisture to the ground. Rather, sleet represents an attack on the life-giving rain, changing its form from nurturing liquid to a near-solid, freezing it into an unpleasant state.

The descriptor *enchanted* echoes the previous word *visionary,* as Caroline admits to herself that her time spent with Robert was more daydream than reality, the state to which she must return. Brontë uses the preposition *for* here to mean "instead of," so that Caroline thinks instead of the lovely summer woods, she sees only the confinement of her room. The woods on a summer day symbolize freedom, while the chamber symbolizes entrapment. The songs of birds—animals who serve as a traditional symbol for women and also for states of independence or the lack thereof—have been traded for sounds of rain, not a happy exchange. Brontë also adds the detail that the rain drops on a casement, meaning a window. That image suggests Caroline trapped inside, looking out at a blurred and melancholy world, the window and autumn weather separating her from the birds and the pleasant summer season spent with Robert that they represent. Whereas the warm summer breeze from the south sighed, much like a lover might, the east wind sobs, mourning like Caroline for something lost.

Finally, having erased Moore's companionship as her dream dissolves, Caroline has to replace it, not with her own presence but with something less, just her shadow. This suggests that Caroline no longer has a full presence but has become a shadow of herself, a popular phrase suggesting a wasting away. Because Caroline's guardian will enforce rules that she may no longer see Robert and she will become ill from the effect of that separation, the reference to a shadow may act as a foreshadowing of future danger to Caroline. A question that leads to a thesis statement based on these observances could be: How do the combined imagery and symbolism in this passage help the reader better understand Caroline? They definitely help the reader understand Caroline's imaginative personality, her romantic inclinations toward Robert, and they also suggest her emotional decline may signal an impending physical decline as well.

You can see how much potential a single paragraph may hold. Many such opportunities will appear as you read through this text. Remember to take notes as you proceed, so that you will not have to waste valuable time and energy searching for passages that you seem to recall but for which you cannot remember page numbers.

Suggestions for topics and strategies to use in investigating topics appear in the sections that follow. These suggestions should be taken as sample ideas, not specific ideas to be adopted in order to complete an essay assignment. The technique of developing questions is crucial to a strong thesis production. After reviewing these suggestions, you may move on to practice this technique on your own.

TOPICS AND STRATEGIES
Themes

Shirley contains several themes that offer promise for an essay. Romance, as in the rituals involved with love, is one possibility. Certainly romance is not treated in the same manner as in Brontë's other novels, since it assumes a secondary importance to the action associated with the Luddite rebellion. At least, that is what a reader believes early on. As time passes, however, Robert Moore, a character deeply involved with the conflict, realizes the importance of love and family. Still, much of the romantic behavior in this novel is determined by the time period and the rebellion, both of which are aspects of setting. The reader observes several individuals who are in love or have been in love, and they each behave in a different manner.

A second interesting topic is education, or more properly, different characters' attitudes toward education. It is specifically involved in several scenes, and Caroline's relationship to her guardian is partially based on her role as student and his role as teacher. In volume 3, chapter 13, Robert

Moore remarks that he would like to find an "orphan girl" for whom he could act as a teacher. Louis Moore is a teacher who has served as tutor to the son of Shirley's former guardian and also to Shirley. He even muses about her while alone in a classroom in volume 3, chapter 6, and the title of chapter 9 in that volume is "The Schoolboy and the Wood-Nymph." Brontë's era did not embrace universal education, which would not arrive until later in the century, despite interest by a limited number of "radicals." For the most part, the upper classes did not desire an education for the lower classes, who also did not see the value of an education. Children worked rather than attend school, helping to support a family that did not want to lose their income in favor of schooling. Religious disputes also delayed the offer of education to all, due to the efforts of special interest groups. In 1843, a factory bill that included education also insisted that all headmasters had to be from the Church of England. Education at last became a reality for all with the 1870 Education Act. Contrary to conventional contemporary attitudes toward education, the Brontë family supported it; all members of their household had some formal education, and three of the daughters attempted to open a school, a venture that was not successful. Thus, Charlotte Brontë's emphasis on education is unusual in its strength, suggesting it is a topic worthy of consideration for an essay.

Sample Topics:

1. **Romance:** Who is in love with whom? For which characters is love unrequited (unreturned)? How do those who love in vain react to that problem? What conflicts of their own making do those in love experience? What conflicts are inflicted upon them by another source? How do they resolve various conflicts? Do the resolutions seem realistic? Does the reader find the fact that two brothers marry the two main female characters satisfactory, or is it a contrived plot aspect? What message does Brontë want to transmit about romance?

   The person who writes about this novel's romance might take a comparison/contrast approach, examining two couples and discussing their similarities and differences and what unites each of the couples. An alternative approach could focus on the fact that some characters must learn certain lessons before they become ready for romance. An interesting scene centering on Caroline's naïve attitude about romance appears in volume 1, chapter 7, as she attempts to speak to her uncle about his dead wife. In contrast to Caroline, Shirley is quite sophisticated and knowledgeable about love and romance. Caroline wants to marry, while Shirley does not initially want to marry. Does their socioeconomic class affect their choices?

2. **Education:** Who is educated? Who is not? What methods are used to educate? How does education seem to affect a character's behavior? Can education ever be negative? Does education affect one's social position? Does education for boys differ from that for girls?

Because Brontë had specific ideas about the need for education, she may tend to cast it in a light that reflects her prejudice. In volume 2, chapter 12, Yorke's daughter Jessie sits beside Caroline, and the two discuss religion and politics, while another daughter, Rose, sits beside a bookcase reading Ann Radcliffe's *The Italian,* a popular early 19th-century romance novel. This scene takes for granted the education of girls and suggests that, at least in private, young women may have intellectual relationships.

Character

All novels offer interesting characters about which to write, most of whom may be classified as major or minor characters, foils, protagonists or antagonists, or types. We enjoy reading about them because of the conflicts they suffer and the way in which they solve their conflicts. Best of all is when a character is somewhat unpredictable. One way to write about characters in *Shirley* would be to consider the female characters as a group. An excellent approach to analyzing a group of characters is through their relationships with one another. For instance, should you choose to focus in an essay on Mrs. Pryor, Hortense, Shirley, and Caroline, you would be able to examine the role of each, determining whether hers is a traditional or a nontraditional role. Mrs. Pryor is quite traditional as the wife deserted by her husband who must sacrifice her child and take a job as a governess. As a single person who must live with her brother, Hortense also represents the traditional world of women. Shirley most certainly represents a nontraditional woman: independent, wealthy, and strong-minded, with little desire to marry. She suggests a new future for women in her outspoken and judgmental manner.

As the younger woman, Caroline should also suggest hope for a better future for women, nicely suspended between the two poles represented by other characters. However, this categorization does not work entirely well. Although well-educated, a boon for a woman, she is also so deeply in love that her passions make her physically ill, and she will be happy only if she can marry Robert Moore, who does not notice or appreciate her. If not for Shirley's taking Moore to task, he would never have recognized how fine a wife Caroline could be. Shirley herself is not left in the single state; instead, she marries Robert's brother, Louis. What, then, does Brontë finally suggest about the situation of women by her novel's conclusion? Attempts to answer this question will move you closer to finding a thesis statement.

Sample Topic:

1. **The female characters:** Who are the novel's most important female characters? Do any cause conflict for the others? Which characters have influence over the men in novel? What does that suggest about those women? What do the women have in common? What traits or powers of understanding do the women not share? Do any occupy the role of foil to Shirley or to Caroline? How does Brontë manage to keep the reader's attention on the women, when the men seem to be so much more active?

   An essay writer brings understanding to a group of characters by examining their relationships to each other. Should they attempt to empower one another, this suggests something quite different than if some of the women work to undermine others. The goal of readers is to reach a sense of familiarity with the characters—their motivations for their actions and their ability to advance plot. As one assigned to write about the novel, your choice of a group of characters can prove challenging but will also lead you to the novel's basic meaning, which you may then share with your own audience.

History and Context

The most important historical matter to consider in *Shirley* is that of the Luddite troubles that occurred in West Yorkshire, among other locations, between 1811 and 1816. The Luddites supposedly named themselves for a fabled character named Ned Ludd, who lived in Sherwood Forest. At the beginning of the 19th century, many workers in England felt threatened by the increase in the use of machinery, which was replacing them in textile factories. Their concerns increased with the passage in 1810 of orders in council (orders issued through the Privy Council, without a parliamentary vote) that contributed to a lowering of standards in the textile industry, further encouraging the adoption of machines that could do the work of multiple workers at great savings in wages. With no particular political goals or any true organization, groups of Luddites intercepted machinery as it traveled to its destination and then destroy it. Others entered factories to smash stocking frames (knitting machines) and other machines already in place. Factory owners defended their property, which led to violence in previously peaceful communities. The attacks escalated to the incident that Brontë adapted in *Shirley*, when approximately 150 workers attacked a mill near Huddersfield protected by soldiers, which resulted in the deaths of two workers. Workers retaliated a week later, attempting to kill one mill owner and succeeding in killing another. The English government, already concerned due to wars with the French and the Americans that had caused an absence of troops and the most serious economic depression since the mid-18th century, began to pass legislation in an attempt to control the outbreaks.

While the Luddite problems, part of the social and economic disturbances labeled the "Condition of England Question," are too large to act as a focus for an essay, one may narrow that focus to examine various aspects of the conflict with the Luddites in relation to the plot of *Shirley*. For example, one could write about the fact that while Robert Moore publicly rejects William Farren's pleas for mercy, he secretly reveals his compassion by asking the merchant, Hiram Yorke, to help find Farren a job. Thus, one topic could be public versus private acts. In addition, Moore's opposition to the war with France, due not to any political leanings but because it disrupted trade, so angers his cousin Caroline's guardian, Mr. Helstone, that Helstone removes Caroline from Moore's home. This plot aspect suggests the topic of the effects of war on the individual. A related subject could be the effect of early 19th-century politics on the working man, such as those featured in the novel. Resources that focus on the Luddite uprisings are readily available, an example being Bryan Bailey's *The Luddite Rebellion*. Many helpful websites also exist, such as "The Luddite's War on Industry" at http://www.insurgentdesire.org.uk/luddites.htm and "The Luddites" at http://www.schoolshistory.org.uk/luddites.htm.

Sample Topics:

1. **Public versus private acts:** Who behaves differently in public than in private? What would cause anyone to do so? What are the consequences of the behavior? What does such behavior suggest about that character?

   The fact that one may behave differently in private than in public may not apply to everyone. Some people exhibit identical personality traits despite the environment. However, others may feel they need to take a public stand against an injustice, but that they may also help others who suffer for their stand. This is true of Moore, because his worker is not a faceless, nameless individual. If writing an essay about this topic, the writer should focus on how that seemingly contradictory behavior helps to define Moore for the reader.

2. **Effects of war:** What are some of the effects of war on those who do not take part in the physical battles? Why do people feel they must defend their stance regarding war? Who suffers due to differences of opinion about war? Can a stance related to war be nonpolitical, assumed simply for practical matters? If so, what might others think about a person whose attitude toward war was based on financial matters?

   Individuals may feel passionately regarding their support of, or opposition to, war waged by their nation. If they feel strongly enough, they may seek retribution against those who do not agree with them, forcing others to become pawns in a political battle of wills. They may not be able to accept that some hold no particular view about war, or they may simply consider other matters, such as personal relationships, more important. If writing an essay about the nonbattlefield effects of war on the individual, one might want to answer the question: What was Brontë trying to say about political ideology in general in her novel?

3. **Politics and the working man:** Which characters in the novel are political? How do you know? Does each view politics in the same way? What are differences and similarities in their viewpoints? How do those differences or similarities help shape their characters? How does social class affect one's politics?

   If you want to write about this topic, then as you read, note passages in which politics are discussed; also note which characters take part in the discussion. For instance, Moses Barraclough is a working man who is arrested for his part in a destructive demonstration. However, this does not necessarily mean that he is a political character. Again, history tells us that what we think of as traditional politics—associated with specific political parties involved in government—seemed to play a small part in the Luddite Rebellion. However, you might define politics in a way that does not focus on specific parties.

Philosophy and Ideas

Crucial to the time period during which Brontë wrote *Shirley* was economist Adam Smith's laissez-faire philosophy, which strongly urged no government intervention in the marketplace. Certain enterprising businessmen used that theory to support abusive behavior toward workers, arguing that labor laws and health regulations were a violation of their right to practice trade. Such attitudes resulted in a loss of compassion for the individual in favor of making a profit. Ironically, Smith never suggested that any businessperson take advantage of another, and he did express deep sympathy for the working man; nevertheless, his ideas were used out of context in order to ruthlessly advance business. An essay that focused on profit at any cost would allow an investigation of such behavior through examination of a character who represents that behavior. One would want to know whether such a person might be persuaded to change his or her conduct, and what would be required to institute such a change.

Another related essay topic might focus on the class and gender divisions produced by the burst of economic activity in England's 19th century. By considering the characters in *Shirley* who represent members of specific classes, an essay might suggest whether any resolutions of their conflicts are realistic or merely convenient to advance the plot. You may also want to review Smith's ideas; resources include Robert Heilbroner's book *The Essential Adam Smith* or Yousuf Dhamee's "Adam Smith's Laissez-Faire Policies" on the Victorian Web.

An additional topic is that of gender equality, or inequality, as it were. As England's march toward industrialization increased, promising wealth and power for certain groups, women did not make large strides in gaining either economic or social power. The fact that Mrs. Pryor has to give up her daughter when her husband deserts her due to economic reasons provides powerful proof of the continued lack of power on the part of women to support themselves in a manner that allowed them some form of independence.

Sample Topics:

1. **Profit at any cost:** Which characters stand to profit from industrialization practices? How much money will they make? Who will not profit? What are the human life "costs" associated with such profit? What choices are left for those who will not profit?

   In considering this topic and how the desire for profit defines a character, a writer will want to investigate whether that character is capable of change. If so, the cause of the change will prove crucial. For instance, if a man loses a game, becomes furious, and then becomes a cheater in order to win, that is not a positive change. However, should he admit his opponent is better than he is, choose to better develop his skills, and return to play an honest game, that man has changed his approach in a way that will prove beneficial to himself and to others with whom he comes into contact. A game may stand as a metaphor for any type of competition, whether focused on money or love.

2. **Class conflict:** Which socioeconomic classes are represented in *Shirley*? Who represents each? What are examples of conflicts the groups encounter with one another? What are examples of conflict encountered within various groups? Who seems to suffer the most conflict? Which groups are able to find resolution to conflict?

Brontë tends to classify individuals according to a number of attributes, including education, family connections, work ethic, and wealth. Not all of the characters allow themselves to be defined by their positions of power or their lack of power due to class membership, but many do. Mr. Yorke believes in a division between his mill workers and himself, but on the other hand, he does not acknowledge any man as his superior and is described in the fourth chapter as a "rebel." Louis Moore tells Shirley in volume 3, chapter 13, "I am a dependent: I know my place. . . . I am poor: I must be proud." Just before that remark, he claims to wish for "a penniless, friendless orphan girl" as a wife, a jest in which Shirley finds little humor. Both Mr. Yorke and Moore clearly acknowledge what amounts to a class position. In an essay based on class conflict, you will want to investigate how an individual's attitude toward class affects his or her personality, and how that effect aids the reader in understanding that character. Such conflicts are also present within the servant class, as Mrs. Pryor is described in volume 3, chapter 2, as cool toward the house servants and naturally "diffident" in personality, causing the servants to perceive her as arrogant, an erroneous perception. She remains aware of the negative effects of her personality, but can do little to alter it.

3. **Gender equality:** What examples of lack of gender equality are evident in the novel? Do any women exhibit any type of power? What type of power might they have, other than economic? Is the lack of equality ever discussed? Do any women yearn for equality?

As noted above, Mrs. Pryor best represents a woman without power, for which she has had to give up her child. The reader learns early on in the fourth chapter that Mr. Yorke talks about equality, is apparently a freethinker, and "is good to all who were beneath him," but women are not involved in that statement. Robert Moore is loved by Caroline, but he does not view her as an equal. She almost dies due to separation from Moore, and he will later confess his love, but only after being first rejected by the independent Shirley. Shirley may not be viewed as equal to men, but she certainly holds power over them through her sexuality and her ability to deny them her favor. In volume 2, chapter 4, she soundly ejects a clergyman from her presence when he behaves haughtily, acting as a social leveler. Her castigation of Moore for seeking to marry for money has the power to change his attitude toward wedlock. Their repartee in volume 3, chapter 13, makes clear that Shirley remains self-confident and self-possessed, showing herself the equal of any man. She may be the character most in control, despite her gender, but her power comes in part from her position as an heiress.

Bibliography and Online Resources for *Shirley*

Bailey, Bryan. *The Luddite Rebellion.* New York: New York UP, 1998.

———. *Shirley.* Ed. Hervert Rosengarten and Margaret Smith. New York: Oxford UP, 2000.

"Charlotte Brontë." The Victorian Web. Available online. URL: http://www.victorianweb.org/authors/bronte/cbronte/bronteov.html. Downloaded November 23, 2007.

Dhamee, Yousuf. "Adam Smith's Laissez-Faire Policies." The Victorian Web. Available online. URL: http://www.victorianweb.org/economics/laissez.html. Downloaded November 25, 2007.

Eagleton, Terry. "Class, Power and Charlotte Brontë." *Critical Quarterly* 14 (Autumn 1972): 223–235.

Giles, Judy. "Shirley." *The Literary Encyclopedia.* Available online. URL: http://www.litencyc.com/php/sworks.php?rec=true&UID=2086. Downloaded November 23, 2007.

Glen, Heather. *Charlotte Brontë, The Imagination in History.* New York: Oxford UP, 2002.

Heilbroner, Robert L., ed. *The Essential Adam Smith.* New York: W.W. Norton, 1987.

Korg, Jacob. "The Problem of Unity in *Shirley.*" *Nineteenth Century Fiction* 12 (Sept. 1957): 125–136.

"The Luddites." Schools History Web site. Available online. URL: http://www. schoolshistory.org.uk/luddites.htm. Downloaded November 24, 2007.

"The Luddites' War on Industry." Insurgent Desire. Available online. URL: http://www.insurgentdesire.org.uk/luddites.htm. Downloaded November 24, 2007.

Rockefeller, Laura Selene. "Shirley and the Politics of Personal Faith." *Brontë Studies* 32.2 (July 2007): 106–115.

Scholes, Robert E. *Elements of Fiction.* New York: Oxford University Press, 1968.

"*Shirley.*" The Literature Network. Available online. URL: http://www.online-literature.com/brontec/shirley/. Downloaded November 23, 2007.

VILLETTE

READING TO WRITE

C HARLOTTE BRONTË published *Villette* in 1853, having already found fame with *Jane Eyre* (1847). The books share several themes, but *Villette* is most closely related to *The Professor*, a novel Brontë wrote prior to *Villette*, but one that would not be published until after her death. In both *Villette* and *The Professor*, Brontë employs her own experiences studying and teaching abroad in Belgium in the creation of her protagonist. However, *Villette's* Lucy Snowe is the more thoroughly rendered character, and much of Brontë's own thoughts and beliefs come to life in her. Lucy's bouts of depression and frequent soul-searching mirror Brontë's own as she continued to suffer from the loss of her sisters and brother. She made attempts to write this novel over two years, but feelings of isolation and loneliness made writing difficult. Finally, in November 1851 she began writing again, but only the following spring did she have enough on the page to send volumes 1 and 2 to her publisher. His encouragement apparently moved her to write more rapidly, and she completed the entire novel by November 1852. Not wanting to compete with her friend Elizabeth Gaskell's novel *Ruth*, Brontë did not allow issue of her novel until January 1853.

The fictional city of Villette clearly represents Brussels, with M. Paul Emanuel based on M. Constantin Heger and Mme Beck based on his wife, Mme Zoë Heger. Like Brontë, Lucy finds herself out of her element and must conquer a multitude of challenges that arise in a foreign culture. Many of those challenges—including loneliness, isolation, despair, abandonment, social class divisions, religious conflict, the use of language, fate, and fortitude—are strong topics for an essay.

As with *The Professor,* Brontë includes much conversation written in French, a language she spoke while in Belgium. Much of the meaning in these instances may be drawn from context, and readers may want to employ a French dictionary. She resisted the sheer romanticism much more familiar to readers and relied on realism as a crucial aspect of her plot. In *Villette's* conclusion, avoiding the happy ending so typical to romance, Brontë leaves readers to wonder along with Lucy whether her love will ever return to marry her. This type of an ending challenged the traditional view of the novel, a challenge Brontë offered in each of her books. *Villette* offers stunning details of Brussels and Belgium as could only be seen through the eyes of a visitor such as Lucy Snowe, as well as a consideration of gender issues appropriate to the mid-19th century. Yet the novel includes much traditional imagery and clearly suggests and alludes to the classical mythological hero's journey.

For instance, in chapter 17, as Lucy recovers from an illness in a strange place, she tells the reader:

> My calm little room seemed somehow like a cave in the sea. There was no colour about it, except that white and pale green, suggestive of foam and deep water; the blanched cornice was adorned with shell-shaped ornaments, and there were white mouldings like dolphins in the ceiling-angles. Even that one touch of colour visible in the red satin pincushion bore affinity to coral; even that dark, shining glass might have mirrored a mermaid. When I closed my eyes, I heard a gale, subsiding at last, bearing upon the house-front like a settling swell upon a rockbase. I heard it drawn and withdrawn far, far off, like a tide retiring from a shore of the upper world—a world so high above, that the rush of its largest waves, the dash of its fiercest breakers could sound down in the submarine home, only like murmurs and a lullaby.

In this scene, Brontë suggests the sea voyage that a traditional hero, such as Homer's Ulysses, undertook as part of an adventure. An enterprising student would see the possibility for an essay topic in the comparison and contrast of Lucy's adventure with that of the classic hero. An important aspect of contrast would be Lucy's gender, as classical hero tales all focused on men. In the quoted scene, Brontë has not only departed from the classic tale's gender aspect but has also employed imagery of safety and protection.

The classic hero's voyage entailed marvelous adventures, but it was also fraught with difficulty and challenge. He met monsters and shape-shifters along the way who attempted to block his successful victory and subsequent return home. He often depended on assistance from a guide to help him meet the many challenges that threatened his success. A reader of this particular scene might first imagine that an adventurer who descended to a "cave in the sea," like the one to which Lucy compares the room, might have died in a storm and sunk to the sea's depths. However, Lucy's description also suggests the classical hero's descent into Hades. In the classical sense, Hades was not hell, where bad people went to be punished. After death, everyone went to Hades, so when the hero descended, it was to consult with the "shades" of dead heroes for wisdom needed in order to continue the journey. Might Lucy be gaining wisdom in her retreat to this "cave"?

Previously in the novel, Lucy felt a miserable sense of isolation that threw her into emotional turmoil; in the quoted scene, she expresses the calming effect of her "cave." All of the imagery points to happiness. Where heroes often encountered monsters, such as the cyclops in *The Odyssey,* she confronts gentle dolphins. In *The Odyssey,* female sea creatures such as the sirens tempted Ulysses and his men and took away their powers. In contrast, Lucy thinks of a mermaid in a positive manner, suggesting that her gender might make her feel more comfortable with that female mythical creature. While a storm rages outside, imitating the force of waves breaking against cliffs, Lucy feels completely safe inside this room. Although her time there will be temporary, the reader understands it acts as respite to help replenish her energies to face the hardships that await her.

One might also base an essay on this scene on the imagery that psychoanalytic critics would find of interest. You can read about 11 different approaches to literary criticism in books such as Charles Bressler's *Literary Criticism: An Introduction to Theory and Practice* or Barry Laga's Web site, "Critical Reading: An Introduction to Literary Theory and Criticism." Psychoanalytic critics would be interested in the fact that Lucy feels as if she is in a protective cave, suggesting that the cave could represent the safety of the womb. Lucy describes the room as "white and pale green, suggestive of foam and deep water," which a psychoanalytic critical approach could claim symbolizes the placental fluids in which the fetus floats prior to birth. Lucy's retreat "back into the womb" suggests that she is preparing for a rebirth, and indeed, she uses this period in her life to prepare for reentry into the normal world of work, teaching at the school. The "red satin" color may symbolize blood, with the pink coral imagery suggesting the flesh of the womb.

Additional symbolic imagery includes the "dark, shining glass." The glass is a mirror, and the mirror is one of many traditional literary images—ones that always have the same symbolic value. Mirrors in literature always suggest a double reflection. The looker sees a physical reflection but generally engages in self-reflection, or consideration associated with self-image, as well. The Bible includes a passage in the Book of Romans that references the speaker seeing in a glass darkly, a popular phrase through the centuries. It means that the normal revealing nature of the glass, or mirror, is not yet functioning. Instead, one who looks into the mirror will only observe darkness, rather than his or her reflection. In the quoted scene, Lucy has not yet developed a clear sense of self-identity; thus, she does not see her own reflection. Instead, she imagines that a mermaid, a mythical female symbol of power and mysticism, might appear there. She suggests some affinity with, or relationship to, that creature and her power over men, which has played a prominent part in many tales of the sea.

The prepared student will understand that in order to write about literature, she or he must study the text carefully, taking notes and asking questions during reading. Knowledge of basic literary criticism techniques proves helpful, as does familiarity with traditional elements of fiction, such as plot, theme, character, setting, and style.

TOPICS AND STRATEGIES

The sections below offer ideas for writing, but they are only ideas. After reading each section thoroughly, you should return to the novel and use your review to spark topic ideas of your own.

Themes

Every work of literature will present multiple themes, or topics, to the alert reader. A topic offers a general focus for an essay. That focus will become much more specific when expressed in a thesis statement for the essay. The thesis statement should be a clear statement that contains some aspect of personal opinion. For instance, one might begin by writing, "In Charlotte Brontë's Villette, specific imagery of the male and the female allows the reader to . . ." The first portion of that sentence puts forth the fact that the novel contains gender imagery. Because this is a fact, it can not stand alone as a thesis statement. However, you may add your opinion as to the importance of the fact to the reader; then you will have a clear, coherent thesis statement that will guide your essay.

Gender issues are important to *Villette*, as they are to all of Brontë's writing. She lived in an age when gender roles were slowly changing but remained, for the most part, traditional. Think of M. Paul, for instance. He is gruff and insensitive and has set beliefs about women's place in the world. While Graham, also called Dr. John, seems more sensitive and romantic, his vision of women and what they may and may not accomplish remains quite traditional. But Lucy is unwilling to observe all of those predestined roles. While she often sits in silence concentrating on needlework, a traditional condition and occupation for a woman, she entertains revolutionary thoughts about the possibilities for women. Brontë clearly reveals the difference between Lucy and Graham in chapter 23, when Lucy reacts to the actress Vashti's power with great emotion and intellect. Graham, however, "could think, and think well . . . but his heart had no chord for enthusiasm." When Lucy asks his opinion of the same performance that has left her breathless, he gives a "terse" and "callous" appraisal; "he judged her as a woman, not an artist; it was a branding judgment." The student wanting to write about gender stereotypes in the novel might ask: Why does Lucy not think in a traditional manner, and what will she gain by thinking this way?

In *Villette*, the reader will immediately notice the importance of certain abstract ideas, such as hope, fate, happiness, and solitude. Their importance is clear due to their repetition in the protagonist's thoughts. For instance, in chapter 15, Lucy thinks, "Fate was of stone, and Hope a false idol." Much of her consideration is about her future and what fate has planned for her, and until chapter 21, she feels quite fatalistic, believing nothing positive awaits her. In that chapter, however, she thinks of how imagination, another promising topic, is the foe to reason and provides "sweet Help, our divine Hope" for humans. She obviously begins to change her mind and to believe she might hope for something better. By chapter 23, she is able to tell the reader, "A new creed became mine—a belief in happiness." A curious reader should ask what has caused Lucy to change her attitude. Will that attitude be permanent, or will she again suffer disappointment?

Solitude is both an abstract idea and a literal state in *Villette* and offers a promising topic for an essay. You should distinguish between loneliness and solitude: Loneliness is not a positive state for anyone, and Lucy is no exception. However, she constantly seeks solitude, as she states at the beginning of chapter 22: "Baffled, but not beaten, I withdrew, bent as resolutely as ever on finding solitude *somewhere*." Her employment brings her an income, but it also causes her to be constantly with the students and prey to Mme Beck's constant surveillance. Readers will naturally wonder why Lucy seems to seek both romance and solitude. Does not one preclude the other?

Closely related to such abstract ideas is the topic of reason versus emotion, seen especially in chapter 21, which is also presented by Brontë as science versus faith in other chapters. This dichotomy has been present in literature since the 17th century and the earliest discoveries by scientists. Because writers are creatures of imagination, they generally champion that approach as a way of knowing, a topic that became crucial to the postmodern discussions of literature popular in the second half of the 20th century. These contradictions are often traditionally associated with gender as well; reason relates to men, while emotion relates to women. Because of this, you would expect Dr. John to be the rational scientist, while Lucy would be the imaginative creative personality. Thus, after Lucy sees the nun's ghost in chapter 22, Dr. John's comfort through the application of reason would be expected. He blames the vision on "nerves," a gender stereotype that was often credited for women's health problems. The term *hysteria*, a state closely related to "nerves," was actually a medical diagnosis applied only to women for several centuries, with the root *hyster* coming from the Greek term for womb. In the next chapter, as Lucy dares to hope that Dr. John might care for her, she states, "Feeling and I turned Reason out of doors, drew against her bar and bolt," as she personifies her emotions and transforms them into her conspirators. Later, with the introduction of Monsieur de Bassompierre, the reader learns he was so preoccupied with "scientific interests" that he did not notice his daughter falling in love with Graham.

Visions and ghosts remain important enough to the novel to also be adopted as an essay topic. Lucy enjoys a rich fantasy life, often seeing true visions of her future and her past. In chapter 22, she believes that she sees the ghost of the nun rumored to have been murdered in the school in its former life as a convent, and she describes various dreams to the reader.

Organized religion provides an additional possible topic, as Lucy frequently considers the conflict between Protestantism and Catholicism. As a Protestant, she is among the minority in *Villette,* and she personally feels a tension caused by the two approaches to faith. On the one hand, she muses about how damaging "popish" or "Romish" rituals and ideas are to her students. On the other hand, she attends confession on one occasion when her desperation for comfort causes her to seek that outlet. Why does she seem to vacillate in chapter 15, when she has felt such strong anti-Catholicism in previous passages? And why does that particular chapter conclude volume 1?

Sample Topics:

1. **Gender issues:** What preconceptions do the genders have about one another? How do the characters' actions reveal their feelings about the opposite sex? Which characters seem to accept their predetermined roles? Which do not? Which characters reflect gender stereotypes? Which do not? What evidence exists that Lucy's more independent attitude causes her conflict?

   Brontë strongly believed that women should have more options than those available in 19th-century England. While she never wrote that women should be equal to men, she did advocate their need for more independence. You may observe Lucy reflecting some of those beliefs. Notice the thoughts that Lucy has about others that pertain to gender roles. Notice her reaction to men whom she believes are too controlling. She gains the respect of both men and women and in the end manages her own school, assuming a role of power. Yet Lucy also engages in various stereotypes of a woman in need of a man, such as crying, longing for love, and injured feelings, and she engages in needlework, sometimes as a distraction from thoughts about men. How is the reader affected by these seeming contradictions? If you choose to write about this topic, you might choose to adopt a feminist view.

2. **Hope/fate/happiness:** In what type of circumstances does Lucy experience hope and happiness? How do those emotions relate to her comments regarding fate? Does she believe that she may escape her fate, or destiny? Do other characters comment about those topics? How do their comments affect Lucy?

On the one hand, Lucy seems to accept that fate cannot be altered by mere humans. On the other hand, she tries to determine her own future. How can you explain this conflict? Her attitude toward both hope and happiness alters several times. Study the circumstances in which they change; is the change a permanent or temporary one? Lucy often personifies her emotions as well as fate or destiny. An essay about these abstractions would necessarily engage and analyze the significance of that type of interaction.

3. **Solitude:** Who wants to be alone? Why can he or she not find any solitude? Does the person's attitude change? Who does not want to be alone? How does he or she differ from those who live lives of solitude?

At times, Lucy feels trapped in the school. She constantly looks out of windows and takes walks outside in order to experience more freedom. She enjoys being alone in the garden or in her dormitory, yet at times she also feels lonely and desires the companionship of certain people. Once again, we see contradictory behavior and thoughts on Lucy's part.

4. **Reason versus emotion:** Which characters represent reason? Which represent emotion? Is reason viewed as superior to emotion, or vice versa? Why? Why was such differentiation important? Do any of the characters ever adopt the opposite approach?

Readers should not be surprised by Brontë's emphasis of the longtime conflict between reason and emotion. They were commonly converted to descriptors of man (rational) and woman (emotional), adding a gendered meaning to each. Brontë seems to have found this dichotomy fascinating, if not frustrating, due to her emphasis on the importance of mutual respect between the sexes. As an artist, Brontë also could identify with the related duality of science versus art. You might examine in an essay why the two terms were accepted as hierarchical—that is, as reason being superior to emotion and science superior to art.

Another related term is *instinct,* attributed more to women than to men as a "natural" way of knowing the world. Brontë writes in chapter 29 that M. Paul at times "had the terrible unerring penetration of instinct." What does this tell the reader about his relationships with women? What does it mean when he attacks the "minds, morals, and manners" of English women a short time later?

5. **Visions and ghosts:** Why is the nun's ghost "haunting" the school? At what times does she appear? Is she frightening? What does her presence mean for Lucy? What do others think of Lucy when she sees the nun? Is the reader supposed to believe in the ghost? How does Lucy discover the nun's true identity? What other visions does Lucy have? Should the visions and the ghost be considered as similar or completely different? Do the visions and the ghost reflect a particular character aspect of Lucy?

Ghosts remain an important aspect of both the gothic romance and the traditional quest adventure tale. Because *Villette* cannot be classified as either of those subgenres or as a ghost or horror story, readers might be surprised by the ghost's appearance. An essay could state an opinion as to the purpose of the ghost in this particular plot. A different essay might show some relationship between the ghost and Lucy's various visions, which begin early in the book. In chapter 6, for instance, Europe appears to be a "wide dream land." But a short time later, Lucy declares daydreams to be "delusions of the demon." How do these varying views of visions and dreams inform the main point of the novel?

6. **Organized religion:** What does Lucy think about Catholicism? Who is Catholic? Who is Protestant? What accounts for Lucy's confusion about her own allegiance? How does religion complicate Lucy's relationship with M. Paul Emmanuel? What message does Lucy's confusion allow Brontë to transmit to readers? Does Brontë seem to believe that one religious practice is superior to the other?

The conflict between Catholics and Protestants had a rich history in England, issuing from King Henry VIII's split with the Roman Catholic Church in the 16th century. People held strong feelings about the two religions, which often resulted in clashes of temperament as well as physical combat. Lucy's combat is an internal psychological and spiritual one. In an essay about organized religion, you will want to carefully analyze scenes in which Lucy feels most strongly anti-Catholic and contrast them with scenes in which she seems to vacillate toward Catholicism. How can you account for these changes in attitude? Note especially the conversation between M. Paul and Lucy about Mlle St. Pierre in chapter 31.

Character

You may also discuss *Villette* in light of its characters. Lucy Snowe, the first-person narrator, is clearly the protagonist. She is not necessarily heroic, although she may exhibit courage from time to time in facing everyday challenges. Like most well-rounded characters, she shows contradictions that make her more interesting. One might examine those contradictions in an essay. Any essay about the protagonist by necessity must identify her moment of realization, or epiphany, which leads to a change in her actions, opinions, or both. Lucy struggles a great deal with developing self-identity, and Brontë includes rich passages that reflect on that struggle. These include scenes that refer to mirrors, but especially Ginevra's confrontation of Lucy in chapter 26, when she asks plainly, "Who *are* you, Miss Snowe?"

You might also be interested in grouping the minor characters in order to write about them. Brontë supplies various antagonists for Lucy in the form of the minor characters, and they could be examined as a group. Examples include M. Paul, Dr. John (Graham), Père Silas, Justine Marie Sauveur, Mme Walravens, and Mme Beck. Her strongest perceived antagonist has to be Ginevra Fanshawe, the person with whom Lucy has several lively debates. She might be considered Lucy's foil and could merit an essay on her own.

Another approach to a discussion of characters would be to analyze the two men in Lucy's life, M. Paul and Dr. John (Graham). What criteria does she employ to evaluate each of these men? Though she comes to accept the fact that Dr. John does not love her, she must experience pain before acceptance; M. Paul is very much involved in that acceptance.

Finally, you might write about the minor female characters. In addition to Mme Beck and Ginevra, these include Polly, Justine Marie Sauveur, and Mrs. Bretton. Do any of these women provide role models for Lucy? If not, to whom does she turn as a model?

Sample Topics:

1. **Lucy Snowe/the protagonist:** What admirable characteristics does Lucy possess? Which characteristics prove less than admirable? Of which personal characteristics is she most and least proud? What conflicts must she overcome? What does she desire in life? What message does Brontë hope to transmit to her readers through Lucy?

   An essay that focuses on Lucy Snowe should enlighten readers on topics they may not have considered. All readers may observe that Lucy enjoys some repartee with M. Paul, but they may not know how to use that fact to better understand her. Her contradictory behavior may confuse some readers who will see it as a character flaw, but that was not Brontë's intention. Rather, her jealousy over not only Polly and Justine Marie Sauveur but even the dead Justine Marie is quite normal. In addition, she conquers most of her base emotions through the application of reason. The fact that Lucy achieves an important status at the book's conclusion by becoming headmistress of a school is obviously Brontë's way of encouraging her female readers. However, Lucy could not have reached that goal without the assistance of a man, M. Paul. Does this diminish her accomplishment?

2. **Minor characters:** What is the purpose of any minor character in fiction? What roles do these characters fulfill in relation to Lucy? Are those roles necessary in order for Lucy to achieve an epiphany? Which minor characters are sympathetic and unsympathetic? Are the minor characters realistic or stereotypical? Do any change from the beginning of the book to its conclusion?

The fact that a character is "minor" does not render him or her unimportant. Generally, minor characters prove crucial to the plot's movement and the protagonist's experiences. An excellent example is Justine Marie Sauveur, who appears only briefly in this novel but excites Lucy's jealousy, until Lucy learns the truth about her relationship with M. Paul. These characters generally do not experience true changes, as the protagonist does. Lucy is in a foreign country, so several of the minor characters act simply to represent Labassecour (Belgium). The care given to shape minor characters reflects the author's intention. Does she create mere "stick figures," stereotypes, or stock characters for the convenience of plot? Or would you describe these characters as more sophisticated developments?

3. **Ginevra Fanshawe:** How does Ginevra serve as a foil for Lucy? Is Ginevra likable? Why or why not? What are the class differences between Ginevra and Lucy? How do those differences lead to expectations on the part of each? Is either surprised by the other's actions, or are those actions too predictable?

Ginevra is most visibly Lucy's competitor for Graham's attention. However, she is important for other reasons as well. She constantly challenges Lucy, both physically and verbally, yet she is the main reason Lucy takes a position with Mme

Beck. She is a recognizable, dependable figure for Lucy from the time she departs London until Ginevra's marriage to the colonel near the book's conclusion. She plays a vital role in manipulation of the nun's tale, as revealed in chapter 39, and also in Lucy's self-realization. Does the reader change opinion about Ginevra by the novel's end? Why?

4. **M. Paul versus Graham/Dr. John:** In what situations does Lucy interact with these two characters? How do they interact with one another? What are their similarities and differences? Which seems to better suit Lucy's personality? How does each compete for Lucy's attention?

Lucy Snowe experiences romantic feelings for both of the male characters in the novel. This plot aspect is a traditional love triangle, but Brontë challenges reader expectations. The manner by which she does so proves important to her development of these lovers' personalities. Neither is completely admirable, nor completely base; they each display rounded personalities. Consider their careers in light of the running conflict between reason and emotion in the novel. Does either occasionally represent a reversal by adopting the "feminine" characteristic of emotion as a way of knowing oneself? Does that recommend him as a partner for Lucy? Should you write about these characters, you will want to consider why one is allowed a "happy ending" and the other is not. How does the culmination of Lucy's relationship with both relate to the topic of fate or destiny that Lucy so often considers?

5. **Female minor characters:** Which female characters are positively shaped? Which seem to be negative characters? Does their negativity equate to evil personalities? How does Lucy's perception of each differ from the reality that readers can see? How does each affect Lucy's destiny? Can the reader understand the motivations of each of these characters? What, if anything, do all of the female characters share?

Female characters in this novel generally exist to either nurture or challenge Lucy. Typically, those who challenge the protagonist are the more strongly defined, interesting characters, and that proves true in *Villete*. An essay about this topic might center on why readers better appreciate the more "evil" characters in literature. Mme Beck provides an excellent example. She is constantly spying on others and puts many obstacles in Lucy's path. However, she also represents a highly successful woman, a rarity in Lucy's time and a characteristic that Lucy hopes to emulate. In your consideration of role models for Lucy, even some of the negative characters can qualify.

History and Context

When Brontë wrote her novel, England was facing incredible change. By the mid-19th century, it had already experienced an enormous shift in population from the country to the city due to the Industrial Revolution. The revolution caused many problems for the working man and woman, but it created a new monied class that Karl Marx labeled the *bourgeoisie*. This group accumulated wealth by acting as a go-between for manufacturers and merchants. They further stratified a social structure set in place centuries earlier. Fewer noblemen and aristocrats occupied the uppermost class than had been the case in centuries past, but many more working poor filled the lower classes. Ironically, middle-class women, such as the Brontë sisters, had fewer choices of work than did their lower-class fellow women. The few choices available to them all involved service as a governess, private companion to the wealthy, or schoolteacher. Brontë had faced these very choices, so she well knew of what she wrote. The class or social structure imagined in *Villette* offers a fine topic for an essay, as Lucy spends a good deal of time musing about class divisions; her thoughts offer strong quoted support for points in an essay.

An additional interesting topic would be that of economics. Lucy thinks a great deal about money, as did nearly everyone in her age. Again, because wealth was redistributed as the country restructured and experienced a boom in trade, many hoped to make their fortunes. The increased trade with other countries resulted in many families' possession of foreign goods. Brontë describes various objects from other countries during her stay in Villette, where inhabitants, although not in England, obviously benefited from the availability of many new types of goods. Those who possess goods also possess power, but such power can be lost.

A third important essay topic that might derive from history and context is that of worldview. Because of the increase in trade and improved transportation, travel between countries and continents increased. Consequently, the world began to metaphorically "shrink," with more people becoming aware of and curious about environments other than their own. Some refused to acknowledge the expanding horizons, remaining provincial, unwilling to accept change or take advantage of new opportunities outside their own circles. Lucy is one who has found the new worldview to her advantage at the beginning of the novel. Ironically, that same view causes her separation from M. Paul at its conclusion. Helpful general sources about history and culture include Michael Rapport's *Nineteenth-Century Europe*; Michael S. Melancon and John C. Swanson's *Nineteenth Century Europe: Sources and Perspectives from History*; and Paul Halsall's internet site "The Long Nineteenth Century," found at http://www.fordham.edu/halsall/mod/modsbook3.html.

Sample Topics:

1. **Class/social structure:** How does Brontë emphasize the importance of class? To which class does Lucy belong? In which classes do other characters fall? Who is able to transcend class differentiation? Who is not? Can the reader sympathize with those for whom class structure is important? What does Lucy think of class divisions? In what ways does the social structure inhibit her fulfillment of her desires? How does social structure affect her behavior?

   All the Brontë sisters feature class differences in their various novels, because they all felt the effects of England's rigid hierarchical structure. Lucy comments on the class and social structure in which she must operate daily. An essay on this topic would include many quotations that capture her thoughts and the remarks of other characters relating to their social positions. Chapter 31 offers special insight into this topic, as Lucy tells herself to take courage and plan a future in Villette, whose inhabitants' lifestyles contrast with those of England. In Villete, they are "infinitely less worried about appearance . . . where nobody is in the least ashamed to be quite as homely and saving as he finds convenient."

2. **Economics:** Which characters are wealthy, and which are not? What does wealth mean to the main characters? How do you know? Who is most vocal about finances? What do the characters' attitudes about money reveal about their personalities? Who suffers or benefits from a change in material status?

All of *Villette*'s characters are concerned about money, but some let their concerns become obsessions. Where so much wealth was available, and people understood the concept of the self-made man or woman for the first time, possibilities seemed to abound. In order to write about the economics of *Villette,* search for comments made about money, but also look for allusions to wealth in the descriptions of goods and settings. In addition, notice the fluid nature of wealth. For instance, the Brettons are wealthy at the novel's beginning, then lose their money and status, but they regain some respect through Graham's practice of medicine and through relocation.

3. **Worldview:** How does Lucy's view of the world change from the beginning to the conclusion of the novel? How do others view the world? Does the world begin and end in Villette? Why would some feel so provincial? Who seems brave and adventurous, expressing desires to travel or move about? How does the emerging worldview of the 19th century relate to Brontë's theme? How does she use it to develop Lucy's character?

Lucy immediately reveals her awareness of a broader world when she leaves England with no resources to begin a new life. Her trust that a better life awaits may seem curious to readers, and the worldview of Brontë's era could help explain that attitude. Some people seem unaware of a broader environment than their own and are happy to live that way. Does Brontë suggest any judgment on that attitude through Lucy or other characters?

Philosophy and Ideas

Religion represents one of the strongest topics related to philosophy and ideas of the era during which *Villette* was produced. The ongoing tension between Catholicism and Protestantism to which Lucy was accustomed in England became even stronger in Labassecour because Villette was in essence a Catholic city. Few fellow Protestants lived there to provide Lucy with support. While Lucy was not a fervent Christian, she did pray and depend on her faith for help. Inhabitants of the fictional Labassecour tried to convert her to Catholicism. The setting for the novel was based on Brussels in Belgium, where Catholicism was the major religion practiced. Catholic lessons were taught in schools, causing foreign instructors some concern over its influence on secular education. The idea of confession was anathema to Protestants, who believed they could achieve grace through direct contact with God.

An additional excellent topic relating to philosophy and ideas is that of the effect of social class on romance. Many held that an individual from one class should not marry one from a lower class. However, if that were to happen, it was more common for a man to marry a woman from a lower class than vice versa. When two people from different socioeconomic levels fell in love, their relationship often led to conflict within their families. A careful consideration of why that should be true would be an important part of an approach to this essay topic.

Sample Topics:

1. **Catholicism versus Protestantism:** In which scenes does Lucy begin to question her faith? What causes her to question it? Does she resolve her conflict? How does her faith affect her relationship with M. Paul? Why does M. Paul eventually accept Lucy as a Protestant?

   Lucy remains skeptical of Catholicism throughout the novel, although in the crucial chapter 15, in which she fears "the sin and weakness of presumption" and labels "Hope a false Idol," she enters a Catholic church and decides to experience confession. She notes that "to take this step could not make me more wretched than I was; it might soothe me." She declines, however, to see the priest again, telling readers she would no more continue that relationship than walk "into a Babylonish furnace." The priest is kind enough to help her when she collapses, suggesting that Catholicism does not restrict one's humanitarian instincts. The reader understands Lucy's attempts not as a lapse but as the result of extreme melancholy and soul searching, which continues in the next two chapters. Later, when the same priest, Père Silas, attempts to derail Lucy's affection for M. Paul by stressing Paul's devotion to his dead fiancée, Brontë again casts Catholicism in an evil role. M. Paul is not innocent of joining the attempt to convert Lucy, yet in the end he becomes more accepting than others. As for Lucy, she considers sharing her life with a Catholic, a fact that an essay about this topic should consider crucial in its analysis.

2. **Social class and relationships:** Who perceives Lucy as a member of a lower class? What effect does that have on Lucy? What does that tell the reader about that character(s)? Do those characters change their attitudes? Why or why not?

    The two characters who obviously hold Lucy in disdain due to her social class are Ginevra and Mme Beck. In Ginevra's case, her attitude is an inherited one in which she does not seem to truly believe. However, Mme Beck will take extreme measures to prevent her cousin's romance with Lucy. In order to write about this topic, one would need to analyze how Lucy copes with relationships that involve class differences, and then decide whether that foretells any specific actions on her part. Also, a writer would need to ask whether Lucy is at fault regarding class differences— that is, does she practice a type of reverse snobbery?

Form and Genre

When discussing the novel as a fiction genre, one may consider the formal elements of fiction, such as plot, characters (discussed above), setting, style, and point of view. While the general elements remain the same from genre to genre, their specific use by each author may vary. For instance, some plots are based on traditional plots familiar to the reader, such as the romantic quest, in which the hero goes on a journey to seek a reward;

this is true in *Villette*. In addition, some authors attribute such prominent characteristics to setting, which can determine many aspects of the plot. *Villette* falls into this category, as Lucy could not have had the same experiences in England that she has in the foreign locale. Whether an author adopts a third- or first-person point of view also greatly affects what the reader may learn about the characters. In *Villette*, the first-person point of view limits the reader's knowledge to the protagonist's thoughts and the information learned from other characters' dialogue. Thus, the reader must determine whether or not the first-person narrator is dependable.

Sample Topics:

1. **Plot:** In what ways does the plot of *Villette* resemble that of a hero's adventure, such as Homer's *Odyssey*? In what ways does it differ? Why does Brontë choose those similarities and differences?

In the specific scene discussed in the first section of this chapter, one could observe similarities between Lucy's situation and that of the classic quest adventure, using the quest as a topic on which to base an essay. One might broaden the approach to consider other aspects of Lucy's adventure by comparing and contrasting them to that of the classic hero. When such a hero received his initial "call to adventure," he generally resisted at first but would often suffer the loss of a loved one, which helped him decide to "cross the threshold" to adventure. During that adventure, he gained a guide and met and battled various monsters and shape-shifters. He eventually became discouraged and descended into Hades to consult with the wise shades, then reemerged, renewed the quest, gained the treasure, and returned home. Lucy also resists the call to adventure, suffering an understandable fear about traveling to an unknown country where she cannot even communicate effectively. However, with the loss of her family, her godmother's reversal of fortunes, and the death of her employer, she decides to answer that call and travels to Labassecour. As she crosses the river to reach the ship that will take her on her ocean voyage, she thinks of the mythological Styx and of Charon rowing a new passenger to the Land of Shades. She confronts many challenges and encounters various obstacles along the way, some of which she overcomes due to the help of various guides, including Graham and M. Paul. Both of these men also may qualify as a type of shape-shifter, as they each undergo a change in Lucy's understanding of them when time passes. She undergoes a loss of a guide when Graham "dies" to her, once she realizes that he does not and will not love her. She eventually claims the hero's reward, or treasure, in form of the school that she gains partly through M Paul's efforts. But in his leaving to search for his own goals, Lucy lacks a romantic partner at the story's conclusion. An essay might develop a thesis around the question: What message does Brontë hope to transmit to readers by altering traditional aspects of the hero's quest tale in her novel?

2. **Setting:** Why does Lucy have to relocate? Why does she select the country of Labassecour? Why does she select the town of Villette? What can she accomplish in Villette that she could not accomplish in London or another English city? What conflicts must Lucy overcome based on the location?

   Specific conditions force Lucy to depart from her home country. Her problem with the language presents an immediate barrier that she must overcome. In addition, living in a Catholic population and serving students from a different social class than hers offer challenges. However, in the end, those very challenges become advantages. The irony in that fact offers an excellent essay topic.

3. **Point of view:** What are the advantages of Brontë's use of a first-person point of view? What are the disadvantages? Is Lucy a dependable narrator? Does she accurately provide "facts" that the reader needs in order to understand the story? Is she honest about her own shortcomings and misjudgment of others?

   While Lucy may make faulty judgments, she is still generous in her consideration of others. Her faulty judgments help provide interest for the reader, who, along with Lucy, may be surprised by various characters' actions as the plot progresses.

Due to her very detailed observations, she does supply much desirable description of her surroundings. One might write about how her occasional shortsightedness enhances the plot for the reader.

Language, Symbols, Imagery

Charlotte Brontë was a master of language, and its importance in this novel is emphasized through the inclusion of much dialogue in French. It is also emphasized through her use of figurative expressions or comparisons, such as similes, metaphors, and personification. In describing the early relationship of Polly with her father, Lucy tells the reader that "her mind had been filled from his, as the cup from the flagon." Personification is clearly used in the naming of the school garden's mighty tree, Methusaleh, and in chapter 13, when Lucy notes that "the eyes of the flowers had gained vision, and the knots in the tree-boles listened like secret ears." Brontë inserts various symbols, both traditional and literary, and her masterful descriptions result in rich imagery. Methusaleh is an example of a symbol. His name is adopted from a biblical character who reportedly lived to be 900 years old and was very wise. Because trees traditionally represent wisdom in literature, Lucy buries her letters beneath Methusaleh, who wisely keeps her secret.

Additional examples of symbols include the seasons. Brontë is careful to mention the seasons consistently as Lucy moves through her first year in Villette. She uses them in the traditional manner, with spring indicating new life; summer a time of flourishing or growth; fall the conclusion of growth and threat of impending problems; and winter the season of death, in a sense both literal and figurative. The seasons are first used metaphorically by Lucy's employer, Miss Marchmont in chapter 4: "What a glorious year I can recall—how bright it comes back to me! What a living spring—what a warm, glad summer—what soft moonlight, silvering the autumn evenings—what strength of hope under the ice-bound waters and frost-hoar fields of that year's winter." In this example, winter is used in an unusual way. Because Miss Marchmont is in love, she sees promise at a time of year when many others would see only death. Also, the moon and the garden both represent the feminine, as does the activity of sewing, embroidery, knitting, and crocheting.

Sample Topics:

1. **Language:** Why must Brontë include so many French phrases? What is the effect of dual languages on the reader? What aspects of Brontë's style are apparent in her expressions?

The French language remains a crucial aspect of the novel. Not only does it represent the setting, it emphasizes Lucy's initial feelings of isolation. As she adjusts to her adopted home, she becomes visibly more comfortable with the use of French. Brontë also makes clear Lucy's attitude through her linguistic style, or choice of vocabulary. An important aspect of style is tone, or the author's attitude toward her subject matter, characters, and readers. For instance, Lucy can adopt a sarcastic or a humble tone through her vocabulary; even her silence can transmit a certain message, depending on her body language. In chapter 28, Lucy explains, "Not that it behoved, or beseemed me to *say* anything; but one can occasionally *look* the opinion it is forbidden to embody in words." Communication occurs in many ways in *Villette*, and language of the heart as well as the mind and mouth unites and divides characters.

2. **Symbols:** Why do authors use symbols, rather than simply depending on the literal understanding of an item or state of being to transmit meaning? What symbols seem to be Brontë's favorites? How do some of these often-used symbols relate to Lucy? Do any come to represent other characters?

Use of symbolism indicates sophistication on the part of a writer, but it also assumes reader sophistication. An essay focusing on symbols in *Villette* could group them for discussion according to which character they were associated with and what type of action was generally occurring when they were used. In chapter 28, M. Paul tells Lucy, "You are well habituated to be passed by as a shadow in Life's sunshine: it is a new thing to see one testily lifting his hand to screen his eyes, because you tease him with an obtrusive ray." Lucy seems to be leaving a shadow state to emerge into the sunshine, generally a male symbol. Thus, the reader understands the symbolism as foreshadowing that Lucy's life may be changing for the good, due to the effect of a man. Some symbols might prove especially related to the 19th century, leading to a better knowledge of that era after the reader completed this novel.

Comparison and Contrast

In the comparison and contrast essay, the student must determine similarities and differences, such as those between two characters or fictional elements within a novel, or between two novels by the same author, or between two novels that share subject matter or theme. But the essay writer must also decide how to discuss those similarities and differences. This essay is challenging in that many students make the mistake of only discussing differences and similarities, forgetting that most readers can also recognize those differences and similarities. The comparison and contrast is only one step in the essay process. The student must also develop a thesis statement based on his or her findings, as in any other essay. In the case of *Villette*, the comparison and contrast essay proves tempting, due to critical claims that Brontë's *The Professor*, also discussed in this volume, provided "practice" for the later more mature novel. Thus, one might find strong supportive material comparing and contrasting her style or the protagonists of each novel. Such an essay would necessitate the reading and study of two novels rather than one, and it might also require instructor permission.

Sample Topics:

1. **Style:** How does the tone of one novel compare to that of the other? Does one seem more mature and polished? Does either seem more reader-accessible than the other? Do you see similarities in the use of vocabulary or the incorporation of imagery? Does the fact that one novel has a female narrator and the other a male narrator distinguish the two in specific ways? Does one point of view appear to be more successful than another?

   Because both *The Professor* and *Villette* are based on the author's real-life experience, one would expect to find certain similarities, and there are many, including the main setting and the abundant use of the French language. An important question to consider would be: Does Brontë use these similar elements for the same purpose? Additionally, such an essay would need to include some evaluative discussion. A thesis statement might boldly proclaim one novel to be superior to the other in matters of style, or it might instead claim that the author's selection of different-gendered points of view makes comparison more difficult than contrast.

2. **Protagonists:** What concerns and desires do Lucy Snowe and William Crimsworth share in common? How do the conflicts that they face differ? What similarities and differences exist in the manner by which they handle those conflicts? Are their goals the same? Does one achieve greater success than the other?

Because we all understand that men and women conduct their lives in quite different ways, the reader is not surprised by the differences between Lucy and William. They may be more intrigued by the similarities. Instinct tells us that Lucy's struggle must be greater, as she has few choices other than to work as a low-level teacher in a school. As a man, William's position has allowed him vastly more choices. However, that instinctive reaction might prove false. Perhaps William's decision to marry a woman others might consider beneath his social rank has caused him more difficulty than that faced by Lucy. You might also write about stereotypical aspects of the protagonists and how they refute or support reader expectations.

Bibliography and Online Resources for *Villette*

Bressler, Charles. *Literary Criticism: An Introduction to Theory and Practice.* 3rd ed. New York: Prentice Hall, 2002.

Brontë, Charlotte. *Villette.* Classic Reader. Available online. URL: http://www. classicreader.com/booktoc.php/sid.1/bookid.1734/. Downloaded July 8, 2007.

———. "Villette." Project Gutenberg. Available online. URL: http://www. gutenberg.org/etext/9182. Downloaded July 8, 2007.

"Charlotte Brontë." The Victorian Web. Available online. URL: http://www. victorianweb.org/authors/bronte/cbronte/bronteov.html. Downloaded April 10, 2007.

Fuller, Margaret. *Woman in the Nineteenth Century.* 1845. Mineola, NY: Dover Publications, 1999.

Gaskell, Elizabeth. *The Life of Charlotte Brontë.* Ed. Angus Easson. New York: Oxford UP, 2002.

Halsall, Paul. "The Long Nineteenth Century." Internet Modern History Sourcebook. Available online. URL: http://www.fordham.edu/halsall/mod/modsbook3.html. Downloaded June 25, 2007.

Laga, Barry. "Critical Reading: An Introduction to Literary Theory and Criticism." Available online. URL: http://mesastate.edu/~blaga/theoryindex/theoryhomex.html. Downloaded July 8, 2007.

Linder, Cynthia A. *Romantic Imagery in the Novels of Charlotte Brontë.* New York: Barnes and Noble, 1978.

Melancon, Michael S., and John C. Swanson. *Nineteenth Century Europe: Sources and Perspectives from History.* New York: Longman, 2007.

Rapport, Michael. *Nineteenth-Century Europe.* New York: Palgrave McMillan, 2005.

Sanders, Andrew. *The Victorian Historical Novel: 1840–1880.* New York: St. Martin's Press, 1979.

Soya, Michiko. "*Villette*: Gothic Literature and the Homely Web of Truth." *Brontë Studies: The Journal of the Brontë Society* 28.1 (2003): 15–24.

Tromly, Annette. *The Cover of the Mask: The Autobiographers in Charlotte Brontë's Fiction.* Victoria, British Columbia, Canada: English Literary Studies, 1982.

Tyler, Irene. *Holy Ghosts: The Male Muses of Emily and Charlotte Brontë.* New York: Columbia UP, 1990.

"Villette." The Literature Network. Available online. URL: http://www.online-literature.com/brontec/villette/. Downloaded July 8, 2007.

"Villette Study Guide." Available online. URL: http://www.bookrags.com/studyguide-villette/. Downloaded July 8, 2007.

Wein, Toni. "Gothic Desire in Charlotte Brontë's *Villette*." *Studies in English Literature, 1500–1900* 39 (1999): 733–746.

AGNES GREY

READING TO WRITE

A NNE BRONTË published *Agnes Grey* in 1847 using the same pseudonym, Acton Bell, that she had used when publishing *Poems* (1846) with her sisters Charlotte and Emily. Although the sisters sold only two or three copies of *Poems,* they became celebrities a short time later upon the publication of their novels. The year 1847 proved crucial for the Brontës, as Charlotte published *Jane Eyre* in October, and in December both *Agnes Grey* and Emily's *Wuthering Heights* were released. While many novels in the period appeared in three volumes, the short length of Anne Brontë's book caused it to be published originally as the third volume of a group of three; Emily's *Wuthering Heights* constituted the first two volumes. Following the deaths of both Emily and Anne, their two novels appeared in an 1850 single-volume edition edited by Charlotte.

All of the sisters' novels contain autobiographical aspects, and *Agnes Grey* is no exception. Anne Brontë based the novel on her own unpleasant experience serving as a governess, first to the Ingham family at Blake Hall, Mirfield, in 1839 and later to the Robinson family at Thorp Green Hall, Little Ouseburn, from 1841 to 1845. The spoiled, aggressive, sometimes violent, and dull personalities of her fictitious characters match those of the real children for whom she cared. So do the attitudes on the part of her employers and young charges, as Anne suffered the abuse that fell on all governesses of her era due to class discrimination. With few employment opportunities available to women from "good" middle-class families, the position of governess was forced on those like the Brontë sisters.

Agnes Grey, like Anne Brontë herself, is from a family whose patriarch is a member of the clergy. Agnes's father falls on hard times through a small income and a doomed investment. The conflict caused by class-consciousness becomes clear in the exposition, or background, to the novel, as Agnes explains that her mother married "beneath" her class when she wed Agnes's father, a church parson. This action angered Agnes's grandfather, who then cut off the income that her mother should have received. The financial crisis suffered by the family moves Agnes to want to help ease their burden. Against her parents' wishes, she takes a job as a governess, planning to contribute her wages to support the family. Dismissed from her initial position, she takes a second position that proves slightly more desirable.

As you read *Agnes Grey*, you should take notes on anything that interests you. Class-consciousness is an obvious choice, as would be family, discipline, education, treatment of the working class, and gender issues, as all of these topics receive repeated emphasis throughout the novel. Several will be discussed below.

Essays may also be written about symbolism and imagery; aspects of Brontë's style, such as tone, irony, and vocabulary selection; a single character or a group of characters; and any of the narrative elements of fiction in addition to character, including plot, point of view, or setting. If you take notes or mark passages as you read, you can easily find those passages again to use for support of your essay's ideas. You must quote directly from the text and cite sources as you try to persuade readers to consider your ideas. A discussion of the correct way to document sources appears in the first chapter.

You will consider many ideas for writing as you complete each chapter of the novel. You do not have to analyze or interpret the entire novel, or even a complete chapter, although you may do so when focusing on a broad topic, such as social class or religion. As a matter of fact, you can write an excellent essay that focuses on one brief passage by utilizing the tools of symbolism and imagery. Here is a sample passage from chapter 1, which is ripe for analysis and interpretation due to the symbolism and foreshadowing a careful reader can identify. The passage concludes the opening chapter as Agnes leaves home for the first time to serve as a governess:

> We crossed the valley, and began to ascend the opposite hill. As we were toiling up, I looked back again: there was the village spire, and the old grey parsonage beyond it, basking in a slanting beam of sunshine—it was

but a sickly ray, but the village and surrounding hills were all in somber shade, and I hailed the wandering beam as a propitious omen to my home. With clasped hands, I fervently implored a blessing on its inhabitants, and hastily turned away; for I saw the sunshine was departing; and I carefully avoided another glance, lest I should see it in gloomy shadow, like the rest of the landscape.

Brontë incorporates many traditional symbols in this passage to help the reader understand the importance of what is happening to Agnes. A traditional symbol is one that has suggested the same idea in literature for ages. For example, the carriage in which Agnes rides is symbolic in that it first goes *across* a valley, meaning it *descends* to a low place, and then must *ascend* in order to leave the valley. Traditionally, a place, or topographical point, located in a lower position than another point carries the connotation of less value within a hierarchy. We see this in terminology such as *lower class,* which describes one's socioeconomic position. A descent, or travel downward, in the classic hero quest indicates the hero is experiencing problems in accomplishing his goal. He must consult with a guide of some type when he descends to learn how to ascend again and win his victory. In Agnes's case, this descent is brief and leads to no learned wisdom. However, her trip *through* the valley suggests some challenge awaits her. Biblically, a valley is a place where either positive or negative things may happen, so the reader does not yet have any foreshadowing clues for Agnes; instead, the suggestion that she faces new challenges is strong. When the cart ascends to the top of another hill, that upward movement suggests that Agnes is moving to a better place. The dark imagery behind her supports this suggestion, as she is moving above the darkness.

After reading further in the book, one discovers the irony in this, as Agnes does not reach a better place during this trip. When Agnes looks back, she sees the church spire, and one may recognize a suggestion that she leaves her strong faith behind. A symbolic challenge to her faith also comes to mind when she sees the old grey parsonage. The parsonage appears ancient, the grey color emphasizing its age as well as a lack of vibrancy, due to the lack of color. This may suggest that Agnes's faith is not as strong as it could be. On the other hand, it may instead suggest that organized religion has weakened as a societal force, yet Anne's faith remains strong. The fact that she prays supports that idea.

A slanting beam falls over the parsonage, illuminating it in an otherwise dark surrounding. Light traditionally suggests goodness and also knowledge, or awareness. But this ray is a sickly one, reminiscent of Agnes's father, who is ill in the parsonage. It also indicates the good or positive aspect is weak, struggling to exist. The dark imagery of the "somber shade" that surrounds it further emphasizes threat or negativity. Agnes realizes this, considering the beam a "propitious" or favorable "omen," but she also immediately prays for her family as the sunshine disappears. Because worldly forces cannot protect her family, she asks spiritual ones to do so. She then prevents herself from looking back, because she does not want to observe her past consumed by the "gloomy shadow" that has already overtaken the rest of the landscape. The ray of light and Agnes's prayer offer hope for her future. However, the consumption of her past by the dark gloom is not an optimistic sign.

In analyzing the symbolic content in this passage, a writer should ask: What is the importance of the contrast of light and dark imagery? What does it mean that the dark is much stronger than the light, actually overpowering it? Agnes does turn away to look ahead to her future, which could be a positive move. Still, the overwhelming tone of this passage is dark, even threatening. Might this foreshadow future problems for Agnes?

TOPICS AND STRATEGIES
Themes

All novels contain many themes, or topics. The term *theme* may more properly be used to discuss the overall meaning the author hopes for readers to take away from her writing. A close examination of topics may lead to a statement of the theme. As already mentioned, social class remains a crucial topic in *Agnes Grey*. Were Agnes not of the middle class, she would not have to take the position of governess in order to help support her family. Her mother is of a social class higher than her father, as Agnes's grandfather was a landowning squire with a steady income. He had intended to give Agnes's mother money when she married, but he feels that she insulted her family by marrying a parson, a person of a lower social class. His strong reaction to her choice causes him to threaten to give her no money if she proceeds with her marriage. She elects to marry, because love is more important to her than money. All readers would agree her choice is admirable, but it proves, quite literally, costly. Her integrity provides an excellent guide for Agnes, who learns that one's actions say far more about one's value than a bank account.

Social class is also prominent in the descriptions of Agnes's experiences as a governess. She comments several times on the conundrum in which she finds herself. Due to her position as a governess being considered lower than that of her student charges, she has no authority over them, yet their parents assign her responsibility for their control. Simultaneously, the parents make clear that she cannot punish nor do more than verbally correct the children, due to the children's alleged superior social position. They also assume she lacks intelligence, when she is actually more intelligent than are her employers. Agnes also knows that she is more ethical and compassionate than her supposed "betters." This leads to great frustration on her part. Due to the large number of references to matters of social class or class-consciousness, one could construct much support for an essay on the topic.

Another strong essay topic would be faith. Agnes exhibits much evidence of religious faith, which is to be expected due to her father's position as a clergyman. However, the subservient positions in which she must work test that faith. When she tries to speak to her young charges regarding proper Christian actions, they constantly disagree or disregard her comments altogether. An example is Tom Bloomfield's dismemberment of birds in chapter 2. Tom defends his actions by telling Agnes, "I'm not a bird, and I can't feel what I do to them." When Agnes tells Tom he will go "where wicked people go to when they die," he explains that he is doing exactly what his Papa did when he was young. When Agnes later defends her own actions in killing some birds in order to prevent their mutilation and slow torture by Tom, Mrs. Bloomfield reminds her that creatures were created for man's "convenience." Agnes quotes from the Bible as her rebuttal, reminding Mrs. Bloomfield, "Blessed are the merciful for they shall obtain mercy." Mrs. Bloomfield refuses to appreciate Agnes's message, probably due to ignorance resulting from her own lack of education.

Education provides another possible topic for an essay. Agnes understands that the value of education is a broadening of one's mind. Her employers do not share this view, nor do they share Agnes's intellectual capacity. They value education simply as a commodity they want to "purchase" for their children with as little expense as possible.

Sample Topics:

1. **Social class:** How does the reader know that Agnes remains aware of class hierarchy? Who else in the novel suffers as a result of class structure? How do Agnes's employers rationalize their children's behavior? How do they rationalize their own behavior? What are some examples that show they disregard Agnes's opinions and feelings?

Agnes liberally shares her thoughts about class divisions with her readers, beginning with the exposition about the class dilemma for which her parents have suffered. She later comments on the repercussions of her own class position. When writing about this topic, you should be able to find an abundance of supportive quotations to incorporate into your essay. You will need to decide exactly what point you want to make, being careful not to oversimplify by villainizing the Bloomfields and the Murrays as Agnes's enemies. Keep in mind their own deeply held view that they have every right to treat Agnes as they do and have received society's approval to do so. Chapter 10 proves useful for an analysis of class in Agnes's description of the new rector's behavior in handing the squire's daughters into the carriage prior to Agnes receiving a seat. In chapter 19, when Agnes's mother has the opportunity to regain her fortune by yielding to her father's repeated demand that she repent her marriage to a man of lower social class, she will not comply. Brontë warns that a loss of ethics may accompany wealth and status. Agnes even remarks in chapter 20 that had her mother remained wealthy, she would have suffered more following her husband's death than she did as a poor person.

2. **Faith:** In what ways does Agnes's faith benefit her? Does it ever seem to work to her detriment? How does she deal with the fact that those who are clearly her moral inferiors have power over her?

An essay that focuses on religious faith should clarify the contrast the reader observes between Agnes and her employers' families. While some of those with whom she interacts, such as Mrs. Bloomfield, and the senior Mrs. Bloomfield, demonstrate obvious familiarity with biblical scripture, they apply that knowledge for a purpose that differs from Agnes's purpose. Matilda and Rosalie Murray exhibit actions that show they do not practice even the simplest of biblical values. In chapter 9, Rosalie goes so far as to make fun of Agnes's sister's selection of a husband and her future life as the wife of a vicar. Chapter 10 opens with a discussion about proper behavior on the part of a rector and the manner with which the rector insults Agnes. What indication do you find that Agnes's faith helps her deal with such obvious insults?

3. **Education:** How does the reader know that Agnes values education? What is the opinion of her employers regarding the education of their children? How might the reader note irony in the fact that they do not value Agnes's education and resulting abilities?

Readers should find a rich irony in the attitudes of Agnes's employers toward education and toward Agnes. While they have hired her to teach their children, they do nothing to support her actions. Instead, they actually undermine her authority and her efforts. In writing an essay on this topic, you will want to ask yourself what type of social creed guides or encourages such actions. For instance, Rosalie Murray remains fixated on marrying a handsome, wealthy man and is more interested in balls and other social activities than in improving her mind, an attitude encouraged by society. Agnes adopts "Patience, Firmness, and Perseverance" as her personal mantra in caring for the children. An examination of the results of this mantra's application to the education of her charges could offer a strong theme for an essay. The attitudes of other characters toward education, such as the views Mr. Weston expresses in chapter 18, also are important to assessing the theme of education. Mrs. Grey's decision to open a school following her husband's death might be viewed by some as a risk to her future happiness. However, in chapter 19, she prefaces the announcement of this decision by marking the fact that she remains grateful for the opportunity she had to educate her own daughters.

4. **Family:** How many different families are there in *Agnes Grey*? How do the family groups resemble and differ from one another? What differences do you detect in the way each group seems to define and value family? Does Agnes's idea of family change as she hopes to create a new family with Edward Weston?

The contrasts between Agnes's own family and the two other families with whom she lives is enormous. Contrasts also exist between the Bloomfields and the Murrays. What might account for these differences among people who share the same social class? A helpful approach to writing an essay about contrasts you identify is to catalog each family's values and note which character best represents those values. In fiction, the reader must be able to detect the motivation for all character actions. Values, or the lack of such, may often motivate and support the attitudes of family members toward one another. Mrs. Murray's insensitivity toward the death of Agnes's father in chapter 18 casts light on her ideas regarding family values. That scene would also be useful in a discussion of the theme of social issues, mentioned above.

5. **Gender issues:** In what situations is a double standard apparent in regard to gender? How does Agnes cope with this double standard? How do some characters use gender inequity to their benefit? Does regard for women change according to their ages?

Because Agnes's family is dominated by women, and her father remains weakened by illness, she matures with the encouragement of her mother and sister. She does not experience this same empowerment in society, where male concerns are given priority over female concerns. The few career options available to women compared to those for men represent a prime example of a double standard where gender is concerned. Students writing an essay on this topic will also find examples of gender preference when studying the attitudes of Agnes's female and male charges in the households where she works. For example, Tom Bloomfield takes as a role model Uncle Robson, a man described by Agnes in chapter 5 as "the scorner of the female sex." Tom's desire to strike his sisters and refusal to obey Agnes would naturally be influenced by the men in his household.

Another approach to this topic would be an analysis of Rosalie Murray. In some ways, Rosalie remains independent, rejecting certain suitors. However, she fixates on making a good marriage. In chapter 9, when Agnes questions why Rosalie values male social conquests, the young woman replies with obvious surprise, "Think of any woman asking that!" That remark would be an important part of an analysis of Rosalie's character, as would Agnes's overall reaction to Rosalie's detailed description of her social "coming-out." Rosalie becomes a much more positive character by the novel's end; an analysis of whether her change affects her gender views could prove revealing. Maggie Berg's article "'Hapless Dependents': Women and Animals in Anne Brontë's *Agnes Grey*" could be of help in writing about this topic.

Character

The characters of any novel provide promising topics for essays once a decision is made regarding the main idea the writer decides to use as a focus. An important starting point is to identify the book's main character, or protagonist, usually a simple task. Next, the antagonist, a major character who causes conflict for the protagonist, should be identified along with the problem that character places in the path of the main character. Additional characters, generally considered minor characters, may be divided into groups for examination based on similarities or differences. For instance, to satisfy an essay assignment, you might choose to write about Agnes's employers or others who serve as authority figures. That would include the Bloomfields, the Murrays, and their various relatives.

An analysis of the children for whom Agnes assumes responsibility also offers rich possibilities for an essay. One way to approach that topic would be to discuss the children's varied effects on Agnes, noting which ones help develop her character. A related topic would be Agnes's effect on the children, as that approach would demonstrate the manner by which the children change due to her presence. That, in turn, would allow reflection on her character as you consider whether her strength and morality act to alter the children in positive ways.

You might also decide to analyze members of Agnes's family, which would include Mary and her parents. Finally, Agnes's love interest, Edward Weston, offers excellent opportunity for analysis. His realistic portrayal counters that of the traditional Victorian fictional romantic hero.

Sample Topics:

1. **Agnes Grey:** How might you describe Agnes's self-image? How does that self-image change throughout the novel? What causes it to change? Is Agnes more content at the novel's conclusion than at its beginning? How do you know? Does the reader realize anything about Agnes later in the novel that was not obvious at the beginning?

   All fictional protagonists face conflict that generally leads to a critical realization, called an *epiphany.* The epiphany subsequently inspires them to change their manner of thinking or behavior. Such a change allows them to become more dynamic, well-rounded characters. Much of this novel centers on the way those with whom Agnes is forced to associate challenge her sense of self. For example, in chapter 7, she admits to feeling degraded by the life she feels forced to lead and refers to "indignities" suffered by governesses in that passage as well as in others. Because Agnes is trapped in that lifestyle, she may not always prevail in her conflict with others. However, the reader should be able to find evidence indicating that although challenged by life, she always retains her high values. Because she is not a member of the upper class and lacks wealth and privilege, Agnes must rely on her strong ethical character to succeed in life.

2. **Agnes's employers and authority figures:** How would you describe the Bloomfields, the Murrays, and their relatives and

friends who are in a position to dominate Agnes? What is the effect of their actions in shaping Agnes's character? Which characters seem helpful at first but ultimately prove to be deceitful or hypocritical? How does Agnes react to such characters? Is her judgment of those characters charitable or harsh? What do her reactions to them reveal about her personality?

Readers come to know the Bloomfields well and the Murrays intimately through Agnes's detailed narrative. Her time spent with the Bloomfields serves as an initiation into the life of a governess, providing an excellent accumulation of information that presages Agnes's future. As readers move further into the novel, they learn that the Bloomfields did not accurately foreshadow Agnes's experience with the Murrays. Should you choose to write about these families and their effects on Agnes, you will naturally engage in some comparison and contrast between the two. You will also notice that Agnes's narrative style shifts somewhat from her account of the Bloomfields, which resembles an objective report, to that of the Murrays, which resembles a more personal narrative.

3. **The children:** How do those children placed in Agnes's care disappoint her? How do they please her? In what ways does Agnes show her displeasure or approval of the children's actions? How does her presence affect their actions? Which children force her to alter her expectations? Do any of the children become important to her future?

While the Bloomfield children prove to be near caricatures in their strident attitudes and behavior, Brontë spends far more time developing the characters of the Misses Murray, who affect Agnes more deeply. The reader follows Rosalie Murray from an arrogant young woman speaking of her power over men in chapter 16 through her transformation into the more sober and realistic Lady Ashby. Rosalie can be seen as a foil for Agnes, in that both seek happiness and fulfillment, although they define those states in very different ways. Thus, an essay based on Rosalie Murray or the children as a group should emphasize the ways in which the children help us better understand the main character, Agnes.

4. **Agnes's family:** In what ways does Agnes resemble her mother and her sister Mary? In what ways does she differ? How do her family members support her desire to be a governess? Why does her mother initially hesitate to approve of Agnes's plan? Does the family benefit or suffer due to her absence? How does her family help Agnes to accomplish her goals? Is Mr. Grey important to the story?

A strong essay may contrast and compare between or among characters. This approach might serve well for an essay based on the Grey family. While Agnes loves and learns from her family members, she also desires separation from them. The essay writer would want to ask why Agnes must leave home in able to realize her own capacities for adventure and love. Her service as a governess proves far more important to her development than she had anticipated. How does it help change her view of family?

5. **Edward Weston:** What are Agnes's early impressions of Edward Weston? Why does he not appear interested in Agnes at first? What causes Agnes to be attracted to him? In what way does he seem a suitable match for Agnes? How does Mr. Weston help Agnes mature? What does Agnes learn about herself from her relationship with Mr. Weston?

Edward Weston does not appear early in the novel, a fact that is important to the story. The student writing about Mr. Weston would want to establish Brontë's reason for "saving" Edward until the point in the story where he appears. She also develops him slowly, as initially he hovers only on the edge of Agnes's consciousness. Readers first learn about him from Rosalie's uncomplimentary description in chapter 9. It is more than balanced by Nancy's description of her interaction with him in chapter 11. Still, Agnes does not know him well for some pages. Does that leisurely character development parallel

Agnes's development of self-awareness? As a major character, Weston's presence in the novel should help Agnes evolve into a new version of herself, better equipped to face the future.

History and Context

Nineteenth-century England was notable for its rapid development in areas including travel, trade, industrialization, communications, and science. Its population shifted from the country to the city as the traditional small farm disappeared, to be replaced by large estates, and factories called for ever more workers. As a direct result of such changes, new wealth developed among those involved in trade and business, while wealth based on land ownership alone decreased. Better facilities for travel led to increased trade and created a new middle-class bourgeoisie, merchants who opened shops and created businesses to offer never-before-available goods to an increasingly wealthy public. Class status shifted to become more focused on materialism than genealogy, and the newly wealthy began to claim privileges previously available only to the aristocracy. Upper middle-class families developed their own social circles and sought education and social training for their children. Literature became more widely available with the use of improved printing methods and the founding of new publishing houses, producing new genres of reading material. As science and materialism became more popular, traditional organized religion reacted to the perceived threat to its influence.

All of these circumstances act as support for topics found in *Agnes Grey* that would be suitable as themes for essays. The topic of materialism might begin with a cataloging of all references to material goods and money, both in a positive and negative manner. An essay on social interaction could focus on the ways in which Agnes is and is not accepted into the activities of the families that she serves. It could examine other activities as well, such as those in which Rosalie Murray engages and her expectations regarding her place in society. Finally, a study of the actions of those engaged in organized religion, most especially the ministers, could engage readers who will observe markedly different role models in Agnes's father, Mr. Richardson, Mr. Hatfield, and Mr. Weston. Christine Colón's article "Enacting the Art of Moral Influence: Religion and Social Reform in the Works of Anne Brontë" could be helpful in an essay about formal religion. Maureen Moran's *Victorian Literature and Culture: A*

Student Guide and Gail Marshall's *Victorian Fiction: Context* provide strong general background for writing about the important historical forces that worked to shape the characters and themes in *Agnes Grey.*

Sample Topics:

1. **Materialism:** How might one define *materialism*? How does materialism tend to define various characters? Who thinks or speaks about material matters? Are such matters referred to in a positive or negative manner? What efforts are made to transfer material comforts from the upper to the lower classes?

Almost all of the characters must deal with material matters. For Agnes and her family, material concerns cause conflict and problems for their day-to-day existence. For Agnes's employers, material matters are a cause for celebration. The laborers featured in the novel constitute the working class. For them, material goods represent the difference between life and death. A good example is the laborer Mark Wood. A contrast between Rosalie's and Agnes's attitudes and actions toward Wood provides an excellent basis for the development of a thesis about 19th-century materialism and its relationship to various classes.

2. **Social interaction:** What types of social interaction occur? Who participates in them? How do the actions of one class differ from those of another? Why is Agnes uninterested in Rosalie's stories about dances and male conquests? Why does Rosalie wish her to be interested? How might their conversations be seen as social interaction?

Social interaction for Agnes and those of her class do not involve dancing and other frivolous celebration. Agnes's visit to Nancy in chapter 11 represents socialization for her. However, not only does she not engage in such playful activity, she tells Rosalie that she does not wish to know any details of Rosalie's social life. The perceptive reader might ask why certain interactions are common to one group but not another. Rosalie views her discussions with Agnes as social chatter, but

Agnes sees them as a chance to educate Rosalie. Does Agnes prove successful in changing Rosalie's social behavior?

3. **Organized religion:** How do the figures representing organized religion resemble one another? How do they vary? What do their parishioners think about them? What do they feel is important for their parishioners? Do the parishioners have different ideas from those of their religious leaders? What traits does Agnes believe to be essential for a good parishioner?

As suggested above, the reader has several characters to observe as examples of religious leaders. Readers view Agnes's father in a private setting, rather than public, but still gain some impression of his beliefs and actions. He might be compared to Mr. Richardson, who will marry Agnes's sister Mary. Although the reader does not know a lot about Mr. Richardson, Agnes provides a description of him for Rosalie at the end of chapter 8. Mr. Hatfield and Mr. Weston are Brontë's most completely developed clerical characters. Chapter 10 supplies details about Mr. Hatfield that are most unflattering, with chapter 14 confirming readers' suspicions regarding his character. Chapters 9 and 10 provide early descriptions of Mr. Weston from both Rosalie's and Agnes's point of view. Nancy's description of Mr. Weston in chapter 11 occurs before Agnes comes to know him and provides the opinion of a cottager, a very different social group than that of Agnes or Rosalie. By analyzing the actions of each character, the only basis on which other characters and the readers have to judge them, you will draw a conclusion about organized religion and its representatives, then you may develop that conclusion into a suitable thesis statement on which to base your essay.

Philosophy and Ideas

When Anne Brontë wrote *Agnes Grey*, England was experiencing an enormous transformation that had begun early in the century. Along with material changes came changes in ideas about the human condition. Increased facilities for travel led to the possibility of a new worldview for people as they moved out of their familiar environments. Increased wealth and the sense of change led to more confidence in the future. Increasing income for those who were not members of the traditional landowning aristocracy allowed some shift from one class to another, and the middle class found their concerns becoming more important as they increased in numbers. Individuals had never before observed such rapid changes in the areas of engineering and manufacturing. Those changes led the British to revise their sense of self, both on an individual level and on a national level. The old England had passed away in a few decades, causing consternation for some but hope for a better future for many. The promise of advancement in life through education began to grow, and more young women were allowed to move beyond the domestic sphere to gain skills. However, those of the upper classes would become more "trapped" by domestic duties than ever before, as young women invested their hopes in a dream of making a wealthy match. The philosophy that one might have some control over one's fate grew as many focused on the material rather than the religious. As seen in Brontë's novel, the old values represented by Agnes and her rural upbringing were challenged by those who lived closer to cities. The wealthier element valued materialism, causing some to reevaluate their definition of success as merely a life lived according to simple biblical rules, rather than an existence imbued with religious faith.

Sample Topics:

1. **Hope for a better future:** What evidence exists that demonstrates Agnes's hope for a better future? Is her hope rational? Is it in line with popular belief? Do other characters encourage or discourage her hope? Why does she succeed in clinging to hope during what appears to be overwhelming conflict?

   While several scenes may be used to support this topic in an essay, those in chapters 20 and 21 should help in developing a thesis. In the latter, Agnes actually speaks to Hope, an emotion that Brontë personifies for effect. Agnes's inner conflict and discussions serve as crucial proof of hope's importance to her peace of mind.

2. **Acceptance of fate:** How does the reader know that Agnes thinks of fate? How does she entertain such thoughts simultaneously

with those of hope? Does her embrace of the theory of fate contradict her Christian faith? If so, in what ways? Does Agnes recognize any contradiction?

A belief in the theory that forces beyond human control direct a person's fate may be seen as contradictory to Christianity. If those beliefs appear in conflict, an essay that focuses on contrasting and comparing those beliefs should also postulate whether that conflict is resolved in this novel. An analysis of characters' attitudes toward fate, particularly Agnes, must also examine other aspects of those characters' lives. For instance, if a belief in fate is tied to one's social class, the class of the character you analyze could prove crucial to that character's attitude.

3. **Importance of education:** Which characters consider themselves "educated"? What criteria do they use to define an education? How does education become a commodity in *Agnes Grey*? In what ways does education reflect social class?

   During the early to mid-19th century, more people had begun to believe that both men and women should be educated, especially if they belonged to the upper class. Education was viewed as a luxury by those who needed to work and who did not have the opportunities to obtain an education. Agnes is an exception to her peers with her excellent education, administered by her mother. What does the source of her education seem to indicate about contemporary society's attitude toward education? Agnes appears to use education as a means of measuring one's behavior toward others. An essay that focuses on education needs to discuss both societal attitudes toward education and the individual attitudes reflected in the novel's characters. Is Agnes correct in her belief that one's level of serious education acts as a predictor of one's moral fiber?

4. **The myth of success:** How does Agnes define success? How do other characters define success? Is it determined by membership in a certain social class? How does Rosalie Murray's posi-

tion as Lady Ashby help support Brontë's message regarding class differences?

In discussing *success,* an essay writer would need to first define that term. In doing so, one might discover that the definition varies from character to character, which is not surprising in a realistic novel based on historical fact. Most did believe that those born into the higher classes would be successful. An essay might investigate that belief through an examination of Rosalie Murray, later Lady Ashby. While she appeared successful to the outer world, she did not enjoy happiness. Does this mean she should be considered unsuccessful? The answer to that question depends on whether one demands happiness as an important element of success.

Form and Genre

As a novel, *Agnes Grey* remains predictable in its general format and in its genre. Novels are divided into chapters. They move forward due to plot, or a series of actions in which the protagonist is challenged through conflict that eventually builds to its highest point, called the climax. Resolution of conflict (not to be confused with solution of conflict) occurs at the climax, with normally very little action following prior to the conclusion. Fiction contains familiar elements, including character, discussed earlier, and plot. Additional elements of fiction include setting, which may involve geography, time period, and culture; author style, discussed below under the subheading "Language, Symbols, and Imagery"; and point of view. Any of these elements can prove appropriate for discussion, or two or more related elements may be written about together in an essay. For instance, plot naturally involves conflict, a crucial aspect of fiction, so those should be discussed together. In analyzing the plot of *Agnes Grey,* one might focus on the speed, or lack of speed, with which the characters progress toward the climax and resolution. Analysis of setting would relate to the above discussion of "History and Context" and "Philosophy and Ideas," as culture remains an important aspect of setting. Finally, one might contrast the realistic nature of *Agnes Grey* with the typical romance novel or domestic fiction to which female readers had become accustomed. Its realistic elements and use of a working middle-class woman as main character surprised many readers in Brontë's day.

Sample Topics:

1. **Plot and conflict:** Who appears to be the antagonist(s) in *Agnes Grey*? How do those antagonists support Agnes's character development? Does each antagonist receive enough "page space" in your opinion? Might the novel's plot have benefited from additional or fewer actions or events? Are the plot's actions realistic and understandable in context?

   Because conflict is an essential factor of plot, analyzing and writing about conflict and plot is a natural process. You should begin by cataloging a list of major events or actions in the story, as these constitute the plot. Then identify how the conflict benefits from each action. Those actions will either introduce new conflict, add extra dimension to an existing conflict, or advance an already existing conflict. As conflict develops, so should the protagonist's character. Characters should react to conflict, and that reaction should be realistic. The reader must understand all the characters' motivations and view those motivations as appropriate for each.

2. **Movement or progression:** How would one describe the plot's momentum or progression in terms of speed? Does the momentum seem suited to the topic? How might an author employ momentum to support character development? Does Agnes's development benefit from momentum? What is the effect of this novel's progression on the reader?

   A skilled author such as Brontë does nothing in error. All aspects of her plotting are by careful design. Therefore, you should be able to analyze the plot, apply labels such as "rapid momentum" or "variable momentum" to the plot's movement, and then suggest a relationship to the development of the main character. How does the slow and at times tedious movement during Agnes's first position as governess complement the later escalating action in her second position?

3. **Setting:** How would you describe the novel's setting in terms of geographical location, culture, and time period or era? What about the setting proves crucial to development of the protagonist? Might this plot have occurred in a different setting?

Like many novels, *Agnes Grey* had to take place during the specific time and in the specific geographic space and culture selected by its author. In order to write about setting, analyze how it supports Brontë's message. In order to accomplish this, after determining what that message is, you will note how it grew from important social issues of the day, and whether those issues would be better emphasized in one setting over another. For instance, the governess position hardly exists in the 21st century; therefore, that type of work would be much less relevant in a novel set during the present day. However, the concern for working people illustrated in the novel would be relevant, as those concerns are timeless and universal. The incorporation of universal, timeless themes is the reason that period novels continue to capture the imagination of readers.

4. **Realism:** What details add realism to *Agnes Grey*? Do any details detract from the realistic portrayal for which Brontë aimed? Which details would have most surprised readers of Brontë's era? What message could Brontë better provide by adopting realism over romanticism?

An essay regarding the realism present in *Agnes Grey* would necessarily need to incorporate some aspects of comparison and contrast to the traditional romantic and domestic novels of her day. Texts such as Gail Marshall's *Victorian Fiction: Context* would again prove crucial to this analysis.

Language, Symbols, and Imagery

The language adopted by a writer is part of her style. She may impose a particular tone or judgment on her subject matter—another aspect of style—through her vocabulary. An important aspect of vocabulary is description through the use of sensory details. An accumulation of such description equates to imagery, as the author draws, through language, a word picture for her reader. Her style may be made more strongly descriptive through the use of symbolism in addition to the incorporation of observable detail. Through its act of comparison, symbolism helps readers better understand a situation or a scene. Anne Brontë used all of these aspects of style with great skill to the benefit of her readers. Her choice to move her protagonist from a familiar surrounding to three different new settings as the novel progresses allows much inclusion of detail about Agnes.

Agnes also spends time outdoors, which permits Brontë to develop a great deal of imagery. Agnes's keen descriptions and her own use of symbolism ring true due to her education and her natural sense of curiosity. For instance, she opens chapter 16 with the statement, "Next Sunday was one of the gloomiest of April days—a day of thick, dark clouds, and heavy showers." Because spring and its showers traditionally signal the promise of new life, this use of April has an ironic tone. Dark clouds generally indicate that something negative will happen to the protagonist. Thus, the reader will understand through symbolism and imagery that Agnes will encounter conflict just when she does not expect it. Such analysis of how Brontë uses symbols or imagery to enhance the reader's understanding of Agnes and the challenges she faces would prove ideal for an essay.

Sample Topics:

1. **Symbols:** How does symbolism aid in the reader's understanding of Agnes? In what types of situations does she tend to use symbolism? Does the use seem to come naturally to her? Why or why not?

   You must continually remind yourself that everything in fiction supports development of the main character, through which the author also develops her novel's main idea, or theme. The first step will be for you to decide what that message might be. Whether you believe that Brontë's message relates to opportunities for women or to the treatment of lower classes by the upper, symbolism can help you make your point. Remember that symbols may be used in traditional ways, but that authors will also include literary symbols, those which prove symbolic only in a particular work.

2. **Imagery:** In what instances does Agnes incorporate imagery into her narration? Does she seem to be more emotional when she does so? What impression does her in-depth description make on her audience?

We have already noted the departure scene, when Agnes first leaves home, for its striking nature imagery. Nature provides much of the imagery for Agnes, but so do interiors. For instance, the details she includes in her first-impression descriptions of the various homes in which she lives prove acute. She also calls upon imagery from nature when she contemplates the values of others. Chapter 17, "Confessions," provides an excellent example. Agnes begins with the use of the traditional symbol of the mirror, "the glass," which always signals that the character who gazes in it is involved in self-contemplation. She continues by constructing near-allegory in her imagery of the fly and the worm to describe the situation of the plain individual, unable to draw attention to herself.

Bibliography and Online Resources for *Agnes Grey*

Alexander, Christine, and Margaret Smith. *The Oxford Companion to the Brontës.* New York: Oxford UP, 2006.

"Anne Bronte." About.com: Women's History. Available online. URL: http://womenshistory.about.com/library/bio/blbio_bronte_anne.htm. Downloaded August 7, 2007.

Armstrong, Nancy. *How Novels Think: The Limits of Individualism from 1719–1900.* New York: Columbia University Press, 2005.

Barker, Juliet. *The Brontës.* New York: St. Martin's Press, 1996.

———. *The Brontës: A Life in Letters.* New York: Overlook Press, 2001.

Berg, Maggie. "'Hapless Dependents': Women and Animals in Anne Brontë's *Agnes Grey.*" *Studies in the Novel* 34.2 (Summer 2002): 177–197.

Brontë, Anne. *Agnes Grey.* Available online. URL: http://digital.library.upenn. edu/women/bronte/agnes/agnes-grey.html. Downloaded August 7, 2007.

Colón, Christine. "Enacting the Art of Moral Influence: Religion and Social Reform in the Works of Anne Brontë." *Women's Writing* 11.3 (October 2004): 399–420.

Langland, Elizabeth. *Anne Brontë: The Other One.* Totowa, NJ: Barnes and Noble, 1989.

Marshall, Gail. *Victorian Fiction: Context.* London: Hodder Arnold, 2002.

Moran, Maureen. *Victorian Literature and Culture: A Student Guide.* London: Continuum International Publishing Group, 2007.

Nash, Julie, and Barbara A. Suess. *New Approaches to the Literary Art of Anne Brontë.* Aldershot and Burlington, VT: Ashgate, 2001.

Winnifrith, Tom. *The Brontës and Their Background.* New York: Palgrave Macmillan, 1988.

THE TENANT OF WILDFELL HALL

READING TO WRITE

THIS WRITING guide features each of the novels written by the Brontë sisters, and you may utilize the "Reading to Write" general discussion sections regardless of which novel you read. Despite a natural variance in some of the narrative elements of fiction, the books share many similarities, particularly that of style. This similarity becomes magnified within works written by the same author, as one might expect. So, as part of your preparation in developing an essay based on Anne Brontë's *The Tenant of Wildfell Hall*, you will also want to read the chapter in this book that considers her other novel, *Agnes Grey*. Critics have noted that Anne learned much from Charlotte, suggesting the potential for comparison and contrast among those novels as well.

The Tenant of Wildfell Hall offers multiple topics on which to build a solid essay. In order to discover a good topic, you should keep a notebook close at hand as you read. You can then record topics as you encounter them. You might create columns headed with topic ideas—for example, family and religion—and then list the page numbers on which you find scenes relevant to each topic. This same approach will work well for quotations that capture your interest and also for any questions that come to mind as you read. Such lists of topics, quotations, and questions will prove invaluable when you settle down to develop an essay. With your lists, you will not have to depend on memory or search through a lengthy novel to find a particular scene or quotation that you remember reading. Because many solid thesis statements are born as answers to questions that you and other readers might have about the novel, your list of questions can be a gold mine.

The Tenant of Wildfell Hall represents realistic fiction, but Brontë also incorporates elements from the gothic fiction genre. As Jan B. Gordon points out in a 1984 article written for *English Literary History,* the use of letters "is a narrative device common to Gothic fiction with its plethora of found letters, scraps of documents in attics, texts as clues to a prior and whole truth which must somehow be pieced together." Gilbert Markham's letters definitely involve the reader in clues and hints at the truth about Helen Graham/Huntingdon. However, of the many elements found in gothic fiction, the mysterious estate is the most recognizable in *The Tenant of Wildfell Hall.* Wildfell Hall, often described in dark, threatening tones, as in Markham's description in chapter 2, bears a name that suggests chaotic conditions, which combine to disrupt order in its tenant's life. Gilbert notes its "dark grey stone," which one might admire, but adds that in reality it must be "cold and gloomy" to inhabit, with "its time-eaten air-holes, and its too lonely, too unsheltered situation." The "gigantic warrior" built to guard its entrance has become overgrown with vegetation, now presenting "a goblinish appearance."

The tenant herself brings mystery to the novel, replacing the traditional gothic hero, generally a dark, brooding male with a mysterious past, popularly labeled a "Byronic hero." Upon examination of this situation, the alert student will note that Brontë's gender twisting in substituting a female (a mother, no less!) for the traditional male suggests a fascinating essay topic. Identity errors, also an element of the gothic novel, add to the mystery. While it lacks the ghosts so popular in gothic fiction, the book's mysterious elements contribute to the reader's early reception of it as a possible gothic novel oeuvre. However, a short way into the novel, the reader understands that it represents realism far more strongly than romanticism. In this aspect, it contrasts greatly with the popular novels written by Brontë's sisters, *Jane Eyre* and *Wuthering Heights.*

The Tenant of Wildfell Hall also incorporates the structure of another popular genre, the epistolary novel. It covers a 20-year period beginning in 1827, and readers learn of events through a series of letters written by Gilbert Markham to his brother-in-law, J. Halford, Esq. His account focuses on his courtship of the beautiful Helen Huntingdon, Wildfell

Hall's mysterious tenant. Gilbert first knows her by her assumed name, Helen Graham. Within this structure, Brontë embeds Helen's diary entries, allowing the reader dual points of view.

Brontë published this novel under her pseudonym, Acton Bell, perhaps to help convince readers of the realistic nature of the male protagonist's voice. Although Anne's sister Charlotte later deemed the subject matter "unfortunate," the novel was popular and enjoyed multiple printings during the 19th century. The three sisters often discussed their work, and critics feel that *The Tenant of Wildfell Hall* offers evidence that Anne learned from her sisters, particularly from Emily's tone and narration in *Wuthering Heights*.

While *The Tenant of Wildfell Hall* might be considered a love story, it is much more, focusing on many different topics, some of which are discussed below. In your essay, you may apply techniques similar to those suggested, regardless of the topic or novel under discussion. One approach involves the most basic of critical schools, known as formalism, which focuses on literary style rather than content to find meaning in any scene. In formalism, elements such as symbols, imagery, irony, and foreshadowing are crucial to reader understanding. Useful sources to refresh your knowledge of formalism and other literary critical approaches include Charles Bressler's *Literary Criticism: An Introduction to Theory and Practice*, Hans Biedermann's *A Dictionary of Literary Symbols*, and Gene Doty's Web site "Signs, Symbols and Interpretations."

For example, in the passage from chapter 12 that follows, Gilbert Markham has just visited Helen at Wildfell Hall. He does not want to return home, where his own family has discussed gossip about Helen that he refuses to believe. He turns back to look at Wildfell Hall and reacts:

> When it rose in sight, I stood still a moment to look, and then continued moving towards the gloomy object of attraction. Something called me nearer—nearer still—and why not, pray? Might I not find more benefit in the contemplation of that venerable pile with the full moon in the cloudless heaven shining so calmly above it—with that warm yellow luster peculiar to an August night—and the mistress of my soul within, than in returning to my home where all comparatively was light, and life, and cheerfulness, and therefore inimical to me in my present frame of mind;—and the more

so that its inmates all were more or less imbued with that detestable belief the very thought of which made my blood boil in my veins—

This passage offers irony, figurative language, symbols, imagery, and foreshadowing for analysis. For example, Gilbert is attracted to a "gloomy object" but repulsed by his home, which he describes with the words *light, life,* and *cheerfulness,* an example of irony. Figurative language appears through the personification of Wildfell Hall as it calls to Gilbert, converting the house into a character in the scene. The descriptive details of the house, the moon, the heaven, the night, and the references to dark and light constitute imagery, details assembled into a word picture that Brontë draws for the reader. The moon is a traditional symbol of woman, and here it symbolizes Helen, the present mistress of Wildfell Hall. The moon's presence above the house, its calm demeanor, and its warm luster all suggest Helen's control not only over Wildfell Hall but also over Gilbert. He calls her "mistress of my soul," suggesting a near-religious experience for him. This alerts the reader that his gazing upon the house in the moonlight greatly stirs his emotions, foreshadowing an upcoming passionate scene. That foreshadowing is supported by his feeling the physical heat that is common to people filled with passion, and he uses figurative language to describe those feelings, comparing his arousal to boiling blood.

The time of year, late summer, is also symbolically important. Late summer suggests an ending of the time of promise, when crops ripen, and the imminent harvesting of those crops. Such imagery leads one to think of the biblical phrase (in paraphrase), "We reap what we sow." The idea inherent in that sentence will reappear multiple times in the novel, particularly in Helen's dialogue. The connotation of late summer as a time of reaping also acts as foreshadowing, alerting the reader that someone will soon reap the consequences of his or her actions.

Such a close reading of a passage can produce ideas for topics about which to write based on the novel's formal elements. You may also begin with questions about your reading and see where the answers take you. For example, a reader might ask whether Helen's being mistress of Gilbert's soul is a good or bad thing and whether that statement might relate to Helen's strong religious faith. Gilbert appears more demon than saint, prompting one to wonder: Does this make him similar to Helen or different from her? Does the fact that he suddenly sees his own happy family as less attractive, choosing to relate more strongly to Helen's gloomy surroundings, suggest that he must separate from his familiar environment in order to discover a primary family of his own? These are only a few of the myriad questions the scene presented in the paragraph above might provoke.

In the discussion that follows you will find many suggestions of topics, and approaches you might take to analyzing them in essays. This guide does not intend for you to adopt these exact approaches; rather, they should act as suggestions to help you develop your own topics and questions. The answers to your questions should help you develop your thesis statement, or statement of your main essay topic. Remember: Your thesis statement cannot simply be a statement of fact; it must contain some element of opinion. It also may not be a question. Review the first chapter if needed for a discussion of strong and weak thesis statements, outlines, and essay formatting.

TOPICS AND STRATEGIES
Themes

The Tenant of Wildfell Hall suggests a number of strong topics from which to develop one thesis statement that may be the focus of your essay. Critics note that Anne Brontë depicts the disaster that results when humans succumb to excess. One example would be the self-indulgence and debauchery of Arthur Huntingdon, who cannot control his addictions and obsessions. His actions result in a life of misery for Helen and their son Arthur. Pride also provides a topic. Most of the families featured practice false pride, holding their social or economic status in too much esteem based on the false values of their culture. In the novel's final chapters, Gilbert Markham hesitates to marry Helen when he learns of her wealth, practicing a type of reverse snobbery that represents false pride. He acts inappropriately and childishly due to his perception that traditional gender roles will not allow him to marry a woman who enjoys wealth equal to or greater than his own.

Another topic is the nature of gossip, which proves harmful both to those who begin false rumors and those who suffer as a result of them. In chapter 10, Markham notes that "vile slander" has been leveled against Helen, and he blames it on "the wickedness and falsehood of the world." Helen understands how such gossip may destroy the most innocent of persons. In chapter 12, she urges Markham to depart Wildfell Hall, as the neighbors will turn his visit against her, meaning they would accuse the couple of immoral behavior, although none has occurred. The Millward and the Wilson families both indulge in gossip that equates to slander, turning their small community against the innocent Helen. Reverend Millward is especially guilty of this, as he acts as a conduit for the slander: In chapter 11, he explains to Mrs. Markham that he confronted the innocent Helen to explain to her what he found "reprehensible" in her "conduct." He depends only on hearsay when making the accusation and then compounds the problem by describing the confrontation to various members of the community, sharing what should remain confidential.

Morality and ethics are also topics worthy of study and are closely connected with the topic of gossip. Helen is highly religious and actively practices her faith, in contrast to the churchgoers of Lindenhope and even the parson and his family. She also contrasts with her husband, a drunk and an adulterer. In an immoral act, his associate, Walter Hargrave, tempts Helen to betray Huntingdon in revenge for Huntingdon's betrayal of her. In chapter 32, Hargrave first tempts Helen to listen to "bad tidings," but she refuses even to hear any accusatory tales, setting her apart from Hargrave in her ethical grounding. Helen's character remains intact, despite exposure to Huntingdon; in chapter 32, she even warns Mr. Hattersley that prolonged exposure to a negative influence, such as her husband, could not help but influence his own behavior. Her counsel and moral behavior helps him mend his relationship with his wife. Markham does not practice ethical behavior when he allows his emotions to send him into a senseless jealous rage against Helen's innocent brother, badly injuring him in an unwarranted attack in chapter 14. At one point in the novel, Helen expresses concern that she may be losing her strong moral center, causing her to run away from Huntingdon and his debauched habits to take refuge at her brother's estate. The attentive reader might ask whether ethics and morality are linked more strongly to one gender than the other, examining multiple characters to determine the answer.

Art and painting also provide worthy linked topics. Helen draws and paints not only to support herself and her son, but also as a means of expressing what she cannot say aloud. In chapter 17, her art acts as a foreshadowing tool when in an early conversation with Huntingdon, he pretends interest in her paintings only as a way to pursue Helen herself.

Through her art, Helen ironically later finds a means to independence apart from Huntingdon.

Brontë emphasizes that education should be equally available to women as well as men, and she focuses on education in the social graces in addition to academic subjects. As Helen writes in her diary in chapter 43, one of her greatest joys is the education of her son. She is taken to task by many observers for this; in particular, her husband's male friends fear she is teaching her son "feminine" traits. Thus, Brontë takes aim at the traditional roles dictated according to gender. She also stresses the act of reading, a direct means to education, in several ways. When Graham first sees Helen, she is bent over her prayer book, and he initiates interaction with her by offering her gifts of books. In chapter 8, they discuss Sir Walter Scott's poetry, and Brontë references Scott's popular poem, *Marmion.* Helen takes refuge in a library as she lays her plot to flee from Huntingdon. In addition, in chapter 33, Brontë makes a sly reference to her own occupation when Helen asks her weeping servant and confidant Rachel if the cause of her consternation is the reading of novels.

Finally, the topic of redemption offers promise for an essay topic, particularly as demonstrated through Helen's act of nursing her profligate husband as he dies. If you select this topic, you will want to consider the meaning of the term *redemption,* who provides the redemption and who receives it, and what effect the act of redemption has on all parties.

Sample Topics:

1. **Individual excess:** Which individuals seem drawn to excess? Which of their actions reveal this? What are the rewards they desire? Why does Brontë indicate that individual excess is an undesirable trait? Does she suggest that such excess may be remedied?

   Brontë's family well knew the challenges to those of modest means. However, the family also observed some of the benefits of poverty, which included a greater appreciation for what small income and possessions they could claim. Anne Brontë no doubt found the increasing focus on material goods in her culture distressing. As a highly religious individual, she valued the spiritual over the physical, as does Helen Huntingdon. Through her novel,

Brontë, like Helen, tried to convince Victorian-era readers of the problems that profligate and excessive living could cause.

2. **False pride:** Who suffers from false pride? Why might you label their pride "false"? What results from false pride? What does the practice of false pride suggest about one's character? Who overcomes this practice and who does not?

In order to discuss this topic in an essay, you will need to differentiate between true pride and false pride. The old adage based on biblical precepts, "Pride goeth before a fall," could apply to several characters in *The Tenant of Wildfell Hall*. Helen, the character who serves as the moral center of the novel, must swallow her pride. How does the contrast between Helen and the other characters lead to clearer reader understanding of the novel's meaning and of the concept of pride?

3. **Gossip and slander:** Who gossips about Helen? Why do they do so? Do any suffer the negative consequences of their own gossip and slander? How does Helen react to the false rumors? What is the source of her strength? Whom does she turn to for help?

Women traditionally had to be concerned about gossip and slander far more than men. In his famous epic tribute to Queen Elizabeth, *The Fairie Queen*, a work no doubt read by the Brontës in their self-education, 16th-century Renaissance poet Edmund Spenser characterized slander as the Blatant Beast who devoured young women. Gossip that connected a woman with a man in a sexual manner outside of the formal relationship of marriage was the most damaging. Even an adult woman such as Helen could not associate with men in a social setting that was not public and populated with chaperones. Rumors could prove deadly to a woman's reputation, because they could be so difficult to disprove. In most instances, lacking civil rights and ownership of property, a woman clung to her good reputation, often her most valuable commodity.

4. **Morality and ethics:** Why does the novel require one character to act as moral center? What characteristics of Helen allow her to be that person? Does her gender determine that role? What does the reader learn about morality and ethics during the Victorian era?

Much of this novel features people acting in an unethical or immoral manner. Helen proves the exception. In order to demonstrate the importance of ethics and morals, Brontë must demonstrate the benefits to Helen of her ethical approach to life. However, the negative consequences remain those most readily identified. Should you choose to write an essay about this topic, you will need to demonstrate why the ethical moral life proves more valuable than one lived for self-indulgence.

5. **Art and painting:** Does Helen view her painting as fine art? What motivates her to pursue it? What does this occupation suggest about her personality? Who else values art? What does that value suggest about the particular person?

As a novelist and poet, Anne Brontë valued all arts, so her emphasis of painting in this novel is not surprising. She repeatedly features Helen painting, causing the reader to connect Helen's high moral character with her art. While you cannot prove a cause-and-effect relationship between them, in an essay on this topic you might focus on Helen's imagination and creativity. They contribute not only to her art but also to her very survival. How are her survival and her art connected?

6. **Education:** In what areas does Helen educate her son? Why does she remain adamant that she educate little Arthur, rather than a governess? Who disagrees with her approach? Do those who disagree with her social education of Arthur make valid points? How does the education of boys differ from that of girls?

The reader observes a number of young people in *The Tenant of Wildfell Hall* in various modes of behavior. Brontë seems to suggest that truly educated young people will view life with an open mind, which will allow them to make measured judgments about others and not leap to incorrect conclusions. Through onlookers' criticism of Helen's guidance of her son, the reader comes to understand that society held differing expectations for the education and behavior of boys and girls. Helen informs her husband that she does not want a governess for Arthur but prefers to instruct him herself. What message does Brontë want the reader to receive from Helen's declaration?

7. **Redemption:** How do you define *redemption*? How does one earn redemption? In the novel, who enjoys redemption? From what is he or she redeemed? Who is the redeemer? Must one be religious in order to practice redemption? How does redemption benefit those involved?

The term *redemption* should be defined as it relates to spiritual faith. Keep in mind that sacrifice is essential to a discussion of redemption. Helen believes nothing is more important than the redemption of one's soul, echoing a core belief of Christianity. In investigating this topic, you will need to decide why Helen takes it upon herself to act as a Christ figure and attempt to redeem her husband. How does she help to redeem additional characters?

Character

Many students enjoy writing about fictional characters because they feel they can identify with some of the characters and understand them better. This act of identification stands as one of the best values of fiction. It also results from perceptive writing, because in order for characters to be believable enough that we can identify with them, we must understand them and find the motivations for their actions to be realistic. A character's behavior may enchant or repel us, and a strong essay will be able to analyze exactly why that is so, whether we consider individuals or groups of characters. Some general approaches, such as evaluating the symbolic meaning of character names, can also prove helpful. For instance, Huntingdon's name may be interpreted as being that of one who pursues prey, and Helen's name is famous in mythology for the beautiful woman, whisked from one country to another, whose husband starts a war in order to bring her home.

The main character, or protagonist, generally offers much about which to write. By definition, he or she occupies the most amount of page space, and readers usually learn what they know about all of the characters from that character's point of view. That does not necessarily mean the character tells the story using a first-person point of view, although Gilbert Markham does so in the case of *The Tenant of Wildfell Hall*. However, Brontë includes a second first-person narration in the form of Helen Huntingdon's diary entries, and her narration occupies greater page space than does Markham's. Who, then, serves as protagonist, Markham or Helen? We might propose that the character who behaves in the most heroic manner, clearly Helen in this novel, is the protagonist. However, 21st-century readers understand that a character need not be a positive one to hold our interest. Another way to attempt to determine the protagonist is to examine who changes from the beginning to the end of the novel. That clearly suggests Markham as the protagonist. Perhaps you want to argue for two protagonists, which would create an interesting topic for a persuasive paper. Markham proves interesting as a "hero" because he has several flaws. He is impatient and often arrogant and rash in his dealings with others, as when he attacks Mr. Lawrence. In chapter 45, Helen accuses him of being her worst enemy as he tries to convince her that her marriage has already ended. He suggests that she should leave her husband, knowing she will view that as an immoral act. This chapter best frames Helen's character due to her strong expression of her religious faith.

Antagonists are characters who cause conflict for the main character(s). Although Markham and Helen create conflict for one another at first, it is based for the most part on misunderstanding and hidden identify. The true source of conflict is the minor characters, all of whom prove crucial to the novel. You can select any of these characters, including the Millwards and the Wilsons, or any of Mr. Huntingdon's drinking companions. An example would be Walter Hargrave, who tempts Helen to take revenge on her husband through a sexual affair of her own. Of course, Arthur Huntingdon is the novel's true antagonist; his actions create the basic conflict that causes Helen to flee her home, ultimately making her available as a love interest for Gilbert Markham. Huntingdon repeatedly mistreats Helen, engaging in patently cruel verbal abuse, as in chapter 43 when he tells her she is not fit to educate her own son. That attitude hurts her almost as much as his infidelity does.

Rachel, Helen's dedicated servant, also offers promise as an essay topic. Rachel's total dedication to Helen not only helps readers better understand Helen's character, it also presents the working person in a positive light. Too often in Brontë's era, the working class was viewed as immoral and ignorant, lacking the intelligence and understanding of the classes its members served. A case can be made that Rachel proves herself superior to others in the novel who view themselves as the superior ones due to their social class. She bears a biblical name, suggesting she may be more spiritual and moral than those who claim to be her "betters."

Gilbert Markham's family is also worthy of analysis. His mother pushes him to marry, and yet she is blind to his desire for love over simply making a worthy match. His younger brother helps heighten the conflict by taunting his brother and teasing him about Helen, although his part in the gossip is more role-playing rather than something he takes seriously. As the friend of Eliza Millward, who desires Markham to marry her, Markham's sister Rose allows herself to be drawn into the gossip and attacks against Helen simply for sport's sake. Markham's family loves him, yet they remain unavailable when he needs their support. For example, in chapter 46, he cannot share with them what he has learned about Helen, for fear that Rose will tell Eliza, who might alert Arthur Huntingdon to Helen's location. Tess O'Toole's 1999 article "Siblings and Suitors in the Narrative Architecture of *The Tenant of Wildfell Hall*" may prove helpful.

Sample Topics:

1. **Gilbert Markham:** What are Markham's distinguishing personality characteristics? Does his behavior fit his elevated social status? Why does Brontë not shape a traditional hero in Markham? What about Markham appeals to the reader? What about him repels or annoys the reader?

   Gilbert Markham is far from the traditional romantic hero, although the alert reader might understand that he would like to be such a hero. A member of the landed class, Markham enjoys status above the era's nouveau riche and is an important element in Brontë's examination of the idea that those of a high social class also had an elevated sense of morality and behaved in an ethical manner. An important question to answer if writing an essay based on Markham would be: What are readers to make of his need for Helen's assistance to become a "better" man?

2. **Helen Huntingdon:** What typical and atypical characteristics of a heroine does Helen possess? What sets her apart from other characters in the novel, particularly the women? What is her social status in relation to those around her? Why is she fixated on the importance of redemption and following biblical precepts? Is her behavior realistic?

When assessing characters in novels written in previous centuries, you must take care not to project your era's and culture's values on those characters. Today many might find Helen too conservative for their tastes. In Brontë's era, readers also found Helen unusual, though not because of her spirituality. Rather, what they found unusual and even disturbing was the way she gave voice to her beliefs, particularly in order to take the men around her to task for their immoral behavior. She contributes the novel's didactic material, which some critics find to be a weakness of the plot, particularly evident in chapter 45.

3. **The antagonist:** Who is the novel's true antagonist? How do you know? Is the conflict he causes for Helen and Markham worse than that caused by others? How do his actions help the reader better understand Helen or other characters?

Arthur Huntingdon obviously challenges Helen, thereby challenging other characters as well, most notably Markham and Lawrence. He also provides another service, supporting Brontë's unwaveringly realistic depiction of debauchery and the dissipation that results from such immoral behavior. That depiction shocked her readers but also intrigued them. Readers enjoy a deliciously bad character, and Huntingdon qualifies; for instance, he is described in chapter 43 as having "a demon in his eye." Other characters may also be seen as antagonists, such as Lowborough, whose name symbolizes his moral character. However, in contrast to Huntingdon, Lowborough enjoys redemption long before the novel's conclusion.

4. **Rachel:** What is Rachel's purpose in the plot? What do readers know about her? How would a reader judge her actions? Why is she so devoted to Helen?

When discussing any character, an important point to make is how that character helps the reader better understand the protagonist. In writing about Rachel, obviously a highly protective and moral figure, you might contrast her with others in the book whose moral code leaves something to be desired. Her faith in Helen sets her in contrast not only to Huntingdon but also to minor characters in the novel, such as Reverend Millward, who in chapter 11 forbids his daughters to associate with Helen. Rachel may be seen as an important character in supporting Brontë's claim through her novel that men share a moral equality with women.

5. **Markham's Family:** Why do Rose's loyalties lie with Eliza, rather than her brother? What values does Mrs. Markham hold that prevent her understanding Gilbert's conflict? Which family member seems most empathetic to Gilbert?

When thinking of Gilbert Markham's relationship with his family, remember that he has no father. He may be using his brother-in-law, to whom he is writing, as a father figure, hoping for advice. As the family's senior male, he is the "man of the house," directing operations on the estate. Because they believe in traditional societal roles, the Markhams envision Gilbert marrying a certain type of woman. In several instances, including the scene in chapter 12 following Gilbert's observation of Lawrence with Helen, he enters a dark mood that his mother does not even recognize.

History and Context

Anne Brontë lived and wrote during a time that was exhilarating for many. England was experiencing extreme upheaval that had begun in the first decades of the 19th century and would extend for several additional decades. The causes of this upheaval were changes that some labeled progress but others considered disastrous. Communication, trade, and travel increased due to the growth of contemporary technologies, the rise of factories and automated manufacturing, and the rapid expansion of the railroad. The fact that Markham's letters move so quickly cross-country, as do several that Helen tells of writing, provides proof of faster modes of communication. Also, during the first part of the 19th century, the small family farm, once so visible in the English countryside, disappeared, subsumed into large estates that efficiently produced more food for a growing nation. New wealth among merchants promoted new social and class divisions; the days when the upper class was occupied only by aristocrats with centuries-old names passed, and the newly rich openly celebrated their wealth with displays of public excess. As men and women of the middle to upper classes gained more time for leisure, some turned to acts of veiled immorality to occupy their energies. While women gained certain freedoms, they remained constrained by a social system that insisted on a stricter moral code for women than for men. Art was not yet considered a serious occupation for a woman, nor was writing, facts reflecting directly on the activities of Brontë and her novel's character, Helen Huntingdon. Improved printing methods made possible a veritable explosion of reading material that members of every class could enjoy; thus, literature grew in popularity. Books and other printed material became abundant, a trend investigated in John O. Jordan and Robert Patten's book *Literature in the Marketplace: Nineteenth-Century British Publishing and Reading Practices*. This resource examines the consumption of print, trends in the literature market, and circulation, offering excellent support for an essay about the importance of reading material in Brontë's novel. In one example of many references to the printed word, Markham and Helen discuss literature, and he orders a book for her.

Fiction gained a huge following in the 19th century, and the novel, still a new genre, continued to evolve, with traditional Victorian romance and domestic fiction giving way to the concept of realism in literature. Realistic fiction and its challenges for readers of the Victorian age would provide a fine topic for an essay about *The Tenant of Wildfell Hall*. Men and women were still expected to marry, but ideas regarding the traditional arranged marriage, or marriage for material benefit, began to shift. As an example, in chapter 42 Helen tells Esther, "You might well sell yourself to slavery at once, as marry a man you dislike." She goes on to caution that a woman can leave her immediate family, but that once married, she must remain with her husband for life. Attitudes toward marriage vary greatly in the novel, depending on the characters considered, offering interesting material to consider for an essay. In selecting historical or political topics about which to write, a source such as Jeremy Black and Donald M. MacRaid's *Nineteenth-Century Britain* will offer excellent support.

Sample Topics:

1. **The printed word:** In which scenes does the printed word play an important role? Which characters have access to reading matter? How do they interact with it? Who reads seriously and who reads for other reasons?

   The fact that books and magazines became popular in the 19th century did not necessarily mean everyone became avid readers. Some people simply carried printed material with them in order to appear educated and well read. Others might collect books in great libraries in instances of excessive materialism. How can the printed word reflect attitudes about materialism and possessions?

2. **Realistic fiction:** How did realistic fiction differ from traditional Victorian romantic fiction? Does Brontë incorporate any aspects of romantic fiction into her novel? In what ways does her subject matter benefit from a realistic versus a romantic presentation?

   In most instances, romantic fiction incorporated a level of sentimentality absent from realistic fiction such as *The Tenant of Wildfell Hall*. An alert reader may notice that Brontë seems to be acutely aware of the differences audiences in her era would notice between her novel and the ones to which they were more accustomed. For instance, in chapter 33 she slyly refers to her own occupation when Helen asks a weeping Rachel if the cause of her consternation is the reading of novels. She may wish readers to understand that she refers to the over-sentimentality of the traditional domestic fiction read by many women, particularly members of the middle class. On the other hand, her wish may be to express ironically the belief held by many that the reading of fiction was detrimental to women.

3. **Marriage:** Who is married in the novel? How would you describe the married characters' relationships? Why does Graham not want to marry? For what reasons do people marry? Which characters are pressured to marry someone not of their choosing?

Many ideas regarding marriage flourished during Brontë's lifetime, and the arranged marriage still existed. However, ideas toward marriage had begun to change. More people supported marriage for the sake of love. Opinions about marriage often grew out of religious beliefs. In order to write about this topic, consider which married characters rely on their spiritual faith to support their marriage. Also consider what different characters do in order to make their marriage relationships healthier.

Form and Genre

As Jan Gordon notes in her article "Gossip, Diary, Letter, Text," *The Tenant of Wildfell Hall* "calls attention to itself as the longest single-narrative, enclosing epistolary novel of the nineteenth century." The term *epistolary* refers to a narrative constructed as letters written from one character to another character. The epistolary narrative in this novel also encloses many pages of diary entries. Gordon claims that these mixed narratives compete for the reader's attention and emphasize the importance of specific voices, as well as the importance of the role of the listener, or reader, in receiving those voices. The novel's audience actually reads over Markham's shoulder throughout the story, first spying on his letters and then joining him in reading Helen's diary. These acts of intrusion on the reader's part were something a Victorian audience would relish, as its members lived under such strict social constraints that they enjoyed such safe "spying" into the private lives of others. However, Brontë did not write with the sentimental overtones that her Victorian reader expected. Helen's private writings reveal nothing scandalous—quite the opposite: They stand as a testimony to her staunch, pure character. And while Markham may dismay some readers with his immature actions, his honesty in admitting them to his brother-in-law in his letters compensates for other character weaknesses. One might examine both the positives and negatives of this narrative formula, interrogating how the format supports or undercuts Brontë's message to readers.

The novel's voices seem well-suited to its dual major settings. Wildfell Hall's gothic characteristics have already been noted, and the setting of Grassdale, Huntingdon's estate, provokes readers' curiosity as they learn that, although it carries a name suggesting peace and even freedom, it does not fulfill that name. An analysis of why the characters fit or do not fit in their various settings provides an interesting essay topic.

One aspect of the Brontë's style worthy of attention is tone, most commonly understood as the author's attitude toward her characters, subject matter, or audience. Throughout the book, Brontë's tone remains somber for the most part, a signal that she considers her subject matter quite serious. One might examine her attitude toward her audience by analyzing the purpose behind her tone. As critics often note, she adopts a didactic tone through Helen, yet they are quick to add that she manages to retain an honest, open approach in Helen's delivery of a high moral message. Through careful shaping of Helen as an admirable character, Brontë manages to remove the sting from her words, edging them instead with an earnest intent. At the simplest level, *style* refers to an author's selection of words, but that selection depends on a careful arrangement and juxtaposition in order to evoke the desired reaction from a reading audience.

Sample Topics:

1. **Format:** What is meant by the term *epistolary novel*? What are the advantages of Brontë's using letters and diary entries as her

format? What are the possible disadvantages? How does this technique differ from the traditional first-person viewpoint, when the narrator simply relates the story for an unidentified audience? What impact does the novel's unusual narrative format have on readers?

An essay that focuses on the known and suggested audience created as part of Brontë's format could prove an enjoyable challenge. In this novel, Markham knows and writes to his audience, J. Halford. Helen ostensibly did not anticipate an audience while writing her diary entries. However, she personally selects an audience when she places her writing in Markham's hands. Does knowledge of an audience make a difference in the way one expresses one's self? Helen is silent on the topic of her personal history to most of those who know her, and her diary speaks on her behalf to Markham. Does this make the "telling" of both stories more or less challenging?

2. **Setting:** How many different settings are featured in the novel? Which ones have names that may be symbolic? What does that symbolism add to the development of the plot? What additional imagery helps support that symbolism? Do Helen's various moods match the settings in which she is placed? Do the settings seem to match their owners' personalities?

Setting is crucial to fiction, often establishing a particular mood that spills over to the characters who occupy that setting. As characters relocate from one setting to another, the astute reader will observe them for changes that take place due to that geographical shift. We discover that Wildfell Hall has already played a crucial role in Helen's life as her birthplace. As in many gothic novels, Wildfell Hall plays such an important role that it becomes a character unto itself. Its name fits the disposition of those who inhabit it, whereas the name Grassdale fits neither Helen's nor her husband's negative moods. Thus, it proves an ironic label.

3. **Tone:** How might one describe Brontë's tone? Does it ever change? If so, what seems to cause the shift? What vocabulary can you identify that best represents her tone? How does her tone help the reader determine the novel's theme?

While Brontë's tone becomes didactic, or preachy, at times in this novel, it resists growing shrill in its insistence through Helen that a moral, ethical life remains the only type desirable. Thus, Brontë keeps her realistic style in place, allowing readers to be able to view Helen without disbelief and without finding her views exaggerated. In chapter 45, when Helen voices her spiritual beliefs to Markham, readers may clearly understand her serious intent. Even the promise of lifelong happiness and complete escape from the torture to which Huntingdon subjects her cannot sway her determination to suffer the consequences of her actions.

Language, Symbols, and Imagery

An author may appeal to readers in several ways. Two of the writer's tools are symbols and imagery. Symbols may be traditional, serving to represent the same emotion or connection over many centuries, or they may be literary, important only to an individual story. Images amount to word pictures, clearly drawn depictions through the use of description, often containing figurative language or comparisons. *The Tenant of Wildfell Hall* contains abundant examples of both symbols and imagery.

An example of a traditional symbol that appears on multiple occasions is the color black. Black and the darkness it evokes are important elements of Brontë's tale. Generally a symbol of death or evil, black automatically marks as suspect anyone who wears it or occupies a space described as dark. When Markham describes Eliza Millward, all is pleasing until he arrives at her eyes, which he terms "remarkable features." They contain "irids" that are black, or very dark brown, and he notes that he could almost describe them as "diabolically—wicked, or irresistibly bewitching." The reader later recognizes this as foreshadowing, rather than the teasing it appears to be at first, as Eliza's true dark character unfolds. Markham first sees Helen after being told that she wears "light mourning," a clue that she will be dressed in dark clothing. Upon observing Helen in the church, Markham notices her "raven black" hair and "long black lashes." He then mitigates against the use of the threatening color by adding that "the forehead was lofty and intellectual." Helen is by no means beautiful, and yet she catches Markham's gaze. The word *raven* used in the description also has a negative connotation, as most people think of that bird as a scavenger and a sign of death.

In chapter 8, a symbol generally reserved for women is used to describe Gilbert Markham. He writes of Helen that she takes pleasure in "mortifying my vanity and crushing my presumption," and that she relentlessly nips them "off bud by bud." Traditionally, a flower in the budding stage represents a virginal woman, still intellectually or sexually naïve to the ways of the world. Brontë cleverly turns this symbol on its head to suggest that for all his self confidence, Gilbert is no match for Helen's true sophistication. Brontë combines symbolism with irony in chapter 32 when Mr. Hargrave, who is sexually pursuing Helen, speaks "with a peculiar emphasis," telling her of the game about to begin that "you are a good player—but I am better; we shall have a long game, and you will give me some trouble; but I can be as patient as you, and, in the end, I shall certainly win." Here Brontë employs figurative language in her use of an extended metaphor, comparing Hargrave's pursuit of Helen to a game. Although a game is generally something pleasurable, it acts as a literary symbol here to represent Helen's precarious state of survival at Grassdale. This passage also represents verbal irony, in that Hargrave does not actually refer to the card game that others believe he does.

Another often-repeated symbolic phrase is that of "reaping and sowing," which gains its symbolism from double sources. It literally describes the act of planting crops and then gathering in the results of the planting. However, it is used biblically to mean that a person will either benefit or suffer from her actions, calling attention to the cause-and-effect nature of our simplest actions.

So many examples of imagery exist that one may be found on almost every page. An image represents much more than simply a series of discreet details. The details must complement and relate to one another in a manner that produces an overall impression in the reader's mind. One particular detail carries no more weight than another. An example appears in chapter 9 when Markham, annoyed by Lawrence's visit and unsettled by the gossip he has heard about Helen, takes refuge in a garden. Most readers recognize that gardens generally symbolize women, and perhaps he goes there to feel closer to Helen. He sits in an enclosure on a seat "embowered in roses and honeysuckles" as he thinks about the "virtues and wrongs of the lady of Wildfell Hall." Soon "voices and laughter" approach, and Markham describes himself as "nestled up in a corner of the bower," hoping "to retain possession of it." But someone begins walking toward him, and he wonders, "Why couldn't they enjoy the flowers and sunshine of the open garden, and leave that sunless nook to me, and the gnats and midges?" Brontë's spectacular imagery offers symbolism and irony and manages also to incorporate dark humor in relation to Markham's predicament. Imagery must support a mood or message in order to be effective.

Sample Topics:

1. **Symbols:** Which symbol does this novel depend on most? Why are certain symbols repeated? Which passages would be more difficult to understand without the symbols? How do specific symbols help Brontë transmit her message?

   Writing about symbols calls for many specific examples from the work of literature that you analyze. In your discussion, you must make clear exactly what each symbol represents. Most importantly, you must analyze why the author selected that symbol to make a certain point or impression.

2. **Imagery:** How does imagery help readers better understand the novel's characters? Which scene best serves to demonstrate the difference between imagery and simple detail? Which character seems most often a part of Brontë's imagery?

   The abundant imagery in *The Tenant of Wildfell Hall* remains a crucial aspect of its narrative. Because the descriptions all come from the two characters who tell the story, what they notice leads to a better understanding of them. The imagery they furnish their readers provides ample evidence that both are creative, imaginative people.

Bibliography and Online Resources for *The Tenant of Wildfell Hall*

Berry, Laura C. "Acts of Custody and Incarceration in *Wuthering Heights* and *The Tenant of Wildfell Hall*. *Novel: A Forum on Fiction* 30.1 (Fall 1996): 32–55.

Biedermann, Hans. *Dictionary of Symbolism*. New York: Facts On File, 1992.

Black, Jeremy, and Donald M. MacRaid. *Nineteenth-Century Britain*. New York: Palgrave McMillan, 2002.

Bressler, Charles. *Literary Criticism: An Introduction to Theory and Practice*. 3rd ed. New York: Prentice Hall, 2002.

Carnell, Rachel K. "Feminism and the Public Sphere in Anne Bronte's *The Tenant of Wildfell Hall*." *Nineteenth Century Literature* 53.1 (June 1998): 24.

Doty, Gene. "Signs, Symbols, Meaning, & Interpretation." Available online. URL: http://web.mst.edu/~gdoty/classes/concepts-practices/symbolism.html. Downloaded August 12, 2007.

Gordon, Jan B. "Gossip, Diary, Letter, Text: Anne Brontë's Narrative Tenant and the Problematic of the Gothic Sequel." *English Literary History* 51.4 (Winter 1984): 719–745.

Jackson, Arlene M. "The Question of Credibility in Anne Brontë's *The Tenant of Wildfell Hall*." *English Studies* 63.3 (June 1982): 198–206.

Jordan, John O., and Robert Patten. *Literature in the Marketplace: Nineteenth-Century British Publishing and Reading Practices*. New York: Cambridge UP, 2003.

Losano, Antonio. "The Professionalization of the Woman Artist in Anne Brontë's *The Tenant of Wildfell Hall*." *Nineteenth Century Literature* 58.1 (June 2003): 1–41.

O'Toole, Tess. "Siblings and Suitors in the Narrative Architecture of *The Tenant of Wildfell Hall*." *Studies in English Literature* 39.4 (Autumn 1999): 715–731.

Poole, Russell. "Cultural Reformation and Cultural Reproduction in Anne Bronte's *The Tenant of Wildfell Hall*." *Studies in English Literature* 33.4 (Autumn 1993): 859–873.

WUTHERING HEIGHTS

READING TO WRITE

E MILY BRONTË wrote a single novel that would become among the most celebrated works in the history of English writing. *Wuthering Heights* joined the equally powerful works of her sisters to make up a compelling group of literary masterpieces, made all the more amazing by the fact they were written by siblings. Notes from the sisters' diaries and letters make clear they discussed their novels with each other, but no specific dates for the writing of *Wuthering Heights* have been discovered. Some literary historians believe Emily may have begun work on her novel as early as 1837, but most believe she probably started in earnest in 1845. Charlotte Brontë wrote to her publisher in 1846 offering three novels for publication: *Wuthering Heights*, her own novel titled *The Professor*, and Anne Brontë's *Agnes Grey. Wuthering Heights* was published in 1847 under the name of Ellis Bell, Emily Brontë's pseudonym. The family had to agree to pay the publisher an advance of £50, the money to be refunded from sale proceeds of the first 250 copies. The novel would revolutionize the gothic genre, but Emily did not live long enough to enjoy its effect. The first of many new editions was issued in 1850, two years following Emily's death; it contained a preface by Charlotte. Charlotte took advantage of that opportunity to attempt to explain to the Victorian readership how such violent subject matter could have been conceived by her sister.

In producing her gothic tale, Emily Brontë used all of the aspects of that genre. A source such as Peter K. Garrett's *Gothic Reflections: Narrative Force in Nineteenth-Century Fiction,* provides an excellent review and discussion of those aspects. Brontë furnished two symbolic houses in her depictions of Wuthering Heights and Thrushcross Grange, but it is the moors that offer the mysterious setting traditional to gothic fiction. While most novels share some things in common, such as an easily recognizable protagonist, symbolism, and irony, some offer something more unusual to the observant reader. In the case of *Wuthering Heights,* the moors act as more than mere setting. They help set the tone of a wild and unpredictable plot, mimicking Heathcliff's moods and tendency toward violence. While nature is technically neutral, never seeking revenge on the humans who expose themselves to its powers, we sometimes tend to attribute such powers to it. Particularly in the case of *Wuthering Heights,* the setting plays such a vital role in shaping the characters that it becomes a character itself. Heathcliff offers readers an essential element of the gothic genre as a dark, brooding Byronic hero, while both Cathy Earnshaw Linton and her daughter Catherine act as gothic heroines finding themselves in need of rescue from danger. Brontë emphasizes the gothic's supernatural aspects by transforming Cathy into a ghost following her death. Her spirit haunts Heathcliff, who, in a macabre act, opens Cathy's coffin to embrace her. He later removes a panel in the coffin so that when he dies and is buried beside Cathy, the couple's spirits may mingle.

At the time of its publication, the novel's hero, or antihero as it were, confused readers who had never encountered a character quite like Heathcliff. He engages in what contemporary readers would have considered immoral actions, seeming to deny his own rational ability. He chooses instead to act upon instinct, leading many to compare him to an animal out of control. Brontë invites that comparison through her description of Heathcliff as a foundling, arriving at Wuthering Heights dirty, ragged, and unable to communicate in anything other than "gibberish."

As you read carefully through each chapter, consider possible writing topics and remember to take notes, especially regarding the characters' relationships. Because the two main female characters share the same first and last names, and the surnames Linton and Earnshaw are shared by several characters, keeping track of the characters can be a challenge; notes will help you to sort them out. While Heathcliff is clearly the novel's most dominant figure, others, including the dual narrators, offer promise as essay topics. The setting also intrigues many readers and for that reason suggests itself as a sound focus for an essay. Brimming with symbolism, irony, foreshadowing, and plot twists, the book offers a wealth of possibilities for the observant reader. In addition, background information may prove helpful, such as that found in Sally Mitchell's *Daily Life in Victorian England* (1996), which helps readers better understand the cultural, social, and political issues during the era in which Brontë wrote.

One approach to note taking involves keeping paper close at hand and developing categories that may be written at the top of columns. The categories could simply be the narrative elements of fiction, such as plot, character, style, and setting, or they might be more detailed. For instance, a column might be headed *protagonist* or *antagonist* instead of *character*, or *tone* and *vocabulary* instead of *style*. Underneath each heading, you should list page numbers on which you note an interesting passage that involves your topics. This approach, or any other organized note-taking system, will prove invaluable when you begin to write an essay, allowing for easy access to important passages without dependence on memory.

As you search for passages of interest, determine elements of the writing that attract you. You can look for similar elements in other passages and analyze those that suggest a deeper meaning than what one gathers at a first quick reading. Finally, ask questions about those passages that may lead to a thesis statement. Consider the passage below, spoken by the Lintons' housekeeper, Nelly, as she tells the story of the Lintons, the Earnshaws, and Heathcliff to Thrushcross Grange's new tenant, Lockwood. She focuses on the return of Heathcliff following a long absence:

> I determined to watch his movements. My heart invariably cleaved to the master's, in preference to Catherine's side; with reason, I imagined, for he was kind, and trustful, and honourable; and she—she could not be called the *opposite,* yet she seemed to allow herself such wide latitude, that I had little faith in her principles, and still less sympathy for her feelings. I wanted something to happen which might have the effect of freeing both Wuthering Heights and the Grange of Mr. Heathcliff,

quietly, leaving us as we had been prior to his advent. His visits were a continual nightmare to me; and, I suspected, to my master also. His abode at the Heights was an oppression past explaining. I felt that God had forsaken the stray sheep there to its own wicked wanderings, and an evil beast prowled between it and the fold, waiting his time to spring and destroy.

One could approach this passage from several angles. A first approach would be to analyze the character of the narrator. Nelly states she prefers Edgar Linton to his new wife, Catherine Earnshaw, and she is quite specific as to why she holds that preference. While her first statement makes her seem prejudiced against Catherine, she defends her viewpoint, appealing to her own honest character. She also can be judged protective of her family, as she wishes for something to free both of the family homes from Heathcliff's evil effect. We would also judge Nelly a fine storyteller, due to her inclusion of details and use of figurative language in describing Heathcliff and his effect on the previously peaceful family.

A second essay approach could involve examining the paragraph for foreshadowing of events and situations to come. Edgar Linton's description as "kind, and trustful, and honourable" could indicate dark days ahead for him, as he may not be a good match if pitted against the "evil beast" Heathcliff. While Nelly admits that Catherine is not Edgar's opposite, meaning she cannot be labeled unkind, distrustful, or without honor, she lacks principles that Nelly finds important. That could predict discord between Catherine and Edgar, and possibly Catherine's being again drawn to Heathcliff. Lacking her husband's principles, she would have not even those weak defenses against Heathcliff. Nelly wishes for "something to happen," which could be a predictor of a future event. However, because Nelly is telling of events in the past, and Heathcliff remains at the Grange during the present, that theory will not hold.

A third method for analysis of this passage results from a study of its symbolism, which appears in the last half of the paragraph. Nelly describes Heathcliff's visits as "a continual nightmare," comparing the invader's presence to a frightening, chaotic experience over which one has no control. His presence is also "an oppression past explaining," again connecting Heathcliff's effect to something unnatural that cannot be dealt with rationally; it even defies Nelly's ability to describe it. In addition, she compares the situation to sheep having been deserted by their shepherd, or caretaker, in noting that God has "forsaken" the sheep, meaning the Lintons, leaving them exposed to danger. That danger comes in the shape of Heathcliff, the "evil beast" who "prowls" around the "fold," or houses, of his victims, preventing its prey from returning home and waiting for the correct time to pounce on them. The verb *prowl* describes the movements of a wolf, a creature who stalks its prey before killing it. The reference to the fold is an important one, as the family homes, Thrushcross Grange and Wuthering Heights, play such crucial roles in the novel. Finally, one might examine the paragraph to reveal mounting conflict between the characters. Nelly seems at conflict with Catherine; Catherine may be in conflict with Edgar, due to their differences in principles; and Heathcliff seems to be in conflict with all of the other characters.

After a close reading of that passage, questions should occur that an essay writer could use to work toward developing a main point. For example, one might ask that if Edgar and Catherine do not share the same principles, why did they marry? A second question could ask: Why does Heathcliff wait to make whatever move against the family he must have planned? A third possible question would be: How could Catherine ever have cared for anyone who is compared to a bloodthirsty beast? Finally, God seems to have deserted this family and left it exposed to evil. Why might that have happened? One can glean many ideas from a single passage.

The sections that follow will offer various suggestions for topic and theme possibilities. However, no thesis statements will be supplied for you. That is because the questions and commentary are meant to spark your own ideas, allowing you to develop a main point about which to write. You are not meant to confine your thoughts to these ideas, but rather to expand beyond them, developing additional suitable topics. *Wuthering Heights* brims with possibilities; you will have little problem finding a topic that you will enjoy. Before you begin to write, you might find helpful a general-discussion Web site, such as publisher Bedford/St. Martin's "Fiction in Depth, or Approaches and Concepts" at http://bcs.bedfordstmartins.com/virtualit/fiction/elements.asp.

TOPICS AND STRATEGIES
Themes

All novels suggest many topics that may form the basis of an essay. While one is not necessarily stronger than any other, more support for one over another may exist, meaning that one may find more passages to use for a particular topic. In *Wuthering Heights,* many possible topics come to mind. Family offers a strong focus, as the novel centers on the relationships between the Lintons and the Earnshaws, and on Heathcliff's relationship to each of those families. Storytelling also could serve as an interesting topic, as the main story has two different storytellers, and the narrator Nelly tells a story within that framed story. Her story is an oral rendition, while Lockwood writes in his journal. Storytelling assumes an audience, and these stories have various audiences, one of which is the novel's readers.

One could also examine morality as a topic. Heathcliff seems to lack a moral core altogether, and yet he differs from the degenerate Hindley. Edgar stands at the opposite extreme, clinging to such a high moral code that he cannot even protect himself. Cathy is somewhere in the middle as far as morality goes, while the children, Catherine and Hareton, seem to fall more into a normal range of moral conflict.

Another topic inherent to the novel is the transcendental concept of "oneness," in which a human may move beyond mortal capacity to join spiritually with another. This idea is brought into sharp focus when considering Cathy's unusual relationship with Heathcliff. One might consider as a topic what happens when one partner desires a union of the couple's personalities, but the other resists.

Finally, landscape offers a promising topic for an essay. Brontë elevates landscape above the traditional element of setting to consider the characters' spiritual identification with nature. She employs description of the landscape as metaphor for both Cathy and Heathcliff. Those characters become inseparable from their surroundings, suggesting again the transcendental importance of nature.

Sample Topics:

1. **Family:** How might one define the term *family*? How many families appear in *Wuthering Heights*? What are their similarities? What are their differences? How are characteristics of

certain families developed? Can one family be judged superior to another? How do families pass their attitudes to each new generation?

One would begin an essay on the topic of families by first defining the term *family* and then moving on to analyze the family members and to interpret the causes of the various fractured relationships. Neither the Lintons nor the Earnshaws appear to be what might be called "normal" families. The Earnshaws gain one member of their family from their father, who brings Heathcliff home with him as he might a lost puppy, an unusual way for a family to expand. Hindley's jealousy reflects a strength extending beyond the sibling rivalry experienced in many families. Cathy feels she cannot marry Heathcliff, suggesting he would not be a proper head of family. Her selection of Edgar Linton as the family head proves more acceptable to the public, yet he is too weak to protect the family properly. Isabella Linton is rebellious against Edgar, paralleling the negative relationship that Hindley has with others. Although Hindley, Cathy, and Isabella all produce children, none thrive within the family community. Nelly also seems a part of the family. Why must these families be so unconventional in order to support the meaning that Brontë wants readers to take away from her novel?

2. **Storytelling:** How many stories are told in *Wuthering Heights*? How many storytellers appear in the novel? Why does Brontë choose to have two specific narrators tell the story? What are the advantages and drawbacks of creating a story with two narrators?

Wuthering Heights could have been told from a third-person point of view, but instead two characters tell the story in first-person point of view. Perhaps Brontë believed that approach made a story from the past seem more immediate, as if it were unfolding in the here and now. She must have had a specific reason for inserting so many layers of storytelling, with Lockwood first relating events to the reading audience, then Nelly telling the story to Lockwood, and then Lockwood again assuming the position as storyteller to conclude the novel. That layering has a particular effect on the reader. Also important is the fact that Nelly's story is oral, while Lockwood records his in writing. Of course, Brontë is the novel's ultimate storyteller. Analysis of the importance of each of these aspects of storytelling offers an interesting prospect for an essay.

3. **Morality:** What is meant by morality? Which characters seem to be guided by morality? Do any seem amoral—that is, without any notion or concern for moral behavior? Which characters are immoral by conscious choice? Do they blame others for their rejection of morality? Who benefits from living a moral or principled life? Why are the moral characters not rewarded for their ethical behavior?

In order to behave in a moral manner, one not only must understand the difference between right and wrong but must believe that right is preferable to wrong. Behaving in a moral manner may be done for personal satisfaction or because such behavior benefits others. In writing an essay on the topic of morality in *Wuthering Heights*, a student might hazard a guess as to why readers often find immoral or amoral characters the most interesting, even though their behavior would be intolerable in the reality of day-to-day living. Morality may have little relation to religion, and the essay writer should be careful not to confuse the two. That writer would want to consider the importance of morality, asking, why must we choose a certain type of behavior, and how do humans learn about those choices? Can morality be intuitive, or must it be learned? German philosopher Friedrich Nietzsche wrote about morality, discussing such topics as guilt, responsibility, and justice. In order to write about those topics, the informed student should study a work such as Nietzsche's *On the Genealogy of Morality* (1887).

4. **Oneness:** What accounts for the popularity of the metaphysical notion that two individuals may become one? Why do people view that notion as a romantic one? How does Brontë subvert the traditional idea of oneness? What do you believe to be the purpose behind her subversion? Why do readers find her technique attractive?

The idea that two souls may mingle to form one is not new. English Renaissance poet John Donne helped make the idea more popular through his metaphysical poetry, although only in later generations would readers appreciate what his contemporaries for the most part viewed as vulgar and outrageous figurative language. The 19th-century romantics espoused imagination as the path to self-knowledge, in reaction to the preceding century in which poets focused on logic during England's Age of Reason. Transcendentalists based their beliefs in part on romantic ideas, believing in the power of intuition as a way of knowing the world, particularly nature. They also recognized an "inward beholding," a process in which one turned the gaze within to discover a reality based on mental and spiritual capacity, rather than material capacity. The thought of souls spiritually mingling to accomplish "oneness" would not surprise those who embraced romanticism or transcendentalism. However, Brontë's suggestion through Cathy and Heathcliff's relationship that a physical oneness could be achieved, particularly in light of Heathcliff's violent nature, would have shocked her readers.

5. **Landscape:** How does landscape differ from setting? In what ways does Brontë make clear the importance of the landscape? Why does Heathcliff find it necessary to transform Cathy into symbolic landscape? How does the concept of Heathcliff and Cathy as landscape support his ultimate desire for the two to become one?

This topic will prove a rich one for the observant student who will have noticed passages in the novel that work to support the idea of Heathcliff and Cathy as landscape. For instance, chapter 9 contains Cathy's impassioned exchange with Nelly, in which she compares both Edgar and Heathcliff to aspects of nature, the figurative language allowing for strong comparison and contrast of the two men. In chapter 10, Cathy compares Heathcliff to "an arid wilderness of furze and whinstone," and during the conversation with Lockwood that concludes chapter 33, Heathcliff notes everything connects him to Cathy, including "every cloud . . . every tree" bearing her features, which fill "the air at night . . . I am surrounded with her image!"

Character

Characters typically offer fine topics for an essay, providing the writer develops a thesis statement that moves beyond an answer to simple "who" and "what" questions about those characters to answer also "why" and "how." Reader interest concerning characters is generally based on their motivations. We do not want to learn only what they do, but why they act in such a way and how they manage to initiate and follow through with plans. A common approach to character analysis is to identify the protagonist, the antagonist, and various minor figures in the book that offer potential for development. For instance, in *Wuthering Heights,* Heathcliff can be seen as the protagonist, as the most page space and attention focuses on him. He may be viewed alternately as romantic and enigmatic or evil and self-serving. None of these adjectives alone does him complete justice, however, which suggests the beginning of a process to develop a thesis. The fact that he has so challenged readers and critics to develop a universal view speaks to his richness as a potential essay subject.

Cathy Earnshaw Linton also is a major character, although not the protagonist. Generally the protagonist undergoes some type of realization, an epiphany, which causes a change in opinion or behavior. We do not see that with Cathy, who dies early in the novel. However, because she causes the most conflict for Heathcliff, she can be termed an antagonist. Not only does she cause conflict prior to her death, but that conflict grows with Heathcliff as Cathy literally haunts him until the end of the novel. Their true love/hate relationship offers an excellent focus for an essay. One might write not about the obvious evidence of the unusual relationship or to explain how it presents itself, but rather the effect it has on the reader or on advancing the plot.

One may also focus on any novel's minor characters, and *Wuthering Heights* offers an interesting array. All characters in the novel, including the children, Nelly, and even the visiting Lockwood, who only briefly makes contact with Heathcliff, are affected by Cathy and Heathcliff's relationship. The Linton siblings both play integral roles as "stand-in" spouses for Cathy and Heathcliff. Edgar Linton offers a strong focus as the true victim of Cathy and Heathcliff's relationship. He actually causes his own early death due to his strong moral character. Isabella Linton stands as testimony to Heathcliff's cruelty and an emblem of what can happen to those who bear the brunt of another's inestimable desire for revenge. Cathy's sibling Hindley offers a balance to Isabella's jealousy and ultimate misery. Obviously, Heathcliff could never have gained control of Wuthering Heights if not for Hindley's degeneracy. Hareton and Catherine could be considered together, as their fates offer a cautionary tale for the suffering of the second generation. After considering all members of the Linton, Earnshaw, and Heathcliff family, an astute essay writer might want to theorize as to which suffers the most due to Heathcliff—that is, which is the greatest victim?

Sample Topics:

1. **Heathcliff:** How does Heathcliff differ from the traditional romantic hero? Why is he classified as a Byronic hero? What facts about his life does the reader never learn? How do other characters react to him? What about Heathcliff causes the reactions that he receives from others? What redeeming characteristics does Heathcliff have?

The popularity of the Byronic hero developed during the time that the Brontës were writing. In order to understand the appeal of this type of character, you should consult a source such as Atara Stein's *The Byronic Hero in Film, Fiction, and Television*. Keep in mind that with any novel as well-known, often-read, and studied as *Wuthering Heights*, you will want to develop a thesis statement that does not simply repeat main points of hundreds of other essays. In writing about Heathcliff, challenge yourself to think of an unpredictable approach to your topic. For instance, you might consider how the reader's attitude toward Heathcliff might have altered had he already been dead at the beginning of the novel. You could begin to narrow this topic by asking a question such as, is he a more potent force in death than life?

2. **Cathy:** Is Cathy a sympathetic character—that is, one for which readers will feel sympathy? Why or why not? How might one describe her flaws? Why does Edgar fall in love with Cathy?

   A crucial passage to aid in your developing an opinion of Cathy is the one quoted above, in which Nelly claims that she "had little faith in her [Cathy's] principles, and still less sympathy for her feelings." An essay focusing on Cathy might quote that sentence and then set about to establish Cathy's principles, determining the motives for her actions as well as her inaction. While Cathy disappears from the plot early as a flesh-and-blood character, her ability to live on through Heathcliff's torment adds to her interest to readers. A careful reading of the first part of the novel might reveal some foreshadowing that suggests Cathy's fate and why she will be able to help the novel's momentum following her demise.

3. **Isabella and Hindley:** How does Isabella help the reader better understand Heathcliff? Does she deserve the reader's pity? What is the explanation for Hindley's despicable manner toward Heathcliff when both are children? What does he contribute toward a better understanding of Heathcliff? Does his death add to the novel's theme in any way, or is he just a plot convenience as a bully turned victim to Heathcliff's desire for revenge?

   Most readers do not view Isabella Linton in a positive light. Her privileged attitude contrasts with the more ethical attitude of her brother, and her inability to welcome Cathy into the Linton family works against reader sympathy. Most readers also can muster little compassion toward her fate, as Edgar tries to warn her about Heathcliff's evil side. While Heathcliff manipulates her into promoting his revenge against her brother, she may appear more favorably to readers when she becomes a mother. As for Hindley, his bullying personality works to turn readers against him as he mistreats Heathcliff early in the novel. However, his father's favoritism toward Heathcliff tempers reader judgment, as does Hindley's strong capacity for love of his wife. When he later becomes a raging alcoholic, so degenerate that he cannot see Heathcliff's plot to own Wuthering Heights, his eventual death comes merely as a relief. Both of these characters, as siblings of two members of the central romantic triangle, offer an admirable symmetry to Brontë's tale and might be analyzed from that angle.

4. **The children:** Why is Catherine so easily manipulated by Heathcliff? Is her entrapment expected? What is the effect on Heathcliff of her forced relationship with Linton? Does Hareton's relationship with Heathcliff help change readers' view of him? What draws Catherine to Hareton?

In writing an essay about Catherine and Hareton, one must carefully consider Catherine's feelings of isolation and loneliness as she matures without a mother or siblings and in the care of a sickly father. Her natural curiosity to know her family better draws her to Heathcliff and Linton, and then Heathcliff manipulates her through emotional blackmail. While the forced marriage of Catherine to Linton may allow Heathcliff to feel he can live vicariously through their relationship to finally experience marriage to the long-dead Cathy, the reader must wonder whether he finds the satisfaction he desired. This essay would require close analysis of the effect of Catherine on Heathcliff's household, and whether Catherine and Hareton's relationship helps Heathcliff to achieve grace before his death.

Philosophy and Ideas

During Emily Brontë's childhood, education had become more widely available for young women. However, the philosophy of children's education was centered strongly on rote learning, an approach that held little appeal for the Brontës. Fortunate enough to have been educated mostly from their father's library, their young minds were able to thrive on more imaginative topics, motivating them to perform original dramas based on historical events. Thus, as an adult, Emily Brontë had little use for the educational programs in place and sought to begin her own school in order to practice her ideas about education. German philosophy and romance writing brought new ideas to England, including an emphasis on the worth of the individual and a belief in the human tendency toward feelings of alienation, a ripe topic for an essay about *Wuthering Heights*. Writing at the end of the 18th century and into the 19th century, Immanuel Kant argued in Analytic of Principles, part of his *The Critique of Pure Reason*, that the mind's role in perceiving nature is not limited to space or time, aspects of the phenomenal world, or the world as it appears to us. He proposed a different concept, the noumenal world, as one where things are unto themselves, a world that lacks space and time. Kant proposed in his Refutation of Material Idealism, "There are objects that exist in space and time outside of me." He believed such objects were necessary to one's understanding of self. These ideas may very well have influenced Brontë's ghostly characterization of Cathy as a detectable force after death, although her material body remained invisible underground. The noumenal world contradicted traditional ideas of the limits of man as set out in biblical teachings. A crisis of faith in English society was supported by a growing doubt in the intellectual strength of Christianity. Adam Smith's *An Inquiry into the Nature and Causes of the Wealth of Nations*, published in 1776, became a guide for more than trade, affecting the treatment of one individual by another. It could be combined with Darwinian theories to rationalize an individual's unethical treatment of his or her fellow humans. Growing theories of trade and adherence to laissez-faire, the absence of social-welfare measures, spread to mistreatment of one individual by another, encouraging the powerful to exploit the weak. An individual could argue that self-interest is a basic human instinct and should guide human action, regardless of its negative effects on others.

Heathcliff may represent such empowered beings, as he gathers material wealth in order to assert his power over others with little concern about the ethics of his actions. However, Adam Smith had contradicted some of the popular ideas derived from *The Wealth of Nations* in *The Theory of Moral Sentiments* (1759). It focused in part on the natural responses of compassion and sympathy that one person should feel for another, as both have shared experiences of pain and disappointment. Web sites such as the Library of Economics and Liberty at http://www.econlib.org/Library/Smith/smMS.html present Smith's writings in full.

A final topic worth considering for an essay about philosophical attitudes is that of fate. Heathcliff and Cathy's fates seem intertwined and predetermined. Nineteenth-century English readers were interested in non-Christian ideas about destiny in *Consolation of Philosophy* (*De consolation philosophiae*) by the classical writer Boethius, who focused on the transitory nature of the material and the superior value of the mind, suggesting that humans need only look within themselves for a satisfaction that Lady Fortune cannot destroy. German philosophers such as Georg Wilhelm Friedrich Hegel broke with the traditional acceptance of the authority of reason, opening the door to consideration of nonrational ways of realization, an idea that could be applied to the relationship of Heathcliff and Cathy and to the determination of their destinies.

Sample Topics:

1. **Alienation:** Which characters appear alienated from others? Which do not? How do some escape alienation? How do they react to or aid those who become its victims? Does it express itself as more a physical or a spiritual phenomenon?

   Feelings of true alienation have a devastating effect on individuals. Alienation differs from depression or simple loneliness, a differentiation that a writer on this topic will take care to make clear. To feel alien or "other," one must conceive oneself to be completely disconnected from the community, with no hope of ever gaining entrance into what appears to be a closed system. Such individuals may see no relationship between themselves and other individuals, sharing no points of reference with their fellow humans. Some may attempt to accept this condition, while others rail against it, never finding their way out of its hold on every aspect of their being.

2. **Ghosts:** How does Brontë challenge traditional expectations of ghost stories? Is the reader convinced that true ghosts exist in this novel? What convinces characters in the story of their existence? Might Heathcliff himself be classified as a type of living ghost in his haunting of the Lintons and the Earnshaws?

Ghost stories maintain an important place in literature, hailing from its oral traditions. Some theories hold that humans need to experience fright in a safe form, such as that offered by stories. It allows them escape from fears they may find difficult to express. Brontë's ghosts have a material presence in the lives of various characters that causes them great discomfort. The ghosts also imbue the moors with a certain personality that further advances the moors' dangers. However, these are the same moors that Cathy and Heathcliff adored, ones that provided them escape from the unpleasantness of the real world. As for Heathcliff, he could almost be classified as a member of the walking dead, with little existence apart from that he shared with Cathy.

3. **Power:** How do different characters in the novel seem to define power? Who is the book's most powerful character? What is the source of his or her power? How does he or she affect others in exercising power? Which emotion appears to be the most powerful in *Wuthering Heights*—revenge or love?

As noted above, many in England confronted a crisis of faith during the 19th century, doubting intellectual aspects of Christianity. As a nonreligious yet powerful person, Heathcliff might have offered an appeal to readers who suffered from that crisis. He does appear to be the character with the most power. He uses both emotional and economic strength to crush the Lintons and the Earnshaws, without regard to their ages or individual characteristics. He is also the most surprising of the characters to end up with power, based on his undistinguished past. His desire for revenge becomes a force that no one can combat. However, one may also see Cathy as a powerful character due to her effect on Heathcliff, both as a living and a dead character. Also, Edgar's love for Cathy basically destroys him, as he becomes embroiled in a love triangle against whose force he has no defense. Boethius believed the power of mind to be superior to that of things material, and Hegel espoused belief in a "nonrational" (not dependent on logic) way of knowledge; those ideas may be seen to play out in *Wuthering Heights*.

4. **Fate/destiny:** Does Brontë suggest through Heathcliff that one can control one's destiny? Or does Heathcliff offer a cautionary tale of the disastrous results that await one who attempts such control? Do Heathcliff and Cathy fulfill their destiny at the novel's conclusion? What aspects of the story suggest that they do or do not?

Many people do not believe in the concept of destiny or fate, choosing rather to embrace the idea that certain natural conditions and our own actions cause reactions that are not predetermined by any particular force. Cathy struggles to determine her destiny, more or less telling Nelly in chapter 9 that both Edgar and Heathcliff are part of her fate. She thus establishes an impossible scenario, as she cannot exist with both of them in her life, which she literally proves when she dies following Heathcliff's return. Edgar assumes his future has been determined, partly by his inherited wealth and position, and he attempts to assist that future through a "good" marriage to Cathy. However, he makes precisely the wrong choice, which leads to his death. Heathcliff carefully plans his revenge in order to force a new fate on Cathy, but he loses her to death, something for which he had not planned. Do these characters actually determine their own fates through bad choices? If you choose to write this essay, you will want to postulate whether Heathcliff does fulfill his destiny after death through reunion with Cathy. You may even postulate that only one of them fulfills a destiny, while the other has no choice.

Form and Genre

Falling as it does into the gothic genre, *Wuthering Heights* could be easily analyzed as an example of that style of writing. As noted in the opening section, it contains all the elements of a gothic work. However, this is such a common approach to writing about the novel that one might develop a more successful essay by selecting a related topic. For instance, reader acceptance of the gothic aspects could prove an interesting subject. As with pure fantasy fiction, the gothic novel often requires suspension of belief on the part of readers. The ghostly aspects especially require that the reader accept, for the purposes of plot, the existence of ghosts. Another approach is the use of setting. While all gothic novels are set in part in a mysterious, sometimes haunted castle, estate, or house, *Wuthering Heights* employs the moors. It is their windswept, wild nature that forms a perfect backdrop for the passion shared by Heathcliff and Cathy. A consideration of how this unusual setting advances the novel's gothic design could result in a fine essay.

Finally, an analysis of the importance of tone to reader understanding of the novel offers a possible essay topic. Brontë's attitude toward her characters and subject matter, like that of all authors, proves crucial to the reader's knowledge of those characters and aids in an understanding of subject matter, such as isolation or the transcendental idea of "oneness" that encapsulates the relationship of Cathy and Heathcliff. In addition, the first-person narration, particularly that of two different individuals, one involved in the plot and one not, may be analyzed for effectiveness.

Sample Topics:

1. **Reader acceptance:** What specific occurrences or ideas in this novel force readers to suspend logic in order to accept those occurrences or ideas? Why might readers enjoy such a challenge?

In writing about reader reaction to any novel, it helps to review reader response to critical theory, such as that discussed in Charles Bressler's *Literary Criticism: An Introduction to Theory and Practice.* Some critics hold that a work of literature does not exist until it finds a reader. *Wuthering Heights* requires a particular type of reader to appreciate what some have seen as Brontë's indulgence of an outrageous imagination. While the story is presented as a serious one and purports to maintain a highly moral message, that message may suffer due to its delivery.

2. **Setting:** In what ways does Wuthering Heights reflect the values and ideals of the Earnshaw family? In what ways does Thrushcross Grange reflect the values and ideals of the Linton family? Which set of values and ideals seems preferable? Do the two locations alter under Heathcliff's ownership? Why do Cathy and Heathcliff identify with the moors? Why do they prefer the wild moors to their homes?

One's home often reflects one's values, desires, and beliefs, and this proves true of the Earnshaw and Linton families. The fact that Heathcliff wants to own the properties is more about his desire to control the members of the families on whom he has vowed revenge than it is to own property, revealing how closely the individuals identify with their homes. Lockwood's exposure to Heathcliff and the details of the families' story would not have occurred without the existence of the two places, as he arrives in the area in order to rent one. One might question how his view of the properties differs from that of the original families, and how that affects his storytelling, versus that of Nelly, who had been raised at the Grange. As for Heathcliff, he has always felt more comfortable on the moors, from which he draws a strong sense of self.

3. **Tone:** Does Brontë's tone change at any points in the novel? What are some specific words or phrases that characterize that change? How does the tone support her theme, or message?

Do the tones of the two narrators contradict or support one another?

At its simplest, *style* may be defined as vocabulary choice on the part of the author, and tone is reflected through that vocabulary. If tone reflects the author's attitude toward her subject matter and readers, the writer of an essay on tone will necessarily want to identify passages projecting that attitude. One must also consider the fact that this story is told by two narrators, whose own attitudes will affect their tones. Thus, *Wuthering Heights* offers a layering of tones that could be analyzed to determine how they support or undercut one another. Theoretically, Lockwood's tone should remain objective, as he is the only character in the novel not personally involved with the family members' interactions. One might look to him for the least biased opinion of Heathcliff, for instance, and the tone he adopts in writing about Heathcliff.

4. **Narration:** Can Lockwood and Nelly be trusted? What are their similarities and differences? What can Lockwood bring to the telling of this story that Nelly lacks? Why is Nelly a likely or unlikely choice as a narrator? Might someone else have told this story better?

The trustworthiness of a first-person narrator often forms an interesting basis for an essay. All a reader can do is gather what seems to be evidence from the story the narrator tells, and also analyze that narrator's motives. For instance, Nelly is certainly biased; she admits early on to a greater devotion to members of the Linton family than the Earnshaws. This would be natural, as she was raised in the Linton household. Why, then, might Brontë have selected her to present the story? Why did she select any involved character at all, rather than telling the story from a third-person point of view, adopting the voice of an unseen and unidentified narrator? Nelly is not a simple observer, as is Lockwood. In addition, she recounts details from the past, while he reports details of the present to the reader.

Bibliography and Online Resources for *Wuthering Heights*

Beiser, Frederick C. *The Fate of Reason: German Philosophy from Kant to Fichte.* Cambridge: Harvard UP, 2006.

Bell, Currer [Brontë, Charlotte]. "Biographical Notice of Ellis and Acton Bell." 1850. Rpt. in Emily Brontë, *Wuthering Heights.* Ed. Linda H. Peterson. Boston: Bedford-St. Martin's, 1992. 15–20.

Benvenuto, Richard. *Emily Brontë.* Boston: Twayne, 1982.

Bressler, Charles. *Literary Criticism: An Introduction to Theory and Practice.* 3rd ed. New York: Prentice Hall, 2002.

Dawson, Terence. *The Effective Protagonist in the Nineteenth-Century British Novel: Scott, Brontë, Eliot, Wilde.* Burlington, VT: Ashgate, 2004.

Dickerson, Vanessa. "Spells and Dreams, Hollows and Moors: Supernaturalism in *Jane Eyre* and *Wuthering Heights.*" *Victorian Ghosts in the Noontide.* Columbia: University of Missouri Press, 1996. 48–79.

"Emily Bronte." About.com: Women's History. Available online. URL: http://womenshistory.about.com/library/bio/blbio_bronte_emily.htm. Downloaded August 7, 2007.

"Fiction in Depth, or Approaches and Concepts." Bedford/St. Martin's VirtuaLit Interactive Fiction Tutorial. Available online. URL: http://bcs.bedfordstmartins.com/Virtualit/fiction/elements.asp. Downloaded November 11, 2007.

Garrett, Peter K. *Gothic Reflections: Narrative Force in Nineteenth-Century Fiction.* Ithaca, NY: Cornell UP, 2003.

Keene, Suzanne. *Victorian Renovations of the Novel: Narrative Annexes and the Boundaries of Representation.* New York: Cambridge UP, 2005.

Larson, Timothy. *Crisis of Doubt: Honest Faith in Nineteenth-Century England.* New York: Oxford UP, 2006.

Mitchell, Sally. *Daily Life in Victorian England.* Westport, CT: Greenwood Press, 1996.

Nietzsche, Friedrich. *Nietzsche: "On the Genealogy of Morality" and Other Writings: Revised Student Edition.* Ed. Keith Ansell-Pearson. New York: Cambridge UP, 2006.

Smith, Adam. *The Theory of Moral Sentiments.* The Library of Economics and Liberty. Available online. URL: http://www.econlib.org/Library/Smith/smMS.html. Downloaded November 11, 2007.

Stein, Atara. *The Byronic Hero in Film, Fiction, and Television.* Carbondale, IL: Southern Illinois UP, 2004.

Stoneman, Patsy. *Brontë Transformations: The Cultural Dissemination of* Jane Eyre *and* Wuthering Heights. Hemel Hempstead, England: Prentice Hall, 1998.

Twitchell, James. "Heathcliff as Vampire." *Southern Humanities Review* 11 (1971): 355–362.

Tytler, Graeme. "'Nelly, I am Heathcliff!': The Problem of 'Identification' in *Wuthering Heights*." *Midwest Quarterly* 47.2 (Winter, 2006): 167–181.

Vitte, Paulette. "Emily Bronte. Rimbaud. Poe and the Gothic." *Brontë Society Transactions* 24 (1999): 182–185.

Winnifrith, Tom. *The Brontës*. New York: Collier Books, 1977.

———. *The Brontës and Their Background*. New York: Palgrave Macmillan, 1988.

———. *Critical Essays on British Literature Series—Emily Brontë*. New York: Twayne Publishers, 1997.

Winnifrith, Tom, and Edward Chiltham. *Macmillan Literary Lives: Charlottë and Emily Brontë*. New York: Palgrave Macmillan, 1994.

"I'M HAPPIEST
WHEN MOST AWAY"

READING TO WRITE

ALL THREE of the Brontë sisters wrote verse, which they compiled into a volume that sold only two copies. Their poetry proved most important for its effect in motivating each of the sisters to write novels. The most often anthologized poetry is that written by Emily, who produced some of it for the Gondal saga she wrote with her sister Anne, a story that chronicled an imaginary island. Two such poems are "Remembrance," discussed elsewhere in this volume, and "The Prisoner. A Fragment," which is not discussed in this volume. Charlotte Brontë would later write a preface to the second edition of poems by her then-deceased sister Emily, telling how she accidentally found Emily's poetry manuscript. Charlotte described the verse as "not common effusions, nor at all like the poetry women generally write." According to Charlotte's account, Emily was the most private of the three sisters, and only with much urging would she consider publication. Critics note that her poetry has a visionary quality that links her to the romantics, and her speaker longs for independence from the material world. Those traits were also apparent in her single novel, *Wuthering Heights*. Several images and ideas appear in all of Emily Brontë's poetry; should you choose to write about her poetry, you will want to note all such recurrences. You should also consult all the chapters in this volume that focus on her poetry.

Poetry contains the most concentrated language and thus, some believe, is the most demanding of the creative genres to write and to understand. Others feel its concise nature causes it to be the most pleasurable. Whatever your past experience in reading poetry for pleasure, reading it in order to write about it demands close attention to both its sound and its sense. Skillful poets never sacrifice one for the other. You will notice that poetry is written in lines, and an essay about poetry discusses it line by line, assigning a number to each line for easy discussion.

One would approach writing about Brontë's poems like that of any poet, considering those elements most important to the understanding of poetry. Some of those elements include figurative language, such as simile, metaphor, and personification; imagery, or word pictures; the use of symbols, words that carry a literal meaning but may suggest an additional meaning; allusion, a reference to a concept, person, or event that is unnamed; tone, or the poet's attitude toward her subject matter; the poem's unseen speaker, or voice; hyperbole, or exaggeration; sounds, such as rhyme, assonance, and alliteration; format, or how the lines appear on the page, including the poem's punctuation; irony, when things are not as they seem; conflict or tension between images or ideas; and paradox, terms generally used in conjunction due to contradictory meaning or implication. Each of these elements is crucial to the theme, or overall message, of each poem.

You should also not fail to begin at the beginning with poetry, which means taking a few moments to consider a poem's title prior to reading it. Make a few notes that describe what you expect from the poem, based on its title. Should you discover that reality contradicts what you imagined, that contradiction may offer a main topic for your essay. Because "I'm Happiest When Most Away" is composed of only eight lines, each line will be considered below.

TOPICS AND STRATEGIES
Themes

When writing about "I'm Happiest When Most Away," one should first analyze the title for a hint as to the theme. The title states that the speaker needs to be "most away" from somewhere in order to feel happiest, which also suggests that she is not optimally happy where she is presently. Her choice of *most* as the adjective that compliments the word *away* is an odd one. A person is generally away or not away; we do not think of away as having degrees. Thus, this state of away may not be a physical one.

You do not yet know the location, which will be important to determine. You also will probably not discover the identity of the speaker, but you will be able to collect clues about her based on her word selection and attitude toward her state of existence. The title serves as the poem's first line. The second line reads: "I can bear my soul from its home of clay." This line alerts the reader that the location the speaker goes away from is probably not a material one, as it is the soul that appears to travel. The time of travel is also important, as expressed in the third line, "On a windy night when the moon is bright," with the choice of time period being the evening or nighttime. The fourth line, "And the eye can wander through worlds of light—," supports the idea that even though travel takes place at night, the moon offers ample light for movement. That suggestion appears ironic, as one would generally travel during the day in the light of the sun. Also important in this line is the fact that the eye appears to be the traveler, along with the soul. This suggests the importance of the imagination in allowing the soul to travel when, perhaps, the body cannot.

The first line of the second stanza, "When I am not and none beside—," suggests that the speaker can exist in a state of nonbeing, a metaphysical description, or conceit, that includes a contradiction. The second extends the metaphysical aspect of the poem in its implication that the universe itself disappears during the speaker's travel: "Nor earth nor sea nor cloudless sky—." The third line reads, "But only spirit wandering wide," including an echo of the term *soul* with the word *spirit*. The verb *wandering* again focuses on a manner of travel. The fourth and final line reads, "Through infinite immensity," introducing another metaphysical concept in the idea of size, breadth, or depth that is so great it defies measure.

In order to write about the metaphysical aspects of the poem, a review of characteristics of metaphysical poetry, such as that found at the Web site "The Metaphysical Poets—Study Guide" (http://www.universalteacher.org.uk/poetry/metaphys.htm) will prove informative, as will a text such as Helen Gardner's *The Metaphysical Poets*. Closely related is the romantic poets' view of the visionary experience, a view known to have informed Brontë's writing. Review particularly the romantic poets Byron and Shelley in a text such as Ian Gilmour's *The Making of the Poets*. The previous observations suggest several possible topics that might develop into a discussion of them, including the speaker's identity, time and manner of travel, light, and metaphysics.

Sample Topics:

1. **Speaker identity:** What clues does the reader have with regard to the speaker's identity? What words reflect on the speaker's personality? What is the speaker's tone? Does the speaker appear to be passive or active? How would the speaker define the term *away*?

   Support for the fact that the speaker's voice is feminine may be found by examining the traditional symbolism of the moon (see below), which is associated with females. As mentioned above, one may also hazard about this speaker that she is not unhappy in her present position; rather, she is happiest when abroad. She prefers to be "not" and "none," indicating a shy or retiring personality that does not want to attract attention to itself. Yet she is courageous enough to send her spirit traveling abroad. Courage as an aspect of the speaker's identity will offer a strong idea for thesis statement development.

2. **Travel:** Why does the speaker seek to travel? Why must she travel at night? Why must she travel only in her imagination? Who is the speaker's audience?

   The writer of an essay about travel will want to investigate facts about Brontë and her era. For instance, was it customary for women to travel? Did Emily travel much? If so, what was the result of that movement beyond her home? If the results were unpleasant, one could support the idea that Brontë preferred imaginary travel to physical movement. The activities of the Brontë children greatly depended on the imagination: Emily wrote some of her poetry about the fictional island of Gondal and thus had experienced the imaginary travel for which her speaker longs. A Web site such as "English Laws for Women" at http://www.indiana.edu/~letrs/vwwp/norton/englaw.html will prove helpful, as will "Victorian Social History" at http://www.victorianweb.org/history/sochistov.html.

3. **Light:** How does Brontë use light imagery in this poem? What might a reference to light refer, other than to the physical characteristic provided by the moon? Why does the speaker not desire daylight travel?

Generally one considers the night to be lacking in light. However, in this poem, moonlight appears to be the most favorable for the speaker's plans. The light from the moon creates quite a different mood than that from the sun. Think about what types of beings move about in the moonlight and how they contrast with those who move about primarily during the day.

4. **Metaphysics:** What is meant by the term *metaphysical poetry*? During what time period was metaphysical poetry the most popular? Why is the metaphysical conceit particularly appropriate for this poem? Can the speaker actually prompt her soul to leave her body temporarily? Why is this such an attractive idea?

Because the speaker describes what we might call an "out of body" experience, metaphysical conceits work well in this poetry. In writing about the metaphysical aspects of "I'm Happiest When Most Away," consider how one would approach the topic of a spiritual journey and why that type of journey might appeal. The romantic idea of the visionary world proved crucial not only to Emily Brontë's poetry but also to her single novel, *Wuthering Heights.* Apply the questions above to the novel as well if you want to consider writing about similar aspects in different genres, constructing a comparison and contrast essay.

Form and Genre

Poetry is the genre in which form proves most crucial. *Form* may be defined simply as the appearance of the poem on the page. A poem may be divided into groups of lines called stanzas, generally separated by white space, which is true of "I'm Happiest When Most Away." Fixed forms in poetry generally contain the repetition of sounds or entire phrases or lines in a set pattern. The most common sound repetition associated with poetry is that of rhyme. Rhyme scheme, or the order in which rhyme is arranged, may be diagrammed through the use of letters that represent each rhyme sound at the end of a line in the order in which the sounds are encountered. In this poem, for instance, because the words at the conclusion of the first two lines rhyme, their scheme is aa. The second two lines also rhyme, using a sound different from that of the first two lines, so their scheme is bb. The rhyme scheme shifts in the second stanza, in which every other line rhymes. Thus, the scheme is cdcd, making the entire rhyme scheme aabbcdcd. Alliteration, when a beginning letter is repeated in several consecutive or near-consecutive words, also acts as important sound repetition. An example in this poem is the *w* in wander, worlds, wandering, and wide; the *n* in not and none; and the *i* in infinite and immensity. Another aspect of repetition in this poem is the fact that the title also serves as its first line.

An additional crucial aspect of format is the poem's use of punctuation. The poem's first line ends in enjambment, meaning it has no punctuation, and the reader moves into the second line with no pause. Enjambment is also present at the end of the third line; thus, all four lines of the first stanza are read in one breath. The fourth line, "And the eye can wander through worlds of light—," concludes with a dash, which indicates one should pause before proceeding. The first line of the second stanza, "When I am not and none beside—," also concludes with a dash, again asking readers to pause, as does the second line in the second stanza, making three consecutive lines that conclude with dashes. White space is used to separate one stanza from another, suggesting transition. A poet never includes any format aspects by mistake; each is important to the transmission of the poem's theme. Thus, when writing about format, your thesis statement could focus on how the format of "I'm Happiest When Most Away" helps the reader understand the poem's theme, the basic message that Brontë hopes to transmit.

Poetry may be the perfect genre for certain topics. In "I'm Happiest When Most Away," the topic is that of spiritual travel in an imaginary world. If you would like to write about why the poetic genre is a good match for such a topic, you will want to consider specific characteristics of poetry, discussed above. The fact that a poem is often brief, compact, and suggests more than it states could make it the perfect vehicle for presentation of ideas regarding the imagination. Poetry also depends on the use of concrete imagery to make its points about abstract ideas. An examination of the concrete imagery in this poem might suggest ideas for a thesis statement. For a quick and simple review of the elements of poetry, visit the Holt, Rinehart and Winston Web site that accompanies its series *Elements of Literature*, at http://eolit.hrw.com/hlla/newmain-links/lit.jsp.

Sample Topics:

1. **Format:** Why does Brontë want to direct where in the poem the reader hesitates? What is the importance of transition from line to line and verse to verse? In what additional ways does the poet guide our reading of her words? What part do rhyme and alliteration play in our gaining meaning from this poem?

   An examination of rhythm and rhyme helps the reader understand the speaker's personality and character. Just as we pause when speaking for certain reasons, so does the poem's speaker. Those reasons could include a lack of confidence about her word choice, a desire to be sure that her audience has received her words as she meant for them to, or simply a desire to rethink and rephrase, or to repeat the main idea in other words. Repetition adds balance to the presentation, which suggests a well-thought-out delivery. Repetition is also pleasing to the ear, so the speaker attempts to entertain, as well as to educate, her listener. The romantic poet Percy Bysshe Shelley, among others, advanced the idea that poetry, or literature, has as its purpose both to entertain and to teach. Should you find that theory helpful to your essay, consult a text about Shelley, such as Reiman's *Shelley's Poetry and Prose,* and read Shelley's "A Defence of Poetry" at http://www.bartleby.com/27/23.html.

2. **Genre:** Could Brontë express the idea(s) of this poem in another genre? If so, why did she select poetry in this case?

We know that Emily Brontë also used the novel form to express her identification with romantic ideals. This means that while the poem may not be the only form, it can accomplish something that the novel cannot, suggesting that Brontë believes those ideas should be featured in line and stanza form. Using what you know about poetic elements, you could argue that while she uses two genres, poetry proves the superior approach.

Language, Symbols and Irony

Symbolism always offers a rich source of ideas for writing about a poem, as it proves crucial to this genre. Symbols may be either traditional, having held a certain meaning over time, or they may be literary, meaning they are used to suggest a certain meaning or connection only in a specific work. Because the meanings of traditional symbols are commonly accepted, a poet may introduce irony into a poem by using a traditional symbol in a nontraditional manner. This poem affords several important symbols in both categories. Traditional symbols include the moon, the night (which is used in a nontraditional manner), and light (discussed above), while a literary symbol is clay. Clay is also an example of an allusion, in this case to the biblical myth of Creation. Irony is present in additional references in this poem, such as in the idea that the speaker refers to being "Away," when in actuality, she never leaves her home, as well in the reference to the state of nonbeing in line 5. A related concept is that of paradox, when a contradictory message is suggested. Paradox is present in the line "When I am not and none beside—," as the speaker suggests a state of nonbeing, normally impossible for a person. The last two lines counter by suggesting that a state of nonbeing is possible through the spirit's wandering.

Sample Topics:

1. **Symbols:** Which symbols are traditional? Which are literary? What is the specific importance of each? What does each symbolize? How do the symbols support the theme of the poem?

   The moon traditionally symbolizes the female, as it gains its light from the sun, a traditional symbol for the male. In the case of this moon, it broadcasts enough light for the speaker to be able to travel. That may be important in determining states of independence for the speaker. The literary symbol in the poem, clay, suggests the clay from which God made the material body of the first man. Thus, if the soul leaves the home of clay, it departs the body. We generally think of that happening only when one dies, so this circumstance is unusual. The symbols suggest a different type of travel, that of the imagination. Such a visionary world is a common topic in romantic poetry.

2. **Irony:** Why are irony and the related element paradox important to the meaning of this poem? Would the poem work without irony and paradox?

   Irony is often crucial to a poem's meaning. Through its use, the poet may suggest that her audience should question what seems to be true, and it also asks the reader to consider how humans judge truth. Generally, we make judgments based on input from our five senses. However, we may need to try other means, such as application of intuition and imagination to discover truth, an idea strongly supported by the romantic poets. Irony may be present in imagery, such as the windy night pictured here. A windy night would seem threatening to some, but to the spirit, it is the optimal time for the spirit and the "eye" to wander. You might also want to consult the chapter in this volume that focuses on Brontë's poem titled "The Night-Wind" to gain some perspective on this image. The verb *wander* is also important, as this trip or voyage is not a hurried or frantic movement, but rather one during which the speaker may take her time.

Bibliography and Online Resources for "I'm Happiest When Most Away"

Benvenuto, Richard. *Emily Brontë.* Boston: Twayne, 1982.

Chapman, Allison, Richard Cronin, and Anthony Harrison, ed. *A Companion to Victorian Poetry.* Oxford: Blackwell, 2002.

Elements of Literature. Holt, Rinehart and Winston. Available online. URL: http://eolit.hrw.com/hlla/newmainlinks/lit.jsp. Downloaded December 9, 2007.

"Emily Brontë." About.com: Women's History. Available online. URL: http://womenshistory.about.com/library/bio/blbio_bronte_emily.htm. Downloaded August 7, 2007.

Gardner, Helen Louise. *The Metaphysical Poets.* New York: Penguin Classics, 1976.

Gilmour, Ian. *The Making of the Poets: Byron and Shelley in Their Time.* New York: Carroll & Graf, 2003.

Leach, Alexandra. "'Escaping the Body's Gaol': The Poetry of Anne Brontë." *Victorian Newsletter* 101 (2002): 27–31.

McHugh, Heather. "Anne Brontë's 'To Cowper'." *Paris Review* 42 (2000): 202–205.

Moore, Andrew. "The Metaphysical Poets—Study Guide." Available online. URL: http://www.universalteacher.org.uk/poetry/metaphys.htm. Downloaded December 9, 2007.

Norton, Caroline. "English Laws for Women (1854)." The Victorian Women Writers Project. Available online. URL: http://www.indiana.edu/~letrs/vwwp/norton/englaw.html. Downloaded December 10, 2007.

"Poems by Emily Brontë." Poetry Archives. Available online. URL: http://www.poetry-archive.com/b/bronte_emily.html. Downloaded August 7, 2007.

Reiman, Donald, ed. *Shelley's Poetry and Prose.* New York: Norton, 2002.

Shelley, Percy Bysshe. "A Defence of Poetry." Available online. URL: http://www.bartleby.com/27/23.html. Downloaded December 17, 2007.

Shorter, Clement, ed. *The Complete Poems of Emily Jane Brontë.* New York: Columbia UP, 1995.

"The Poems of Anne Brontë." Available online. URL: http://mick-armitage.staff. shef.ac.uk/anne/poems/an-poems.html. Downloaded August 7, 2007.

"Victorian Social History: An Overview." The Victorian Web. Available online. URL: http://www.victorianweb.org/history/sochistov.html. Downloaded December 9, 2007.

Winnifrith, Tom. *The Poems of Charlotte Brontë: A New Annotated and Enlarged Edition of the Shakespeare Head Brontë*. Oxford: Blackwell, 1984.

"THE NIGHT-WIND"

READING TO WRITE

E MILY BRONTË published poetry along with her sisters under their pseud-onyms—Currer, Ellis, and Acton Bell—in a volume that sold only two copies. According to statements by Charlotte and others, Emily was the most sensitive of the sisters and the most private. Her widely anthologized poems project a tone of longing, as their speakers express a yearning for a life they cannot inhabit materially but must instead seek through their imagination. The poetry shares much in common in addition to tone, including nature imagery such as the moon, stars, wind, and night. For instance, in "I'm Happiest When Most Away," also discussed in this volume, Brontë includes a specific reference to "a windy night when the moon is bright."

Imagery is only one aspect of poetry to notice as you study any poem for possible writing topics. Other elements of poetry include figurative language, symbolism, irony, paradox, sound, repetition, allusions, and for-mat; several of those elements will be discussed specifically below. Like all literature, poetry projects a particular theme, or message, that the author hopes the audience will take away with them. One approach to establish-ing a theme for a poem is to study its basic topics. Please review the chapter focusing on "I'm Happiest When Most Away" for a detailed discussion of elements of poetry and Brontë's debt to ideas of the romantic poets and to metaphysical poetry. Those discussions apply to each of her poems.

TOPICS AND STRATEGIES
Theme

Poetry offers various clues to meaning, often evident through the poet's emphasis of certain elements or technique. A crucial element for poetry is figurative language, also called figures of speech, or the use of comparisons. Common figures of speech include metaphor and simile, as well as personification. Brontë employs all three in this poem. Probably the most notable is the personification of the "soft wind," mentioned in line 7, as it converses with the speaker, assuring her of Heaven's glory and the fact that Earth, also personified when described as "sleeping," is "fair." In the third stanza, the speaker states: "I needed not its breathing / to bring such thoughts to me," but the wind continues to whisper to her. She later uses metaphor to compare the wind to a "wooing voice" and to music, protesting that the wind's music lacks the power to "reach my mind." These comparisons suggest that the poet focuses on inspiration, a term that literally means to breathe in. Poets often write of their muse, of what inspires them, and the night wind of this poem clearly represents inspiration. The speaker attempts to deny that her inspiration reaches her mind, yet as the poem continues, her tone loses that confidence.

Other repetition occurs in imagery, as Brontë constructs a warm summer's night scene, described as "mellow," lacking clouds, with bright moonlight that shines into the speaker's window. The moon serves as a traditional symbol for woman, who in that era commonly spent much time indoors, as does this speaker, in what feminist critics refer to as the domestic sphere. She muses silently inside as the wind comes indoors to tempt her outside. As the poem continues, temptation is reemphasized when the speaker states in the seventh stanza that the "wanderer," or wind, refuses to depart, and his kisses grow warmer. The wind also claims it will win her, taking her against her will, extending a sexual reference and imagery of temptation.

A closely related topic is that of *carpe diem*, a concept common to Renaissance poetry. The phrase means "seize the day," and it was an approach employed by poets to win the hearts of young women. For example, a courtier attempted to persuade a young woman to yield her virginity to him, as within a short time the beauty and purity she had so carefully preserved would age and eventually die. Brontë's reference to the grave as "beneath the church-yard stone" in the final stanza accomplishes the same purpose.

Sample Topics:

1. **Inspiration:** How does the wind inspire the speaker? What does Brontë suggest about her own work by focusing on a

source of inspiration? Does the poem suggest anything about how a poet relates to her muse or source of inspiration? Why does the reader need to learn in the penultimate stanza that the speaker and the wind have remained friends since her childhood?

Ultimately, inspiration is all-important to a poet. Brontë may suggest that her own inspiration comes from unusual sources. The fact that the wind refers to the "dark winds" and "thick leaves" as attractive things, rather than frightening in the traditional sense, is unusual. The dream imagery and reference to human feelings may suggest that inspiration cannot come from everyday activities. It comes to this speaker only when she sits alone, and it has been a frequent visitor for some time. Perhaps Brontë suggests that some poets understand their muse and know how to call it forth, or at least understand the best circumstances to encourage it.

2. **Temptation:** Why does the wind tempt the speaker? What action does the wind desire the speaker to take? Why is imagery of sexual seduction appropriate to the poem's theme?

The speaker safely at home at night may have to depart her secure surroundings in order to take advantage of inspiration. Perhaps her creativity is closely associated with nature. Her room may be a metaphor for her mind, with the window imagination that allows her to see beyond her constrained world. She may, on the other hand, require the nighttime silence in order to discover the song to which the wind refers. Temptation may be necessary in order to move her beyond her daily routine and to open her ears to the song that symbolizes poetry.

3. **Carpe diem:** Why does the wind argue using the carpe diem theme? Why is that always an effective argument, regardless of the circumstance, speaker, or listener? Can the reader identify signs of passion in the poem that become associated with the wind?

Everyone fears death, and to be reminded that all sensory input ceases with death is to be reminded that one should spend this day as if it were the last. The wind wants the speaker to understand that future opportunities are not guaranteed. She must leave her confinement, whether it be spiritual, mental, emotional, or physical, and yield to the inspiration that seeks to possess her. Poets find immortality through their words. Thus, the speaker can avoid death, in a manner of speaking, if she yields to her muse.

Bibliography and Online Resources for "The Night-Wind"

"Emily Bronte." About.com: Women's History. Available online. URL: http://womenshistory.about.com/library/bio/blbio_bronte_emily.htm. Downloaded August 7, 2007.

Benvenuto, Richard. *Emily Brontë*. Boston: Twayne, 1982.

Chapman, Allison, Richard Cronin, and Anthony Harrison, ed. *A Companion to Victorian Poetry*. Oxford: Blackwell, 2002.

Elements of Literature. Holt, Rinehart and Winston. Available online. URL: http://eolit.hrw.com/hlla/newmainlinks/lit.jsp. Downloaded December 9, 2007.

Gardner, Helen Louise. *The Metaphysical Poets*. New York: Penguin Classics, 1976.

Gilmour, Ian. *The Making of the Poets: Byron and Shelley in Their Time*. New York: Carroll & Graf, 2003.

McHugh, Heather. "Anne Brontë's 'To Cowper'." *Paris Review*. 42 (2000): 202–205.

Leach, Alexandra. "'Escaping the Body's Gaol': The Poetry of Anne Brontë." *Victorian Newsletter*. 101 (2002): 27–31.

Moore, Andrew. "The Metaphysical Poets—Study Guide." Available online. URL: http://www.universalteacher.org.uk/poetry/metaphys.htm. Downloaded December 9, 2007.

"Poems by Emily Brontë." Poetry Archives. Available online. URL: http://www.poetry-archive.com/b/bronte_emily.html. Downloaded August 7, 2007.

Reiman, Donald, ed. *Shelley's Poetry and Prose*. New York: Norton, 2002.

Shelley, Percy Bysshe. "A Defence of Poetry." Available online. URL: http://www.bartleby.com/27/23.html. Downloaded December 17, 2007.

Shorter, Clement, ed. *The Complete Poems of Emily Jane Brontë*. New York: Columbia UP, 1995.

Winnifrith, Tom. *The Poems of Charlotte Brontë: A New Annotated and Enlarged Edition of the Shakespeare Head Brontë*. Oxford: Blackwell, 1984.

"REMEMBRANCE"

READING TO WRITE

A S A YOUNG person who spent most of her time with her siblings, Emily Brontë worked with her sister Anne to construct stories about the imaginary world of Gondal. Her poetry is generally categorized by critics into two groups: the Gondal poems and the non-Gondal poetry. In February 1844, Emily copied her poems into two notebooks that represent those two divisions. The Gondal notebook contains groupings of poems that focus on certain characters from the fantasy, while the non-Gondal poetry is more personal, in the lyric form that would be so admired by later English writers. She continued to add to the collections through May 13, 1848. Today, approximately 168 of her 200 known poems exist in manuscript form, almost all belonging to the era previous to her writing of her novel *Wuthering Heights.*

"Remembrance" derives from the manuscript titled "R" and is the lament of the Gondal saga's heroine for her hero's death. Originally titled "Alcona to J. Breznaida," the poem's initial gloomy tone reflects its subject matter. Peppered with words such as *cold, grave, despair, destroy,* and *tears,* the poem still has an underlying suggestion of grace, as its speaker has drawn strength from her grief. The fact that Brontë never uses the word *death* throughout the poem works to keep the reader's focus not on the loss of the loved one but on the fact that he is remembered. However, the poem's conclusion with a question that must forever stand unanswered makes clear that the loss of her first and true love will haunt her through eternity. That question balances one that concludes the first stanza, thus framing the poem in interrogation. Brontë may suggest to the reader that there are no clear answers to questions about death, separation, and the strength of selective memory. As you read, you will search for such clues as to the poem's meaning, using each of the elements of poetry to do so. Keep in mind that a poet rarely states a poem's theme. Rather, it is suggested, and the reader must remain observant to identify and act upon such suggestions.

Before completing this chapter, please review the chapter that focuses on Brontë's poem "I'm Happiest When Most Away." It contains a detailed discussion of elements of poetry that applies to each of her poems. In addition, that entry discusses the influence on Brontë of the romantic and metaphysical poets.

TOPICS AND STRATEGIES
Theme

Poetry offers various clues to meaning, often evident in the poet's emphasis of certain elements or technique. Repetition is a technique the observant student will be aware of, as through repetition the poet calls attention to words, patterns, or rhythms. The most repeated term in this poem is *cold,* contained in a repeated phrase, "cold in the earth." The speaker substitutes that phrase for the word *death,* a word that she never speaks. In this case, what is not said may be important, because it is such an obvious omission. The poem focuses on the death of a loved one, and death offers promise as development into a theme. To say that death is the theme would not be quite correct. Rather, the theme must relate intimately to death. That theme, which one who wishes to write about this poem must discover, would offer a fine focus for an essay.

An additional obvious topic is that of loyalty. The speaker notes in the third stanza's first line that "fifteen wild Decembers" have "melted into spring" since her lover's death. Even after all those years, she still suffers acute grief over his loss and remains loyal to his memory. The third line of that same stanza notes that such devoted spirits are "faithful indeed." That line also describes the speaker as having endured "years of change and suffering!"—making clear that other changes have taken place in her life, yet her attitude toward her dead lover has not changed. In the fourth stanza, she does mention having forgotten the "Sweet Love of youth," or the dead man, due to the demands of everyday life, as "Other desires and other hopes beset me," but they only "obscure" her dead love; they do not remove him from her mind completely and forever. She has enjoyed no "later light" or "second morn" to compare to her time with him.

A related topic is that of change over time, suggested in the lines just discussed, because the speaker has not changed in her attitude toward the lost love. However, 15 years inevitably changes anyone, and the speaker refers to her youth as having passed while, in the sixth stanza, "the days of golden dreams had perished." Brontë includes past-tense verbs later in the poem that emphasize the passage of time, including *perished, cherished, strengthened,* and *weaned.*

An additional topic that offers strong possibilities is that of grief. The stanzas project a keening tone that supports the connotation of mourning, emphasized through the repetition of the lines "Cold in the earth" and "All my life's bliss," as well as words such as *cold* and *far.* That repetition in the first two stanzas projects a rhythm suggestive of that in elegy. The speaker has suffered for 15 years, part of that time spent in thought about her loved one. Her loss remains acute because she has never experienced another true love. She describes the days spent with the dead man as "golden," emphasizing the degree of her loss of such value.

A final topic could be that of strength. The persona in this poem is not a passive woman. While she has grieved for her loss, she has also experienced "wild" winters and has marked each spring well, spring being a traditional time of rebirth. She has changed and suffered and yet kept her wits about her when the "World's tide" has borne her along. She also notes in the sixth stanza that despair did not have the power to destroy her memories. Its attack helped her learn to cherish life, even though she had no joy. She overcame the urge to commit suicide, "Weaned my young soul from yearning after thine; / Sternly denied its burning wish to hasten / Down to that tomb" to join her dead love. She remains strong in part by denying herself the pleasure of recalling "Memory's rapturous pain" and the "divinest anguish," lest she not be able to continue in the world of the living. These topics strongly relate to one another, and you may want to consider an essay that focuses on more than one.

After considering each topic carefully, remember to develop a clear focused thesis statement, which will be supported by each of your discussion paragraphs. That thesis may suggest a meaning or theme for the poem, based on the topics that the poem reveals. As you identify your own topics, remember to develop questions like the ones below that will help lead you to a thesis statement.

Sample Topics:

1. **Death:** What is the speaker's attitude toward death? Does she continue to rebel against it, accept it, or remain ambivalent? How can you discern her attitude? Why does Brontë not allow the speaker to ever use the specific word *death*?

   The speaker appears to rail against the state of death in the poem's opening, because of its ability to remove her "Only Love" from her. The physical separation brings great pain, as does the separation over time, both serious effects of death. However, it has been suggested that death does not end a relationship, but instead merely changes it. Perhaps through use of terms other than *death*, Brontë suggests that the reader should think of death in a nontraditional way.

2. **Loyalty:** What reason(s) does the speaker supply for having remained loyal? Why does she value loyalty? What evidence does she give that proves her loyalty? Do you think she would expect the same loyalty from her lover, were their roles reversed?

   Loyalty and faithfulness remain important to this speaker, and she takes comfort in being able to place herself in the category of the faithful, yet she does question her own loyalty.

3. **Time:** Has the passing of time healed the speaker's wounds? How has it changed her? Does she blame or credit her lover for any of the results of time's passing?

   The writer who constructs an essay on the topic of time must keep in mind the poem's title, "Remembrance." This poem is all about how the speaker remembers her lost love and the fact that she even remembers him after 15 years. Time generally throws obstacles into the human path that weaken memory.

Keep in mind that over time, imagination may transform a memory into something greater than reality. Brontë opens her poem with a question about time, a crucial fact.

4. **Grief:** How might one describe this speaker's grief? Is it pure? Does it seem forced? Can she freely express it? For what, precisely, does she grieve?

The reader understands that the speaker misses her lover, as any lover would. However, many people would move on to find another companion, particularly after 15 years. Is it the speaker's grief that has prevented her doing that, or something else? While grief makes anyone suffer, the speaker seems to benefit in some ways due to her grief. Suggesting any benefit could greatly strengthen an essay on this topic.

5. **Strength:** Does the speaker project a strong image? If so, how is that accomplished? Does anything about her strength surprise the reader? Is it a mental, physical, or emotional strength? What seems to be its source? Why does she require strength?

The speaker may show evidence of strength in various ways, including in her choice of terminology. She also shows strength in the fact that she chooses to remember her dead lover when forgetting would prove the easier choice. Memory can take a toll on humans, turning them bitter and even weakening them physically. The manner with which the speaker chooses to remember her lover may relate to her retention of strength, or it may even be responsible for her strength in the face of various challenges she must face over the 15 years of their separation. Her choice to live has also required a great deal of strength, as is evident in her description of struggling against the inclination to join her lover in the grave.

Comparison and Contrast

Emily Brontë also dealt with the haunting aspects and effects of grief in her novel *Wuthering Heights.* Her poem's speaker eerily predicts Heathcliff's mourning for Cathy. The speaker has longed to join her dead lover in the grave, as does Healthcliff. This poem does not rely as heavily on the romantic idea of the power of imagination and spiritual vision as some of Brontë's others. However, in its final stanza it definitely suggests the power of the imagination through memory to transform suffering into something magnificent, evident in the paradox that appears in the phrase *rapturous pain*. That type of suffering is also endured by Heathcliff, who refuses to release Cathy from his passionate claim on her. If you want to write about these similarities through a comparison essay, you should read carefully detailed critical analyses of Emily Brontë's poetry, such as Christine Anderson and Margaret Smith's *The Oxford Companion to the Brontës*. A student or an inexperienced writer should take care not to suggest a cause-and-effect relationship between two works, such as the idea that Brontë's early poetry caused her to write about Heathcliff in the manner that she chose. However, one may certainly conclude that the two share similar approaches, based on ideas of the romantics and the metaphysical poets.

Bibliography and Online Resources for "Remembrance"

Anderson, Christine, and Margaret Smith. *The Oxford Companion to the Brontës*. New York: Oxford UP, 2006.

Chapman, Allison, Richard Cronin, and Anthony Harrison, ed. *A Companion to Victorian Poetry*. Oxford: Blackwell, 2002.

Davies, Stevie. *Emily Brontë: Heretic*. London: The Women's Press, 1997.

Elements of Literature. Holt, Rinehart and Winston. Available online. URL: http://eolit.hrw.com/hlla/newmainlinks/lit.jsp. Downloaded December 9, 2007.

Gardner, Helen Louise. *The Metaphysical Poets*. New York: Penguin Classics, 1976.

Gilmour, Ian. *The Making of the Poets: Byron and Shelley in Their Time*. New York: Carroll & Graf, 2003.

Moore, Andrew. "The Metaphysical Poets—Study Guide." Available online. URL: http://www.universalteacher.org.uk/poetry/metaphys.htm. Downloaded December 9, 2007.

Reiman, Donald, ed. *Shelley's Poetry and Prose*. New York: Norton, 2002.

Shorter, Clement, ed. *The Complete Poems of Emily Jane Brontë*. New York: Columbia UP, 1995.

"STARS"

READING TO WRITE

A S THE MOST private of the Brontë sisters, Emily Brontë did not share her poetry until Charlotte discovered it. Like her sisters, she published under a pseudonym, partly because the reading public was not accustomed to women writers, but also probably to preserve her privacy. At first glance, a knowledge of Emily's private and retiring demeanor seems to offer assistance in helping a reader understand the speaker of "Stars," who prefers the obscurity of night to the revealing light of day. The speaker offers a paradox in noting in the first two lines that the "dazzling sun / Restored our earth to joy," yet in line 19 she claims that the sun could "scorch with fire" her "tranquil cheek." That contrast could represent Brontë's attitude toward self-exposure and has done so in other poems discussed in this volume.

However, a closer reading of the poem reveals that this persona desires the stars more than the sun not to enjoy peaceful isolation but, rather, because she spends the time that the stars are in the sky with her lover. Brontë routinely adopted ideas from the romantic poets, who believed nature to be inspiring and instructive, and in this poem her speaker feels that way about the stars but not the sun. Her passion acts as inspiration in this particular poem, as she sees the sun as a negative force rather than a positive one. Brontë's style was affected by that of the metaphysical poets, and this poem echoes feelings from John Donne's "The Sun Rising," which opens with an address to the sun: "Busy old fool, unruly sun / Why dost thou thus / Through windows and curtains call on us?" The imagery of curtains also appears in Brontë's 10th stanza.

Please review the chapter on "I'm Happiest When Most Away" for a detailed discussion of elements of poetry as well as of Brontë's debt to ideas of the romantic poets and to metaphysical poetry. Those discussions apply to each of her poems.

TOPICS AND STRATEGIES
Theme

In her poem "Stars," Brontë focuses on a favorite topic, that of self-imprisonment. The voice of her poem prefers night to day and so establishes herself as a nontraditional persona. Most people prefer daylight, feeling too much is hidden by the darkness. But as noted in line 9, this speaker is most at peace when the stars provide her light. She feels a kinship with them, revealed when Brontë employs personification in the fifth line in referring to the stars' eyes and equating them to her own. She chooses to stay indoors, hiding from the fire that burns her skin. Once one establishes the presence of a lover, however, that fire could also relate to the heat of passion. Lines 19–20 read: "And scorch with fire the tranquil cheek / Where your cool radiance fell?" The "cool radiance" could be that of the stars or of her lover. That the persona could depart if she so desired is made evident when she frees the flies that are imprisoned with her, described in lines 37–38.

Dreams or fantasy also make good topics for writing. Like all poets, Brontë depended on inspiration to give her ideas and to guide her pen. In line 41, her speaker appears to equate Dreams with the Stars and the Night. She capitalizes the first letter of each word for emphasis and may suggest that inspiration comes to her at night, rather than during the day. Particularly as one notes the presence of a lover with the speaker, his attentions could equate to that nighttime inspiration. One might also suggest that the Dreams mean that the speaker only imagines her lover. Poetry has traditionally been used to describe romantic fantasies.

While romance may not seem a likely topic at first, an observant reader notices the clues that indicate the speaker is in love. In lines 16–17, the speaker states that a "sweet influence" "proved us one," attesting to the presence of a second person who becomes one with her. The trope of two becoming one is a familiar aspect of metaphysical poetry. In addition, in lines 31–32, she tells her audience, whether lover or stars, that she wants to recall Night in order to see "Your worlds of solemn light, again / Throb with my heart and me!" This is a passionate declaration, and the speaker probably does not mean Night when she says "Your worlds." Rather, she refers to a lover whom she invites to "throb" with her. At the poem's conclusion, the reason for the speaker's desire for night becomes clear. She concludes by addressing a loved one, asking to sleep through the sun's "blinding reign" to "only wake with you!" Thus, the night brings physical interaction with one the speaker loves; that one may have to depart with the sun. The speaker may also mean that she dreams of her love at night, rather than that he is physically present with her.

Sample Topics:

1. **Self-imprisonment:** How do we know the speaker imprisons herself? Why would she do that? Can readers relate to her state of isolation? How does her choice of isolation help shape her character? How might one define isolation in terms of this particular speaker?

While self-imprisonment often acted as a poetic theme for Brontë, her speaker is generally alone. This poem suggests a lover, either real or imagined, who joins the speaker in her imprisonment. When writing about literature, as long as you can defend your ideas with directly quoted material from the poetry, your essay will be acceptable; rarely can readers and critics be absolutely certain of their interpretation. Only if the poet has written about the poem can the reader be confident in identifying her intention or the meaning of the verses.

2. **Dreams/fantasies:** Why does the idea of dreams seem more appropriate for the night than for day? Why is it easier to dream under stars than the sun? Why must the speaker dream when she has a lover who comes to her at night? How does the dream or fantasy state relate to poetry in general?

While humans may also enjoy daytime dreams, in the instance of this poem, the night is preferable for dreaming. One accomplishes that type of dreaming in bed, and line 47, among others, confirms that this speaker focuses on sleep. When in line 29 the speaker turns to her pillow to recall night, we know that she wants to experience the sensation of night through sleep during the daytime. Only then can she see "Your worlds of solemn light," which can mean either the light of the stars or the light produced by her lover, or perhaps the act of loving.

3. **Romance:** Can the reader be sure that the speaker refers to a lover and not just to the stars? How does the poem's meaning alter if one accepts that the speaker addresses only the stars, and not a lover? How does it change if the lover is a product of fantasy? Can one enjoy and benefit from such a romance?

This poem focuses on romance, with the night better accommodating to the lovers. The speaker prefers the stars because when they are in the sky, she will be one with her love. However, the speaker may possibly conjure a fantasy lover during the night, as dreams are also emphasized. The imagery of flies (line 37) clashes with that of romantic dreams and has a jarring effect that serves to make readers wonder whether the lover exists in reality.

Language, Symbols, and Irony

One can never go wrong in writing about a poem when selecting language elements for one's focus. Poets celebrate language and word choice with every term, phrase, and line, often challenging readers to reach beyond the accepted meaning of words generally found in a dictionary. Because language remains a fluid concept, with new terms constantly entering and exiting everyday usage, our vocabulary should not be perceived as static. Poets remain famous for playing with language, suggesting second and even third meanings through figures of speech, symbolism, and irony. For instance, Brontë appears to employ personification in referring to the stars, such as in lines 1–2, when she writes, "your glorious eyes / Were gazing down in mine," and in line 9: "and drank your beams / As they were life to me." In actuality, she may be speaking of her lover, or a lover about whom she dreams at night.

Examples of symbols include the sun, typically a symbol of the male, and the dawn, which traditionally symbolizes rebirth or a new beginning. Irony remains strongly suggested in Brontë's unclear references to her lover: Does he exist or not?

Another important aspect of language is the sound it produces, such as rhyme and alliteration. "Stars" contains rhymes at the end of every other line, giving the poem a balance seen in the opposing concepts of night and day and the sun and the stars. Alliteration is present in stanza 10 in the words *waved* and *wakened* and *room, rise,* and *roam.* Brontë includes interesting and unusual sound repetition, such as that in the fourth stanza when the *th* combination is heard in "Thought," "Through," and "Thrilled," with the words *thought* and *through* each repeated in the stanza. In stanza 9, "glowed" is repeated, and the word *And* begins lines 34, 35, and 36, calling attention to that series.

Rhythm also includes repetition, as the first and third lines of each stanza contain four beats, while the second and fourth lines contain three beats. Like rhyme, the rhythm accentuates the poem's balance, which mirrors the constant cycle of day and night, life and death. The emphasis of particular ideas in words, phrases, and references that reappear focuses the readers' attention and acts as clues to the poem's overall meaning.

Sample Topics:

1. **Figurative language:** Why do poets in general seem to prefer indirect references, such as figurative language? Why do readers enjoy such comparisons? How does figurative language in "Stars" affect its reading? What clues to meaning can the reader gain through figurative language?

A major comparison the reader of this poem should notice is that of stars to the speaker's lover. Brontë seems to use them interchangeably, sometimes confusing the reader as to which she refers. Worthy of notice is the fact that while the sun is a traditional symbol for the male, the speaker's lover is identified with stars instead. The sun's warmth, generally deemed to produce a positive effect on the Earth, becomes negative through comparisons. In the final two verses, its effects are destructive rather than nurturing.

2. **Symbolism:** What symbols exist in the poem? Which seem the most important? What is the literal meaning of the objects or persons that also act as symbols? What is surprising about the symbols?

Brontë uses many aspects of nature in her poem. The dawn, the sun, birds, and the wind generally represent positives. However, the glow that the sun brings proves invasive, intruding into the speaker's sanctuary. The birds' songs are not soothing or beautiful, but loud, while the winds are not gentle but instead shake the door, as if demanding that it be opened. The imagery of flies is harsh, as they are generally considered nasty creatures, not to be encountered in a poem about love. The fact that they traditionally symbolize death and decay should trip an alarm in the mind of the observant reader. What might the juxtaposition of the lowly fly with the magnificent night sky mean? Perhaps Brontë further emphasizes the deathblow the sun deals to her dreams and imagination through the fly imagery.

3. **Irony:** Where does irony appear in "Stars"? How does it help shape the speaker's personality? Is the speaker purposefully ironic, or is the situation simply ironic in a manner outside her awareness? In other words, is she trying to mislead her audience?

We may return to the imagery of the flies to investigate irony. The sun awakens them, just as it does the speaker. They feel imprisoned in the room and seek release, contrary to the speaker who must get out of bed against her wishes to "give them leave to roam." Flies are unlikely representatives of freedom or romance, and yet Brontë uses them that way in this poem. In addition, the sun in this poem takes life, rather than giving it in the manner we traditionally associate with the sun. The image of death is strong in the final two stanzas, where it not only burns the speaker, but also "drains the blood of suffering men" and drinks their tears. The irony, or the unexpected, is quite strong throughout the poem, offering an excellent essay focus.

4. **Repetition:** What phrases and terms are repeated? What is the effect in each case of that repetition? Does one phrase seem more strongly emphasized than another? Do any of the sound repetitions cause the reader to linger over certain lines at an important moment in the poem?

Brontë employs the traditional instance of repetition referenced in the above discussion, but she also includes some not-so-traditional approaches to repetition. For instance, in stanza 11, she reverses the order of the words *Stars* and *Night* when she repeats them in lines 41–42: "O Stars and Dreams and Gentle Night; / O Night and Stars return!" The constant repeated rhythm also mimics the rocking lilt of a lullaby, important imagery when related to sleep and dreams.

Bibliography and Online Resources for "Stars"

Chapman, Allison, Richard Cronin, and Anthony Harrison, ed. *A Companion to Victorian Poetry*. Oxford: Blackwell, 2002.

Elements of Literature. Holt, Rinehart and Winston. Available online. URL: http://eolit.hrw.com/hlla/newmainlinks/lit.jsp. Downloaded December 9, 2007.

Gardner, Helen Louise. *The Metaphysical Poets*. New York: Penguin Classics, 1976.

Gilmour, Ian. *The Making of the Poets: Byron and Shelley in Their Time*. New York: Carroll & Graf, 2003.

Moore, Andrew. "The Metaphysical Poets—Study Guide." Available online. URL: http://www.universalteacher.org.uk/poetry/metaphys.htm. Downloaded December 9, 2007.

Norton, Caroline. "English Laws for Women." The Victorian Women Writers Project. Available online. URL: http://www.indiana.edu/~letrs/vwwp/norton/englaw.html. Downloaded December 10, 2007.

Reiman, Donald, ed. *Shelley's Poetry and Prose*. New York: Norton, 2002.

Shelley, Percy Bysshe. "A Defence of Poetry." Available online.URL: http://www.bartleby.com/27/23.html. Downloaded December 17, 2007.

Shorter, Clement, ed. *The Complete Poems of Emily Jane Brontë.* New York: Columbia UP, 1995.

"Victorian Social History: An Overview." The Victorian Web. Available Online. URL: http://www.victorianweb.org/history/sochistov.html. Downloaded December 9, 2007.

Winnifrith, Tom. *The Brontës and Their Background: Romance and Reality.* London: Macmillan, 1973.

"NO COWARD SOUL
IS MINE"

READING TO WRITE

EMILY BRONTË and her sisters published a collection of poems in 1846, paid for by Charlotte Brontë. Published under their pseudonyms of Currer, Ellis, and Acton Bell, the volume contained 21 poems written by Charlotte and 19 written by Emily and Anne. Emily selected her poems from two manuscript notebooks, one that contained her lyric poetry and the other containing poetry associated with the Gondal fantasy that she wrote as a child with Anne. Emily Brontë's poems were later hailed as some of the best of the lyric poets, grouped with those of Elizabeth Barrett Browning, Christina Rossetti, and Emily Dickinson. Dickinson so admired Brontë's "No Coward Soul Is Mine" that she asked that it be read at her funeral. Like others of Brontë's poems, "No Coward Soul" has a musical quality common to her lyrics, a quality described by Charlotte as "wild, melancholy, and elevating." According to Charlotte, this poem was the last written by Emily just prior to her untimely death.

While many of Emily Brontë's poems reflect a persona who feels imprisoned, sometimes by her own choosing, they generally also contain a theme of release through the imagination. She sometimes worked with the traditional idea of immortality available to the poet through the permanence of the printed word, which allows triumph over death. However, in this poem her speaker clearly turns to God for the promise of immortality. The speaker of "No Coward Soul" gains her power of resistance from God, denying death the pleasure of claiming her soul along with her body. Critics point out that Catherine Earnshaw Linton's deathbed speech in Emily's novel *Wuthering Heights* also focuses on release through death from a life that imprisoned her within her own body. That fact suggests the possibility of a comparison/contrast piece, although that type of essay will not be discussed here. As one reads this poem in preparation for writing an essay, careful notation of the importance of faith to the speaker will also prove crucial.

Before proceeding to the material below, please take time to review the chapter in this volume that focuses on Brontë's poem "I'm Happiest When Most Away." It contains a detailed discussion of elements of poetry and of Brontë's debt to ideas of the romantic poets and to metaphysical poetry that also relate to this chapter. You may perform a Web search for "romantic poetry characteristics" that will take you to sites such as Al Drake's "Romantic and Victorian Characteristics" (see the bibliography) for an in-depth review. Texts such as M. H. Abrams's seminal edition of *English Romantic Poets: Modern Essays in Criticism* will provide an excellent background on aspects of romantic poetry. Remember that when writing about poetry, one refers to specific line numbers. Should a line be quoted, the line number generally follows that line and is enclosed in parentheses.

TOPICS AND STRATEGIES
Theme

As noted above, God is a crucial topic in this poem. That topic is noticeable in the title and first line, when the speaker states that her soul is no coward. Because one relates the soul to religious belief in God, that connection is made immediately. Stanza 1 refers to "Heaven's glories" and the fact that the speaker is armed by Faith against Fear. God is mentioned in three different ways: by the name *God,* the term *Deity,* and the pronoun *Thee* in the second stanza, as the speaker directly addresses the source of her strength. Stanza 5 describes God's spirit as an active one that "Pervades and broods" and "Changes, sustains, dissolves, creates and rears." In the final stanza, God is addressed as "Being and Breath"—in other words, the essence of life for the speaker. Brontë's references are specifically spiritual more than religious, and thus they relate to the romantic idea of a visionary world, one that this speaker imagines as being superior to her mortal world. She even imagines that the material earth disappears, yet the visionary world of God remains. That "Every Existence would exist in thee" is an idea also imagined in *Wuthering Heights*.

A related topic is that of faith. The speaker's belief does not ground itself in any of "the thousand creeds / That move men's hearts." Rather, it grows directly from God, with no need of men's vain beliefs. The speaker's tone turns bitter in the third stanza as she labels such creeds "Worthless as withered weeds" and compares them to idle froth on the seas. Such froth lacks the strength to cause doubt in one who has strong faith. The reference to creeds may mean general beliefs of various religious groups, and it may also mean other types of beliefs that serve as religion for some, such as wealth or power.

Immortality could be another topic, and it is referred to in the final line of the fourth stanza. Those with faith in God believe in an afterlife where they will exist until infinity. That existence will remain when all material resemblance, including all heavenly bodies, disappear, as noted in the penultimate stanza. Existence after the end of existence is a metaphysical idea, and Brontë offers a metaphysical paradox in lines 23 and 24. The speaker states unequivocally that although "thou," or God, were "left alone," all existence would yet exist. You may review metaphysical ideas at Andrew Moore's Web site on "The Metaphysical Poets" or in any texts that discuss metaphysical poetry.

Brontë addresses death, another possible topic, in a manner resembling that in the Bible's New Testament. Her final stanza echoes 1 Corinthians 15:55: "O Death where is thy Victory? Death where is thy sting?" Death's destructive nature is mentioned in the poem, but only in order to emphasize that it cannot destroy God; therefore, it also cannot destroy those who have faith in God.

Sample Topics:

1. **God:** According to the speaker, what proof of God's existence does she have? Why does he inspire her belief? What characteristics of her God inspire such confidence in the speaker?

   The speaker not only praises God's glories in the first stanza, she affirms he is the source of her strength. He never leaves her, as he is "ever-present" in her breast. She describes him as "Almighty" and a deity of "wide-embracing love." Brontë focuses on the New Testament God, a kinder, gentler deity than the vengeful God of the Old Testament, but certainly not a weak one. He offers her a "steadfast rock of Immortality" to which she may securely cling.

2. **Faith:** How do we know that the speaker has faith? To what is faith compared? Why does the speaker require faith? Why is what appears to be a natural faith superior to organized religion? What is the importance of the references to the celestial bodies?

The speaker makes the point that human creeds are built upon a vanity so distressing that she cannot even express its impact, made clear in her description of the creeds as "unutterably vain." The creeds lack even the value of weeds, a reference to plants that have no value. Not only do weeds lack worth, in large numbers they may crush those plants which are valuable, cheating them of the water and nutrients they require in order to flourish. Her faith separates her from such vain men, allowing her to conquer the fear of death. Her belief is more everlasting than the universe from which heavenly bodies could disappear, and still her faith would remain intact. Such hyperbole marks poetry by the metaphysical writers.

3. **Immortality:** Why is immortality important to the speaker? What assurance does she have that it awaits her? Why would readers be interested in such immortality?

Brontë includes various terminology that focuses on everlasting life, such as *Undying Life, eternal,* and *Immortality.* Because death ends an earthly life, the speaker must demonstrate that her spiritual life is not restricted by time. All humans fear death, and the poem's speaker acts as an apostle, a witness for God who perhaps wins other souls with the promise of immortality. Brontë may also suggest the immortality that the poet gains through her work, as God is referred to as "Breath," and the term *inspiration* literally means "to breathe in." If God, and nature through God, have inspired her to write, and that writing will live on after she dies, then God's promise of immortality assumes a double meaning. That double meaning lends itself to the ideas of romanticism.

4. **Death:** Why does death fascinate humans? How has man attempted to conquer death?

Death has been a topic of literature for as long as literature has existed. The great leveler, it remains important because it affects everyone in precisely the same manner. This poem suggests that belief in God can vanquish death, rendering it powerless. God can never be destroyed, nor can humankind, who are his creation, unless God so deems it. For those frightened by the idea of complete removal from existence, the speaker comforts them with the promise of an existence that humans can only imagine.

Language, Symbols, and Irony

Word selection in any poem is crucial due to poetry's concentrated character. One approach to the use of figurative language, or words that introduce comparison, is personification, or assigning human attributes to things not human. In "No Coward Soul Is Mine," personification occurs frequently and thus would attract the attention of a writer as a potential essay topic. The poem's title begins the act of personification by designating the soul as not cowardly, meaning that it is brave; it is described as "No trembler." Rather than the speaker referring to herself as courageous, she attributes that characteristic only to her spirit. Other personified abstract ideas may be recognized by the uppercase letter that begins their name, denoting a proper name as attributed to humans. Examples include Faith, Fear, Death, Being, and Breath. An essay about personification might adopt a different approach and focus on the differences in the poem had the poet not included personification.

Sound and its repetition are crucial aspects of word choice for the poet. A poet emphasizes sound through rhyme and through the repetition of sounds by use of alliteration, or repeating a sound in different parts of words placed in a series. Poets and critics note that repetition heightens the emotional effect of poetry, particularly when read aloud. A Web site such as PoetryPoetry's "Using Repetition in Poetry," which is directed at those who write poetry, is also interesting for readers of poetry in its emphasis on the use of repetition. Brontë's poem contains abundant repetition, which is worth investigating in an essay.

Sample Topics:

1. **Personification:** Which objects or ideas are personified? What is the effect on the reader of thinking of these ideas in terms of personification? How does the personification heighten the emotional effect of Brontë's message to her readers? How would the effect of the poem change if Brontë had not employed personification?

   Use of the uppercase letter at the beginning of terms produces an immediate effect for the reader. Readers are used to interpreting uppercase letters in a particular way, and all poets depend on that interpretation when using uppercase letters. If we know a person's formal name, that knowledge adds significance to the person's identity which may or may not be deserved. A formal name also gives the reader something to relate to. One might suggest that each capitalized term, through its capitalization, is raised to the level of God, which also begins with an uppercase letter.

2. **Sound repetition:** Why are repeated sounds pleasing or effective? Which repeated sounds in this poem result in reader pleasure? Why would that pleasurable effect on a reader be important to a writer focusing on a serious topic in her poem?

   Brontë inserts several sound-effect terms in her poem in addition to rhyme. The repetition of *s* and *t* sounds calls attention to the words containing them. Examples include the poem's second line, in which "trembler in the world's storm-troubled sphere" makes noticeable use of those sounds. An additional example appears in the skillfully crafted word series in line 20: "Changes, sustains, dissolves, creates, and rears." Repetition of the *s* sound promotes the momentum of the series and also suggests a connection between the words in the series. The use of alliteration is most noticeable in line 11 in the phrase "Worthless as withered weeds," where the repetition of *w* calls attention to the words. When readers focus on alliteration, they will also focus on the meaning of the terms, and all of these *w* words describe the vain (also a repeated word) creeds "that move men's hearts." That phrase also contains alliteration in the repetition of *m*, and the *s* sound is prominent. The word *vain* represents two types of repetition, that of sound but also that of meaning, because it can have two meanings. Both may apply to Brontë's usage.

Bibliography and Online Resources for "No Coward Soul Is Mine"

Abrams, M. H. *English Romantic Poets: Modern Essays in Criticism.* New York: Oxford UP, 1975.

Chapman, Allison, Richard Cronin, and Anthony Harrison, ed. *A Companion to Victorian Poetry.* Oxford: Blackwell, 2002.

Drake, Al. "Romantic and Victorian Characteristics." *E212: British Literature since 1760.* Available online. URL: http://www.ajdrake.com/e212_sum_04/materials/guides/rom_romvic_character.htm. Downloaded December 19, 2007.

Elements of Literature. Holt, Rinehart and Winston. Available online. URL: http://eolit.hrw.com/hlla/newmainlinks/lit.jsp. Downloaded December 9, 2007.

Gardner, Helen Louise. *The Metaphysical Poets.* New York: Penguin Classics, 1976.

Gilmour, Ian. *The Making of the Poets: Byron and Shelley in Their Time.* New York: Carroll & Graf, 2003.

Homans, Margaret. *Women Writers and Poetic Identity: Dorothy Wordsworth, Emily Brontë, and Emily Dickinson.* Princeton, NJ: Princeton UP, 1980.

Moore, Andrew. "The Metaphysical Poets—Study Guide." Available online. URL: http://www.universalteacher.org.uk/poetry/metaphys.htm. Downloaded December 9, 2007.

Shorter, Clement, ed. *The Complete Poems of Emily Jane Brontë*. New York: Columbia UP, 1995.

Thormahlen, Marianne. *The Brontës and Religion*. Cambridge: Cambridge University Press, 1999.

"Using Repetition in Poetry." PoetryPoetry Workshop. Available online. URL: http://www.poetrypoetry.com/Workshops/00-07/RepWorkshop.html. Downloaded December 19, 2007.

INDEX